JIM FISK: *The Career of an Improbable Rascal*

JIM FISK:
The Career of
an Improbable Rascal

BY W. A. SWANBERG

CHARLES SCRIBNER'S SONS · New York

QUOTATIONS FROM COPYRIGHTED SOURCES

Direct quotations from the following copyrighted books have been included in *Jim Fisk—The Career of an Improbable Rascal*, on pages
indicated in parentheses following each source. These quotations are used
by special permission of the publishers and copyright holders listed
below.

Fuller, Robert H.—*Jubilee Jim: The Life of Colonel James Fisk, Jr.*,
The Macmillan Co., New York, 1928. Used by permission of Mrs.
Frances H. Savage. (P. 272)

Grodinsky, Julius—*Jay Gould: His Business Career, 1867-1892*, University
of Pennsylvania Press, Philadelphia, 1957. (P. 89)

Hesseltine, William B.—*Ulysses S. Grant, Politician*, Dodd, Mead & Co.,
New York, 1935. Used by permission of Professor William B. Hesseltine. (Pp. 127, 144)

Lane, Wheaton J.—*Commodore Vanderbilt: An Epic of the Steam Age*,
Alfred A. Knopf, New York, 1942. (Pp. 29-30, 42)

Nevins, Allan and Thomas, Milton Halsey, editors—*The Diary of
George Templeton Strong*, The Macmillan Co., New York, 1952.
Pp. 1, 260, 279, 285)

Sachs, Emanie—*"The Terrible Siren," Victoria Woodhull*, Harper &
Brothers, New York, 1926. Used by permission of Mrs. Emanie Arling.
(P. 113)

Van Wyck, Frederick—*Recollections of an Old New Yorker*, Liveright
Publishing Corp., New York, 1932. (P. 173)

Warshow, Robert Irving—*Jay Gould*, (Greenberg, New York, 1928).
Used by permission of the present publisher, Chilton Company,
Philadelphia. (P. 46)

White, Bouck—*The Book of Daniel Drew*, copyright 1910 by Double-
day & Co., Inc. Reprinted by permission. (P. 28)

FOR Sara Valborg

SOME STUDIED OPINIONS OF *James Fisk, Jr.*

"I was born to be bad."—*Fisk himself*.

"He was such a good boy!"—*his wife*.

"Morals! The man never had any; hasn't got any now, and will never have any this side of the bottomless pit."—*Attorney Thomas W. Pittman*.

". . . his whole life, even those phases of life which decorum veils, [was] an acted comedy—no more striking phenomenon of human nature has been seen in our time. . . ."—*The New York Herald*.

"What a scamp he was, but what a curious and scientifically interesting scamp!"—*George Templeton Strong*.

". . . as absolutely devoid of shame as the desert of Sahara is of grass."—*Rev. Henry Ward Beecher*.

"He has done more good turns for worthy but embarrassed men than all the clergymen in New York."—*Boss Tweed*.

"Perhaps of him it may one day be said that he was first in war, first in peace and first in the pockets of his countrymen."—*The New York Times*.

"Colonel Fisk was generous to a fault."—*Rev. Edward O. Flagg*.

Contents

viii   *Contents*

JIM FISK: *The Career of an Improbable Rascal*

1 *All Aboard!*

EARLY in 1869, the more sensitive citizens of New York became aware that an insufferable hayseed from Vermont named James Fisk Jr. was exceeding even his previous demonstrations of vulgarity. For two years he had done so well in this line that improvement was thought impossible. Yet, by fertile imagination and earnest effort, he had succeeded. Just as some men are born athletes or intellectuals, Fisk seemed divinely fashioned for the function of giving offense to people of taste. Manhattan's upper crust was wounded to discover that such a buffoon could not only win wealth in the metropolis but could trample on men with college degrees and social prestige in pushing himself to frightening financial and political power. The elite would have liked to ignore him, but he could no more be ignored than a holdup man or a discordant brass band. The well-bred lawyer George Templeton Strong viewed him with revulsion:

"Illiterate, vulgar, unprincipled, profligate, [he is] always making himself conspicuously ridiculous by some piece of flagrant ostentation. . . ."

Fisk was thirty-three, short, rotund, merry and utterly shameless. His broad face, though the wide-set eyes were somewhat protuberant, was saved from unhandsomeness by its expression of twinkling humor. His reddish-yellow hair was parted just west of center, to flare at the temples into curls that looked like a barber's handiwork. His generous mustache, described as being "the color of a Jersey cow," was waxed at the ends to dangerous keenness. It was said that he used perfume. Far from playing down his portly figure, he dramatized it with fancy suits and low-cut vests that allowed the cherry-sized diamond in his shirt bosom to blind the onlooker.

While his appearance gave injury to men of discrimination, his conduct added insult. He was noisy. He murdered the king's English. He went to fantastic lengths to get public attention—he who should have sought merciful concealment. His open affair with an opportunistic beauty named Josie Mansfield was already the talk of the town. For him to keep a mistress in oriental splendor while his wife lived conveniently distant in Boston was only one of his transgressions. Everybody knew how he and his quiet crony, Jay Gould, had stolen the Erie Railway, bribed judges and legislators to make the robbery legal, and since then had milked millions out of the road and its stockholders. Gould at any rate had the grace to shun publicity. Fisk wallowed in it.

Now he was splashing into a new sensation. He was moving the Erie offices uptown to Eighth Avenue and Twenty-third Street into the former Pike's Opera House, a four-story marble palace with 2600 seats.

No one had ever heard of a railroad being run from an opera house, although it was conceded that the Erie, for all its size, was a comic-opera carrier with more farce than freight in its makeup. The former owner, S. N. Pike, had lost heavily in presenting grand and light opera and was glad to sell the building to Fisk and Gould for $820,000. Fisk was enthusiastic about the deal, pointing out that the building contained three floors of offices on the Eighth Avenue side that would accommodate the Erie staff at the same time as he was indulging his taste for the drama in the theater on the main floor. Workmen streamed into the place in January, and by the time they finished they had consumed $250,000 more, changed the name on the lintel to "Grand Opera House," installed a bronze bust of Shakespeare in the entrance, built a great staircase from the marble-paved lobby, frescoed the walls and ceilings, and all in all transformed a building which at its completion only two years earlier had been thought the last word in splendor.

Indignant shareholders, who should have known better than to think they had any voice in affairs, were writing in to protest that holding Erie stock was gamble enough without getting involved in opera. Fisk brushed this aside as a misconception. The building, he repeated, was his property and Gould's. The railroad was merely renting the offices on a nineteen-year lease at $75,000 a year, the theater section being separate, his own private enterprise and responsibility.

Still, there were critics who asserted that serving as vice-president and managing director of Erie ought to be a full-time job, and how could he conscientiously have the leisure to conduct real-estate and theatrical promotions on the side? Others, who construed an office as a mere shelter, grumbled at the expense of the new layout. Being a minor Erie stockholder in 1869 was such a misfortune that none of them could be expected to take a bright view of things.

Indeed, Vice-President Fisk's new office on the second floor gave no hint that Erie was too destitute to pay dividends. It was a great hall, entered through carved oak doors that led into an anteroom protected by a bronze gate guarded by ushers. In the inner sanctum Fisk sat enthroned in a huge chair studded with gold nails, before a broad desk raised on a dais, surrounded by mirrors and silken hangings. The cerulean ceiling was splashed with crimson ovals emblazoned with the word "Erie" in gold. A gold-and-brown rug sank under the feet. Even the wash stand in the corner was a $1000 affair of marble and porcelain, a reporter noted, "the bowl being tinted with rose and gold, and displaying the figures of lovely nymphs in disporting attitudes." While Fisk obviously enjoyed this luxury, he seemed equally proud of the fine employees' dining hall, and the Erie safe, an innovation costing $60,000. Rising seven stories in height from sub-basement to roof, it was an individual safe on each floor, said to be so fireproof that if the entire building should burn down, the safe would remain standing, blackened but intact. Faultfinders sneered at this. Of what use was a mighty safe so long as Fisk and Gould knew the combination?

The Vermonter seemed impervious to criticism. If there was one facet of his personality that galled the sedate more than any other, it was a love of notoriety so extravagant that he preferred to be insulted than ignored. Strangely, the most important Erie property of all, a steam-operated printing press, was hidden away in the basement and not even mentioned. This press, the foundation of the wealth of Fisk and Gould, had already printed upwards of $23,000,000 of counterfeit money in the form of watered Erie shares with which the two predators had slain uncounted lambs in Wall Street and fattened their own purses. It would print more. The ability of this machine to transform blank sheets of paper into certificates worth from fifty to seventy-five dollars each was a secret weapon that Fisk, always a joker, liked to call "the freedom of the press."

He now went ahead with a series of moves calculated to show the big city what an up-and-coming country boy could do. Although he had never finished grammar school and had trouble with his spelling, he announced that the Opera House would present Shakespeare in March. He lured the producer C. W. Tayleure away from a profitable connection with the Olympic Theater and sent him to Europe in search of talent. He next leased Brougham's Theater, an intimate little playhouse on West Twenty-fourth Street just behind the Fifth Avenue Hotel, where Fisk was living at the time. With it he acquired the services of the skilful actor-playwright-producer John Brougham, who stepped aside while the house was renovated with plush and gilt. Moving down to Fourteenth Street, Fisk leased the great Academy of Music, where the impresario Max Maretzek had been presenting grand opera during the winter. He hired Maretzek as well. Within a few months his dollars had made him the biggest theater magnate in New York, owner or lessee of the three finest entertainment places in the city, boss of three producers of acknowledged prestige, a greasepaint guerilla ready to pick Europe clean.

"With most of the past achievements of Fisk, jr., we have little sympathy," huffed Horace Greeley's *Tribune*. ". . . As to his opera-houses and the like, we don't feel the need of any more. Our French theater evinces such ability and skill in commending Adultery as a Fine Art, that it don't seem to need any assistance."

Possibly this was a double-edged thrust by Greeley, for Fisk had long commended adultery as a fine art. While living at the Fifth Avenue Hotel, a hostelry opposed to sin, he had kept Miss Mansfield three minutes distant in a comfortable house just around the corner at 18 West Twenty-fourth, hard by Brougham's Theater. On establishing Erie in the Opera House he took steps to keep his massive business and private activities centralized. He installed Josie in a four-story brownstone dwelling a half-block west of the Opera House at 359 West Twenty-third, spending a fortune in decorating the place in Erie style. Knowing her aversion to toil, he supplied her with a butler, cook, chambermaid and coachman.

Having bought a dozen houses adjacent to the Opera House along Twenty-third Street, he fitted up the second floor of 313 West Twenty-third, three doors removed from his office, as his own diggings. A lover of canaries, he had one in every corner. Being about halfway between the Erie palace and Josie's home, he lived midway between business and pleasure. He was content with this modest arrangement because 313 was used only during legal or romantic emergencies and he could usually be found at 359.

In his brief New York career, Fisk repeatedly had been threatened with arrest and had been served with scores of

summonses, some of them costly and all of them causing in-
convenience. At times he had been forced to lock himself
in his office to escape process servers intent on dragging him
into court. With this in mind he had carpenters build him
an enclosed passageway that led from the back door of
his home, across two intervening yards and into the Grand
Opera House—a contrivance some naive observers thought
was designed to protect him from inclement weather. His
domestic austerity ended at the threshold, for his stables
behind the Opera House on Twenty-fourth Street were
in the grand manner. This was an era when a man of fashion
was marked by the smartness of his rig. Fisk had six, including a barouche, a phaeton and two clarences, one of the
latter lined with gold cloth. He kept fifteen horses, all
blacks and whites, requiring the attentions of five stablemen.
A canary above each stall filled the steeds' leisure hours with
song. A good reinsman, Fisk liked to drive six-in-hand, with
black horses and white harnessed together in pairs, two
Negro footmen in white livery at the front, two white
footmen in black livery at the rear—an outfit sure to be
recognized when he rolled up the avenue with Miss Mansfield or a few chorus girls as passengers.

At the time he acquired the Opera House, Offenbach's
naughty opera bouffe, *La Périchole*, was on the boards
with enough success so that Fisk continued it while Tayleure was abroad planning greater things. He often doffed
the cares of Erie to rush into the theater and give Adolph
Birgfeld, the interim director, the benefit of his experience
as a one-time circus menagerie helper. Since Mlle. De Rosa
and her ballet troupe were part of the cast, along with
several ingénues and soubrettes, he bossed a whole posse
of women performers. What with his free-and-easy way
with females and his already gamy reputation, it was inevitable that rumor should invest him with a bevy of
theatrical concubines. Wide-eyed tales flew of Fisk inviting
a score or more of half-naked dancers into his office, order-

ing champagne and pickled oysters from Delmonico's, and indulging in orgies of the kind that brought Rome to ruin. It was generally believed that his licentiousness had so infected large segments of the railroad's personnel that the place was a nest of debauchery. Broadway jokesters had Erie clerks singing timetables drunkenly to opera-bouffe melodies.

One stockholder brought suit against Fisk, asking his removal on the ground that he was simultaneously wrecking the railroad and all conceptions of decency in housing the line's main offices in a building devoted to song and dance, where hussies of the stage were as likely as not to seduce impressionable young male employes from their true allegiance to Erie and send them straight down the primrose path. The complaint read in part:

". . . that it is injurious to the business of said corporation [Erie] to have its offices in a building which in part is almost nightly occupied for operatic and dramatic performances; that the frequenting of said building and its approaches by the large number of young clerks in the employment of said Company, and by opera and theatre women at the same time, and the musical and dancing rehearsals by day, with the tread of ballet girls and the echoes of operas and songs, and of all sorts of string and wind instruments resounding in said building, within hearing and almost within sight of numerous young clerks at their desks . . . are demoralizing to said young men, destructive of the interests of said Company, and without a parallel in rail-road history."

The plaintiff further alleged that this mixture of railroad administration with lutes, dulcimers and lovely women had "caused to be so confused and mingled in the thoughts and associations, especially of the New-York clerks . . . the ideas of 'Erie' and 'Grand Opera,' of work and amusement, of ballet girls and operatic spectacles, with trains, telegraphs and time tables, as to impair the sense of duty, and to injure

the business efficiency of said clerks and employees, and
the good repute of said Company." He charged that Fisk
himself, the author of all this delinquency, was adding to
Erie's disgrace "by bringing or allowing to come into, and
tolerating in the offices of said Company, and appearing with
in said Grand Opera House, females of bad repute. . . ."

Fisk was indifferent to such lawsuits, having the best
attorneys in town to handle them. While the portrayals of
sin in the Erie menage were exaggerated, a fair appraisal of
his weaknesses would favor the opinion that improprieties
occasionally took place. All questions of morality aside, the
unanimous opinion in town was that Fisk, whose ability to
assimilate corporations had set some sort of gastric record,
was courting trouble in trying to swallow three theaters on a
full stomach. Most New Yorkers, visualizing him at his Erie
desk with a showgirl on each knee, never dreamed that
when he put fun aside he worked with speed and efficiency
in managing his complicated enterprises.

"He comes to his office at 9½ in the morning with the
promptness of a patrolman on his beat," wrote Matthew
Hale Smith. "He takes off his coat and is prepared for his
day's work. There are sixteen apartments in the Central
Office, and by the side of his chair are sixteen telegraph
wires, so that he can call any person into his presence whom
he may wish to see. Telegraphic communication with every
station on the Erie Road is complete. Jersey City and Wall
Street are also connected with the Erie office. Letters are
read the first thing in the morning and answers dictated. It
is no uncommon thing for Mr. Fisk to dictate three letters
at one time. . . ."

Josie Mansfield heard the showgirl rumors and evinced
some jealousy, although she well knew that she was the
apple of Fisk's eye, the recipient of a large share of his
immense fortune, and that if his esteem could be measured
in dollars she was far ahead of the field. Known behind
Fisk's back as the Cleopatra of Twenty-third Street, she

admitted to twenty-two years. She had successfully concealed a vivid past. Yet she managed to convey an impression of soft innocence, and when it came to beauty she was more than a match for the Opera House belles.

"Miss Mansfield is of full, dashing figure . . ." another journalist commented. "Her eyes are large, deep and bright, and inclined to Chinese in type. Her purple-black hair, worn in massive coils over a well-shaped head is a wonder in its luxuriance and native gloss . . . Her voice is very soft and sweet, but her smile that of a woman who grants it only after measuring its width and depth, and calculating its results to a nicety before bestowing it."

Insofar as he could get away with it, Fisk treated Josie precisely as if she were his legal wife, even to the point of leaving her to make frequent business trips. When he was in town he took her on occasional drives in Central Park, shopping tours or excursions to Long Branch. But for all his brass, his social appearances with her were limited by the rigid code of the day. He did not dare to share his great proscenium box with her at the Opera House, since such open wickedness would drive away customers. She had her own private box directly above his. He could not take her to fashionable places like Delmonico's or the Fifth Avenue Hotel, knowing that if he did so he would no longer be welcome there himself. Since fashionable places had a magnetic attraction for him, this meant that he moved freely in circles where she was barred, further restricting their time together. As a fallen woman, she was sometimes put in the humiliating position of having to wait outside the door while Fisk quaffed champagne or transacted business in staid company, as evidenced by one of the notes he dashed off to her: "Dear Josie—Get ready and come to the Twenty-third Street entrance of the hotel and take me down town. . . ."

Having fair intelligence, Miss Mansfield must have understood that while Fisk was faithful to her in his fashion, she would ever come second to his enormous ambition, which was the mistress that never left his side. Now that he had three theaters to operate in addition to a railroad and other enterprises, he was busier than ever, rushing from place to place, carrying the details of many diverse projects in his mind, a sharp fellow bristling with plots to get ahead of other sharp fellows. He often communicated with Josie by note, keeping a messenger handy for the purpose. But he still breakfasted and lunched with her whenever possible, and he made frequent use of her brownstone house as a place to entertain business and political associates at dinner and cards, with Josie acting as hostess.

Thus she met privately many of the great and notorious with whom Fisk rubbed elbows publicly. But these occasional entertainments were scarcely enough for an adventuress who craved continuous excitement. There were signs, unseen by the preoccupied Fisk, that Miss Mansfield was growing bored. Emancipated from housework by a staff of servants, she was often faced by leisure she was not equipped to cope with, having little taste for reading or meditation. While it was true that Fisk had rescued her from poverty and decorated her with diamonds and sables, these adornments were like the lady herself, useless unless they were *seen* by somebody. Fisk, who had an uncanny ability to foresee pitfalls in business, never suspected that his gorgeous plaything might be a source of trouble.

2

Prince of Peddlers

EVEN as a boy in Brattleboro, Vermont, James Fisk Jr. was regarded as a curiosity, a character, a smart aleck who would have been annoying but for his boundless good nature. He was born on All Fool's Day, 1835, on the other side of the Green Mountains at Pownal. Possibly the date was significant, as people said with a wink, but in later years no one could explain how such a person as Fisk could be the product of a center of New England honesty and thrift. His mother died when he was a baby, his father marrying Love Ryan of Putney after no more than a decent interval, and the family moved to Brattleboro, the bustling Connecticut River village that framed the boy's earliest memories and which he ever afterward looked back on fondly as his home town.

The senior Fisk, always known as Pop, was pure Yankee descended from English forbears, an itinerant peddler who left with a loaded wagon on Mondays to return at week's end with diminished cargo but thicker wallet. In his spare time he invented contraptions, among them a copper lightning rod and a safety device whereby a driver could pull a lever releasing the harness on runaway horses, thus freeing the wagon. His inventions were more singular than remunerative. On one peddling trip, when he ran out of shawls and had an excess of small flowered tablecloths, he assured housewives that the tablecloths were the latest Boston style in shawls and sold them all.

In Love Fisk he had a wife of warm maternal affection who reared young Jim as if she had borne him herself. "To the stepson," records a Brattleboro historian, "Mrs. Fisk gave a mother's unstinted love and devotion, and in his mature years he repaid it with a devotion as strong." In 1843, when he was eight, she had her own child, Mary Grace, whom Jim adored.

While he was remarkable in filial attachment, without a mean bone in his body, he was a problem at school—good only at arithmetic, execrable in spelling, grammar and general deportment. At twelve he quit or was ousted from school and began accompanying his father on peddling trips. He charmed rustics with a ready spiel and an endless stock of jokes. When a woman customer complained that his father had deceived her as to the value of a twelve-and-one-half cent piece of calico, he had an answer.

"Well, now," he said, "I don't think father would tell a lie for twelve and one-half cents, though he might tell eight of 'em for a dollar."

In 1849 Pop Fisk, an abstainer, showed a gambling streak by building a temperance hotel, the Revere House, on Main and Elliot Streets in Brattleboro, thereby saddling himself with an oppressive mortgage. Continuing his peddling, he hired a manager to run the hostelry, where young Jim often waited on table and regaled the guests with witticisms. "Jim was fond of reading the few papers that reached the village," relates a biographer, "and as his memory was good he always mastered their contents and could entertain a select company of travelers with an unfailing stream of news-items from all parts of the world, seasoned and spiced with his quaint comments."

A born salesman and innkeeper, he had less taste for the concomitant chores—cleaning the barn, washing dishes. He wanted to see the world. When he was fifteen, Van Amberg's Mammoth Circus and Menagerie played at Brattleboro, and when Van Amberg left town, so did Jim Fisk. For two or three years—the records are vague—he traveled with the show, helping tend the animals, doing roustabout work and eventually rising to ticket collector on tours reaching as far west as Illinois. Gaudy by nature, he enjoyed the blare and bunting as well as the hokum of circus life. A willing twig, he was bent into permanent peculiarity by this road-show interlude so that ever afterward he seemed to regard the whole world as a circus, with all the people in it merely clowns, and Jim Fisk the biggest clown of all. While nothing on earth could have shaped him into conventional lines, it would seem that Van Amberg must share responsibility for the fashioning of one of the nation's most awe-inspiring eccentrics.

About eighteen when he quit the circus and returned home, Fisk was a genial, stocky young man who favored blinding checked suits and bristled with get-up. Right away he rejoined Pop on the peddling route, and right away he let Pop know he was conducting his enterprise with a lamentable lack of acumen. His horses were spavined. His wagon, which had not been painted for years, could easily be mistaken for a manure hauler. The thing to do, Jim urged, was to spruce up the rig, make it visible from afar, a thing to excite admiration and promote sales. Besides, to his way of thinking the old man was too content with covering his same old route within spitting distance of Brattleboro when he could easily add a couple of wagons, cover more towns, sell more goods and make higher profits. And why should he dress in farmers' overalls, giving people the impression that he was an ordinary tin peddler, when he could as well wear store clothes and uphold his dignity as a merchant of the road?

Being an amiable man, Fisk *père* did not clout his son, who offered these suggestions and many others with the best of humor. Pop allowed that he had been in business quite a spell, knew a thing or two about it, and considered the idea of primping a peddler's cart not worth a second thought. Jim proved his point by buying his own wagon, painting it red with yellow wheels, installing a bright yellow umbrella over the spring seat, donning top hat and striped coat and striking out on a route of his own. He so quickly outstripped his father in sales that the omen was plain to read. Pop Fisk bowed to progress and painted *his* wagon the same way. Business boomed so that they added a third wagon.

Simultaneously Jim was courting Lucy Moore, a winsome, dark-haired girl a shade taller than he, who had come from Springfield, Massachusetts, to attend the Brattleboro Female Seminary. An orphan who was reared by an uncle, Lucy fell prey to the lively Fisk sales pitch. In 1854, when he was nineteen and she only a month over fifteen, they were married—a union that did not unite but was fated to set some sort of record in continuous yet amicable separation. During the eighteen years of their marriage, Lucy would see her husband only occasionally, becoming in fact a spinster with benefit of clergy. Fisk showered her with gifts and there seems no doubt that he loved her tenderly, though not exclusively.

While the bride settled in Brattleboro, the groom was coining money on the road and spending it at country taverns where rustics hailed him with glee as a fellow who could make things crackle. His humor was so benign and free from malice that it filled any room with warmth. He delighted in telling jokes on himself, heaping ridicule on his own ineptitude until listeners were in stitches. His father, worried about the hotel, sold him his interest in the peddling business and retired to run the Revere House. Folks in Brattleboro, who always considered Jim likeable but loony, predicted his early failure. On the contrary, Pop Fisk's harebrained boy combined shrewd management with medicine-show display to create markets for goods thrifty Yankees had got along without before. By 1856 he had five wagons on the road, each sporting the circus paint scheme, each drawn by four spirited horses with polished harness, spreading new tinware, yard goods, jews-harps and jewelry over southern Vermont and New Hampshire and northern Massachusetts. In the circus tradition, he had placards printed announcing the date of arrival of a Fisk wagon at all towns on the route—cause for excitement in any backwater village. He made frequent overnight buying trips to Boston. He originated an "Annual Spring Exhibit of Fisk's Peddlers," parading his decorated wagons down Main Street to the tune of the Brattleboro Cornet Band. Jim Fisk, it was said, would rather listen to a band than eat, especially if it was playing for Jim Fisk.

What with his racetrack attire and endless japery, the buffoon in him was so visible that even men who thought they knew him well were unaware of the driving efficiency underneath. His four hired salesmen were not unaware of it. They had been coached in the Fisk method of merchandising: If you can't sell them silks, sell them calico, or a frying pan, or a thimble—but *sell.* He reserved the main highways for himself, sending the others on branch roads as skirmishers. The five wagons would separate for a week, each man on his own, to meet at a pre-selected railhead where Fisk took inventory, made each driver account for every penny, and had replenishments ready. The boss was a taskmaster with a long memory for detail, a rapid-calculating brain, warm approval for good work and little patience for failure.

As time went on he branched out as a jobber, obtaining much of his goods from the large Boston house of Jordan, Marsh & Company, selling direct to small-town retailers. "He always drove in a dashing style at the rate of ten miles an hour," one historian commented, "and never failed to attract everybody's attention." Although he was a canny bargainer, he never sold wooden nutmegs or cheated anyone. The Fisk enterprise became a back-country institution, the flashy young proprietor being known as the Prince of Peddlers, "always jocose, scattering pennies and candy among the children, bewitching smiles among the sweetsixteens, and consternation among their mammas." His steady increase in sales made such an impression on Eben Jordan, president of Jordan, Marsh, that in mid-1860 Jordan offered him a job as a salesman in Boston.

Ever stirred by restless ambition, Fisk snatched the opportunity after only a show of deliberation. Since he could not possibly supervise more than five wagons, his peddling enterprise had reached its limit of expansion—a limit that never in his life would he believe he personally had reached. Expansion was as necessary to him as breathing. Selling his business to a promoter from Troy, he moved with Lucy to Boston, taking with him a reputation for honesty that would never be the same again. In later years, he came to look back on his peddling career with a nostalgia similar to that of the fallen woman recalling her innocent youth.

"Happy!" he said long afterward. "By George, them was the happiest days of my life! I had everything I hankered after, money, friends, stock, trade, credit, and the best horses in New England. Besides, by God, I had a reputation. There wasn't no man that could throw dirt onto Jim Fisk."

Taking rooms at the fashionable Tremont House, the Fisk couple lived together as Mr. and Mrs. for some six months—the longest period of conventional connubiality Lucy would ever know. Strangely, the man who had pried open the wallets of frugal Yankees was a failure as a wholesale salesman. The glittering ringmaster of a merchandising circus had become a mere drummer among other drummers, a center-ring performer suddenly deprived of the spotlight, wheedling retailers who had no proper understanding of his importance. The congenital show-off was thrust into unhappy anonymity. "Unless nature has borned you with a dry-goods mark onto your back," he later said with scorn, "don't be a salesman."

Jordan told him kindly he had better go back to peddling. Fisk, who would have preferred slow torture to returning to the home folks in defeat, did some fast talking to avert this humiliation. Unlike Jordan and most other Bostonians, he sensed that the South would not swallow Lincoln, that a war was coming. In the merits of the North-South quarrel he took little interest, but it struck him that whatever they were fighting about would open vast new merchandising opportunities. When Sumter fell and the war did come, he persuaded Jordan to send him to Washington to see if the government might be interested in textiles. Lucy remained in Boston while Fisk took the best suite at Willard's Hotel, installed a bar and buffet and invited Congressmen and generals to enjoy the hospitality of Jordan, Marsh & Company.

No one could entertain with the rollicking bonhomie of James Fisk Jr., one of the first of the war profiteers. Jordan, Marsh had several thousand blankets which, though serviceable, were of unappetizing color and somewhat mildewed. Retailers spurned them, but Uncle Sam snapped them up. Fisk began telegraphing orders for woollens, cottons, uniforms, socks, underwear and other items that had Jordan goggle-eyed. The mill expanded, hired more help, but still it could not keep up. *Buy more mills*, Fisk wired. Jordan bought more mills, to find new orders swamping him. Fisk was living up $1000 a day in the capital and consummating deals in the hundreds of thousands. "It has always been shrewdly guessed," one observer commented, "that he paid liberally for the favors granted him, knowing that the profits on the transactions would be immense." Learning that a mill in Gaysville, Vermont, was the only producer of a type of needed textiles, he bought the mill for Jordan, Marsh and secured a monopoly—his first corner. Perfectly aware of his importance to the firm, he let Jordan know that he would be pleased to become a partner. Jordan complied instanter. Fisk got jobs with the firm for dozens of Brattleboro friends. His success in wangling government contracts was due only in part to his free-handed entertaining, for quartermasters found him a work-horse—efficient, conscientious, a get-it-done man who would have 10,000 shirts ready on the day they were promised, shirts that would not melt in rain. "The man that will take the upper hand of a soldier in the field, is worse than a thief," he said with virtuous scorn for contractors who sold shoddy.

In 1862, with cotton rotting in Southern warehouses and hard to come by in the North even at two dollars a pound, he set about to remedy the imbalance. While getting cotton out of the South involved trading with the enemy, violating the blockade, smuggling and possibly other illegalities, he justified it on the ground of patriotism, reasoning that it was ridiculous that soldiers should be deprived of essential clothing—and merchants of profit—because of a mere technicality. The details of this bootleg operation, with its attendant stratagems and bribes, remain dim, for he said little about it after the war. It is known that he continued it on an immense scale for two years. Already well liked by Washington officialdom, he threw glamour into the breach by hiring an adventurous actress named Lottie Hough to wheedle passes through the Union lines. Whether Miss Hough's methods were strictly proper is not known, but her success was so complete that she retired with a fortune after the war.

Fisk had a platoon of agents risking their skins to buy cotton for him in Tennessee and Louisiana, one of them his own father, who was admirably trained for the job by years of Yankee bargaining. The senior Fisk headed a buying group in Tennessee until the heat proved too much for him. He suffered a sunstroke and had to be sent home to Brattleboro on a litter with icepacks on his head. Although he recovered physical health, his mind was affected, and he spent much of the rest of his life in a Brattleboro asylum, a plaintive lunatic attended by two nurses hired by his son. Fisk himself, never lacking in courage if there was money in it, made several buying trips into the Dixie No Man's Land, once narrowly escaping capture by a Confederate patrol. He was sending cotton north by the boatload, cargoes of fabulous value that kept the spindles whirring at Jordan, Marsh, now the nation's biggest enterprise of its kind. One of his biographers solemnly avers that his purchases of contraband cotton reached peaks as high as $800,000 a day.

Fisk was indeed useful to Jordan, Marsh, but by 1864, with the war's end in sight, government buying tapered off. Possibly the Green Mountain boy would have stayed on had he not persisted in giving the impression, to Jordan as well as everybody else, that he and not Jordan was running the show. While they were still good friends, and remained so until Fisk's violent death, Jordan saw that one or the other would have to go. He bought out the younger man's interest for $65,000, and Fisk was a free agent again.

Always a big spender, he had seen enough of frenzied wartime finance to develop contempt for a thousand-dollar bill. His taste for diamonds, waffle-weave suits and boned turkey had grown, as had his girth. Nowhere along the line had he felt any itch to shoulder a musket and help save the Union. The war was fought by enthusiastic volunteers and reluctant draftees, and he fell in neither category, possibly being one of those who bought his way out. The feeling of common responsibility to win victory was far from universal, so that his non-participation implied a lack of national zeal, an unwillingness to trade beans in the ranks for luxury and champagne, rather than cowardice, which was not among his weaknesses. Now twenty-nine, soft but enormously vital and healthy, he seemed to feel he had made an adequate contribution to the war effort by furnishing clothing to the troops and by supervising a great Boston rally that sent food and bandages to the survivors at Antietam. Since his lifelong aim was to win fame and attention, he might have taken a flyer in soldiering if he could have done so with suitable panoply—say, as a general. Anything less was not for him. Other young men were doing the fighting around Richmond when Fisk opened his own textile jobbing house on Sumner Street in Boston, found business poor and closed up in a few months.

This was Lucy's second experience with conventional married life—namely, having a husband who lived in and could be seen and spoken to. It was to be her last of any duration, for late in 1864 Fisk was off to New York. With his sublime self-confidence, his innate love of gambling and his experience at swinging heavy deals in Washington, he had no doubt that he could crack Wall Street like a nut.

Opening gaudy brokerage offices on Broad Street, he followed his usual routine of holding open house and treating fellow speculators to choice liquors. Possibly he was too breezy in his talk of bending the stock market to his will, for it seems that some of his listeners felt an impulse to ambush him if occasion offered. This was one of the few times when his confidence outrode his ability. He was ignorant of the pitfalls of speculation, a lamb fraternizing with wolves. It is written that "He launched out boldly and almost haphazardly in all the leading stocks." Caught napping in a sudden bear movement, by winter's end he was all but fleeced.

Having fought the war with telegrams, he saw an opportunity to recoup his losses by capitalizing in a similar way on victory. Confederate bonds had fallen on the London exchange with Southern losses but were still selling at some eighty cents on the dollar. Grant now had Richmond in a vise. Victory seemed certain, and when the Confederacy met defeat her bonds would plummet in value. Not yet was there an Atlantic cable, so it would take more than a week for news of the war's end to reach England by fast steamship. If anyone could get to London *before* the news, he could sell Confederate bonds short like mad at eighty cents on the dollar and reap a harvest when they sank. Fisk resolved to get there first.

Forming a pool with three capitalists, he furnished the scheme while they supplied the money. Chartering a fast steamer, he sent it to Halifax, the nearest North American port to England, with orders to keep up steam for instant departure. Aboard the ship was his agent, a knowing New York broker named Hargreaves, who had instructions to speed to England when given the signal. One obstacle was the telegraph, which then fell fifty miles short of reaching Halifax. Fisk had the last fifty miles strung at his colleagues' expense, then watched Richmond with a cold, profiteering eye.

On the historic day when Lee surrendered, the word sped over the wires to Hargreaves: "Go!" Hargreaves went. He reached Liverpool in six days and a half—two days ahead of the arrival of the first ship from New York with the news. Speeding to London, he kept mum about defeat and dutifully sold Confederate bonds short to all buyers. Alas!— one of Fisk's partners, a conservative man, had privately telegraphed Hargreaves at Halifax not to sell more than five millions in bonds, so he limited his sales to that amount. When news of the surrender reached London, the bonds tumbled to $22. Hargreaves therefore collected the difference between $22 and $80, making a handsome profit for his employers but missing the downright killing that would have been possible.

Fisk, whose intention was to follow the London market clear down to zero, ever afterward lamented the timorousness he felt had deprived him of millions. He took his winnings, entered the Wall Street lists with more boldness than discretion, and quickly lost every penny. Money *per se* meant little to him, but humiliation and defeat were galling. As he closed up shop and borrowed cash to get back to Boston, he let it be known that his retreat was only temporary.

"I'll be back in Wall Street inside of twenty days," he said, "and if I don't make things squirm I'll eat nothing but bone button soup till Judgment Day."

3 *The Scarlet Woman of Wall Street*

So SOCIABLE that he would talk to himself if no one else was handy, Fisk struck up a conversation with a dejected-looking man aboard the Boston-bound train. The man turned out to be John Goulding, inventor of an improved device for the weaving of textiles whose value no one seemed to comprehend but he. Immediately interested, Fisk scanned Goulding's drawings, listened while the inventor described the advantages of his idea, and became convinced that its possibilities were enormous. In Boston he borrowed money to buy out Goulding's patent—a purchase that would involve him in lawsuits for seven years but nevertheless would bring in a fortune on its own account.

He also borrowed money from Eben Jordan and others to make a new start in Wall Street. Unlike many spendthrifts, he had always paid his bills, building a credit rating so solid that no one seemed to regard him as a risk. Although he was known as a likeable, high-powered freak, his personal reputation was undamaged, for, to quote one biographer, "his contempt for the most cardinal laws of decent social life had not then been openly manifested." He spent less than a month in Boston this time, so involved with the patent, the loans, a side trip to Brattleboro and in laying the groundwork for his counter-attack against Wall Street that Lucy probably saw little of him. Alert to all financial scuttlebutt, he learned that a group of Boston capitalists were anxious to buy the Stonington line of steamers, a fleet of nine vessels owned by Daniel Drew of New York that plied Long Island Sound between New York and Stonington, Connecticut, connecting there with the railroad to Boston. He matched this with a rumor he had heard in New York—that Drew wanted to sell if he could get a fair price —and smelled a deal in the offing, with himself as middleman.

Returning to New York late in 1865, Fisk put up at the expensive Fifth Avenue Hotel, a hostelry favored by financial moguls, and called on Daniel Drew. Drew was sixty-eight, tall, spare, illiterate, shaggy-browed and black-haired despite his years, the possessor of an expression of near-sighted venerability that concealed a killer instinct. A Wall Street original never duplicated, he was a multimillionaire gambler notorious for his willingness to break a promise or betray a friend if he could profit thereby. After a colorful career as menagerie flunky, drover, innkeeper and loan shark, he had emerged as a steamboat magnate, expanded to become the presiding desecrator of the Erie Railway, and found his true genius in gouging the stock market, leaving windrows of ruined speculators in his wake. Stooped, shabby, he lived in a mansion on Union Square, attended church faithfully, carried the stripped shaft of an old umbrella as a cane, and abused grammar whenever he opened his mouth. "I was wonderfully blessed in money-making," he later said. "I got to be a millionaire afore I know'd it, hardly." Now he was laying secret plans for another stock coup that would take extra capital—hence his desire to sell the Stonington line, which was unprofitable anyway.

Here Fisk struck a piece of luck. It happened that Drew had been born and raised at Carmel, New York, a vicinity used by a number of circuses as winter quarters. As a young man he worked for Howe's circus and later knew Isaac Van Amberg, with whose show Fisk had traveled. Drew, who loved to reminisce about his circus days, was delighted to find a man who knew the smell of tanbark and the pitchman's lingo. He was further pleased when Fisk managed to sell his nine steamers to the Boston syndicate for \$2,300,-000. Fisk wound up with a fat commission and, what was more important, the temporary blessing of the most powerful and unscrupulous operator in Wall Street.

Drew knew a shrewd fellow when he saw one. In his speculative machinations he could use another friendly broker. Shortly thereafter, Fisk joined forces with William Belden, son of an old friend of Drew's, and opened the brokerage offices of Fisk & Belden. Formerly an outsider in the Street, he was now an insider, an ally of Drew, which meant entrée into the councils of Erie. With Fisk and Drew aboard, Erie was steaming up for a wild ride to places no respectable railroad ever went before.

For more than a decade Drew had been a director of Erie, never once regarding it as an instrument of transportation with a responsibility toward the public and its stockholders. In his view Erie, which he called "Airy," was simply a financial fig tree to be shaken regularly so that its fruit fell into the waiting Drew baskets. One of the first of the robber barons—a breed rapidly becoming numerous —he had of late years been treasurer and acknowledged dictator of the road, subjecting it to awful abuse. Its schedules were fictional, its rolling stock ruinous, its iron rails so worn and chipped as to invite derailment. It was Drew's habit to issue new capital stock "to install steel rails," then use the stock for speculative profit and let the rails go hang. Steel rails were expensive. He instructed his general superintendent to turn the old iron rails so that their chipped edges were outside, the less eroded edges inside to present some show of resistance to wheel flanges. Erie engineers complained that they were obliged to travel over two thin streaks of rust.

If it was dangerous to ride Drew's railroad, it was as risky to joust with him in stocks. Known as Uncle Daniel or The Deacon, he was such a confirmed bear operator that he was also called The Great Bear, Ursus Major, The Speculative Director, and many unprintable appellations. His soul, it was said, bore the exact shape of a dollar sign. A psalm-singer every Sunday, he put aside all mercy the rest of the week. He had given the Methodist Church $250,000 to found the Drew Theological Seminary in New Jersey, not to soothe his conscience, critics said, since he had none, but to ingratiate himself with certain wealthy religious people whom he could use in his speculations. Fisk knew precisely the character of his elderly playfellow. Treacherous or not, Uncle Daniel was a power in the Street, a man with good coat-tails to cling to until Fisk could develop his own momentum. He took a good hold and clung.

Early in 1866, Drew staged his coup. Erie as usual needed money, so he loaned his own road $3,500,000, taking as collateral 58,000 shares of Erie stock. Unknown to out-siders, he now had a huge block of shares for use as ammunition in manipulating the market. Using Fisk as one of his brokers, he promptly launched a bear raid, dumping his shares and selling Erie short with such telling effect that its price plummeted from 80 to 55½ while unfortunate bulls caught in the squeeze roared in agony. Ursus Major then bought back at low prices the stocks he had sold high, milking the Street for a fortune in the process. He was delighted that one of the heaviest losers was crusty Commodore Cornelius Vanderbilt, who had stung him for nearly a million in a similar ambush in 1863.

Fisk rode the Drew coat-tails merrily, making a handsome profit in broker's fees and a far bigger one in "inside" speculation of his own. Erie, already known as the Scarlet Woman of Wall Street, found its reputation more lurid than ever. While Vanderbilt pondered revenge, there was a loud newspaper outcry against Drew that bothered the old sinner not a whit, since the stock market at the time was an unregulated financial jungle ruled by the sharpest tooth and claw.

The Vermont lamb who had been clipped clean only a year earlier was learning the tricks fast. At the same time he was displaying an uninhibited eccentricity of behavior that startled, annoyed or amused his sedate fellow speculators. To the stiff-collared gentry he was like a man who, looking for a saloon, had stumbled into church instead without discovering his error. Among the conservative financial tribe he stood out like a racetrack tout, his clothing vivid, his fingers flashing with rings, a huge diamond centered in his shirtfront. He was genial, uproarious, dripping with a patter of jokes good and bad, belching cigar smoke through brushy red mustaches. To watch Fisk in action was to develop an impression of being a spectator munching peanuts inside a tent. W. W. Fowler, a literate broker of the day, put this impression into words:

"The blonde, bustling and rollicking James Fisk, Jr. . . . came bounding into the Wall Street circus like a star-acrobat, fresh, exuberant, glittering with spangles, and turning double-summersets, apparently as much for his own amusement as for that of a large circle of spectators. He is first, last and always a man of theatrical effects, of grand transformations, and blue fire."

Another broker who watched the Fisk antics with some wonder was a slight, intense-eyed, black-bearded man named Jay Gould. Gould had no blue fire at all, although a childhood of grinding poverty on the far side of the Catskills had made him burn with one inner determination: to get rich. Frail, quiet, shy, he had just turned thirty, a year younger than Fisk. As a boy he had written an essay titled "Honesty is the Best Policy," an admirable effort he soon forgot. He had invented an efficient mousetrap, worked as a surveyor, then entered the tannery business in Pennsylvania with a wealthy merchant named Charles Leupp. He speculated so heavily with his partner's money that when Leupp found out about it he feared he was ruined and shot himself dead. Coming to New York in 1859, Gould married the daughter of a well-heeled grocer and discovered a fine source of quick gain—railroads. Aided by his father-in-law's capital, he bought cheap control of several rusting short lines, worked hard to give them an appearance of solvency, then sold them at a profit. Like Fisk, he had been deaf to the call to arms, spending the war years comfortably in Broad Street as a member of the brokerage firm of Smith, Gould & Martin.

Otherwise faithful to his wife, Gould was now entering into a liaison with the Scarlet Woman. Like Fisk, he was trading briskly in Erie shares, seeking full entry into the boudoir where Daniel Drew was practically a fixture.

In 1867 this got to be dangerous sport because several others were courting the hussy, topmost among them Commodore Vanderbilt. When the burly Commodore headed somewhere, most men had sense enough to get out of the way. The former circus helper and the one-time mousetrap inventor seemed lacking in this elemental sense of self-preservation. They had an idea that they could lick Vanderbilt and lick Drew too.

4

The Gentle
Double-Cross

Cornelius, the great Cornerer,
A solemn oath he swore,
That in his trousers pocket he
Would put one railroad more.
And when he swears he means it,
The stout old Commodore.

By 1867, Drew's young man Fisk was said to be a million-aire. Whether this was true or not, he acted like one. He owned a sizeable block of Erie stock, sported a gold-headed cane, became a regular at Delmonico's and bought his wife a $75,000, four-story mansion at 74 Chester Square in Boston so that she could be comfortable though solitary. By this time he had not only entrenched himself in New York but had so fallen in love with the metropolis that it was clear he would stay there. Lucy's continued residence in Boston constituted an odd marital arrangement that caused comment. It was said that she liked Boston and had such an aversion for New York that the separation was her own choice. It is also possible that Lucy, being of a retiring disposition, decided that daily life with the rumbustical Fisk would be more than her nerves could stand and preferred distant harmony to connubial chaos. Intelligible though this decision was, it placed on her some responsibility for the stupendous folly into which her footloose spouse would plunge. In Boston Lucy had an inseparable companion in Fanny Harrod, a childhood friend, while in New York Fisk was busy turning double-summersets and contemplating battle with some formidable adversaries, all of them with designs on Erie no more honorable than his own.

That unfortunate road was one of the biggest of the day. It had 773 miles of broad-gauge track, its 459-mile main line starting at Jersey City, across the Hudson from Manhattan, to wind northeastward along Pennsylvania's corner boundary, swinging westward near Binghamton and traversing upstate New York's southern tier of counties to end at terminals in Buffalo and Dunkirk. Its 371 locomotives hauled more than two million passengers a year and almost three and a half million tons of freight in operations that employed more than 7000 people. The road even had a folklore, one of its items being the heroism of Mrs. Silas Horton, who lived beside the main line in Owego. Seeing a great tree fallen across the track, Mrs. Horton in 1854 sacrificed modesty in favor of humanity, stepped out of her red flannel drawers and waved them to flag down a speeding express, saving it from certain disaster—a feat for which she was awarded a lifelong free pass.

This kind of selfless devotion was unknown among the road's directors. The Erie was a misused giant, and no one knew it better than Commodore Vanderbilt. More to the point, Erie had become his direct competitor. Vanderbilt had recently gained control of the New York Central line, running between Albany and Buffalo. Since he already controlled the Hudson River and Harlem lines, both of them connecting New York with Albany, he was now a New York-to-Buffalo railroader just like Erie, with hopes of grabbing more lines reaching to Chicago. Being a man who liked to set his rates as high as the traffic would bear, he had an aversion for competition. He resolved to swallow Erie, and at the same time settle accounts with his old enemy, Daniel Drew.

"I use the Harlem Road just as though it all belonged to me," he once told a friend, "and that is the way I shall control every other road as long as I control any, as though it all belonged to me."

White-haired at seventy-two, Vanderbilt carried his tall frame as erect as if he were thirty years younger. He was profane, efficient, ruthless in a direct and honest way, a man with a habit of kicking all obstacles aside. Heroically self-made, he had been fighting competitors ever since boyhood when he operated a small ferry from his native Staten Island, winning success in driblets, buying more vessels until he became the biggest of the steamship moguls. Of late years he had moved in on railroads with the same relentless power. Unlike Drew, he would buy steel rails and make the customers pay for them. He could not spell to save his neck, but he was one of the three richest men in the country with something like thirty millions, and he could write a check on a piece of butcher's paper which any knowing banker would honor. He once tried to cheat his son William in a contract for hauling manure to Staten Island, just to teach the young man a business lesson. Later, when his wife Sofia protested nervously against moving to a mansion on Washington Place, he had her committed to an asylum for several months to eliminate her objections. He had known Daniel Drew for a quarter-century, since the time when both were in the Hudson River steamboat business, and the two men occasionally played whist together despite the Deacon's pious protests at Vanderbilt's swearing. Now Drew was in the way, and Vanderbilt was out to crush him.

As the 1867 election for the Erie board of directors approached, there were three parties jockeying for control of the road, each of them owning large blocks of stock but none of them alone possessing enough to assure a voting majority.

The first was headed by Drew, who had looted the road for years and had a clique of shareholding directors on his side in addition to the support of a character new to railroad combat—James Fisk Jr.

The second was led by Vanderbilt, an Erie director for seven years whose millions made him a potent contender.

The third was a group of Boston speculators steered by John S. Eldridge and including Fisk's old friend Eben Jordan, who already controlled the unfinished and debt-ridden Boston, Hartford & Erie Railroad. The B., H. & E. had been completed from Boston to Hartford, with fine maps to show how it would push westward to Fishkill Landing, New York, where it would make connections via ferry across the Hudson with an Erie branch at Newburgh. This connection was entirely a paper myth of the future, never to be realized. The B., H. & E. was in corporate nightmare, gasping under ten mortgages it could never pay without manna from somewhere. The Boston capitalists had come up with a solution to their dilemma typical of the foxy financing of the time. They aimed to gain control of Erie, then let Erie assume the debt in the dubious expectation that the B., H. & E. would give Erie a gateway to New England and a thriving business with Yankeeland when, and if, it was finished. In the beginning, Jay Gould was cooperating with the Boston group. However, the lines of battle were anything but clearly drawn, since many of the skirmishers were glancing uneasily over their shoulders, ready to jump to another side if they found it to their advantage.

In this fluid struggle for power, any two of the contending parties could combine to slaughter the third. Uncle Daniel, for a wonder, was caught napping. Behind his back, Vanderbilt conferred with Eldridge and his Boston cronies and formed a coalition with them aimed at kicking Drew clear out of Erie. The agreement between them was perfected in detail, the Boston sharpshooters insisting on ousting the malodorous Drew as a move which in itself would lift much of the stigma from Erie's soiled reputation. A slate of directors was drawn up, omitting Drew and including Vanderbilt and Boston representatives.

When the Great Bear learned of this, he was in panic at

the thought of losing his chief source of plunder. Although he never extended mercy to others, he was not too proud to beg for it himself when in travail. On the Sunday before the Erie election, Drew called at Vanderbilt's Washington Place home, asked him plaintively how he could be so hard on an old colleague and pointed out how profitably the two of them could work together.

Drew could be persuasive when money was at stake. Vanderbilt, at first contemptuous, listened to the old buccaneer's representations and began to alter his Erie scheme. It struck him that it might be more advantageous to have Drew on his side as a lieutenant than on the outside as a sworn enemy, for with his large Erie holdings and his known speculative trickery he could cause trouble. In the end, Vanderbilt made one of his rare errors in judgment. He agreed to let Drew stay on the board if he would stop his infernal bear raids and join the Commodore in a bullish movement of the market. To this Uncle Daniel readily assented. Vanderbilt knew that a Drew promise was worthless, but he felt he had his rival in his power and could make use of him.

When news of this reached Eldridge and his Boston mates, they were outraged. Vanderbilt had abrogated his bargain with them and was playing railroad whist with Drew, whom he had pledged to scuttle. They called on Vanderbilt to protest, and he joined them in a visit to Drew's Fourteenth Street residence, where the talk and the cigar smoke grew thicker as the night wore on. Things reached such a state that Vanderbilt and Drew got to hinting how they could freeze out the Bostonians entirely if they did not come to time. Eldridge and his partners surrendered. The three parties drew up an agreement whereby all of them would have a hand in Erie, although the Commodore fondly believed that *his* hand would be uppermost. However, since the Bostonians had been howling for Drew's scalp and had let it be known that he would be ejected, a bit of fakery was hit on to save them face. The slate of directors already framed, free from the Drew contamination, would be elected. Then one of them, a Vanderbilt man named Levi Underwood, would resign, whereupon Drew would be elected in his place.

This little hoax was enacted according to script when the election was held at the Erie offices at West and Chambers Streets on October 8, 1867. Underwood remained a straw-man director for two hours, when he dutifully withdrew because of "pressing obligations" and Drew was named for the vacancy. Erie stock rose at the news that Uncle Daniel was ousted, only to slump again when it was learned that he had wormed his way back in via the trapdoor. There was a fluctuation of 3½ percent in the stock quotations during the day, in which the connivers in the deal made fine speculative profits both on the rise and the fall. John Eldridge was made president, an office which in his hands would mean little, and Erie assumed the debts of the B., H. & E., while Drew was again named to his old post as treasurer.

"The Erie election yesterday turned out to have been something very like a farce," snapped the *Herald*, not at all deceived; ". . . the new board of directors . . .is positively worse than the old one."

By this the *Herald* meant no direct insult to two of the seventeen new directors, James Fisk Jr. and Jay Gould. In fact, this pair were so little known in railroad circles that the papers referred to Gould simply as "J. Gould," while Fisk was named as "Fiske" and even "Fish"—an obscurity that would not cloud them for long. Vanderbilt himself was not a member of the new board, being satisfied to boss it from without. His nephew and broker, Frank Work, was a director, but Work was merely padding, for the Commodore felt he had the other two factions headed by Drew and Eldridge securely under his thumb.

In this smug view he failed to take into account the capacity for intrigue of the Messrs. Drew and Eldridge, neither of whom was content to dance to the Vanderbilt tune.

Uncle Daniel, who had seen all along that if he could join forces with the Boston crowd he could freeze out Vanderbilt and once more run the Erie show, was busily buttering up Eldridge. Eldridge, still incensed at being euchred by Vanderbilt in the pre-election wirepulling, began to see useful qualities in the old gambler he had so righteously denounced. Within a few weeks the two were all but holding hands.

The Commodore did not discover this until midwinter, when strange things began to happen to Erie stock on the market. According to the agreement, Drew was to combine with him in bulling Erie shares and taking profits on the rise. Frank Work and another Vanderbilt lieutenant, Richard Schell, enthusiastically joined in a stock-buying pool with Drew aimed at kiting the price for their mutual advantage. Work and Schell soon were puzzled because the Erie quotation showed no sustained advance. The price would rise a few points, then sag again in a most annoying way. When they consulted Drew about this, the old man made out to be innocently perplexed at the fluctuation.

"I never seen sich a queer performance in my life," he said. "But keep on buying, boys, for it's sartain to raise. Don't be skeered."

When another fortnight passed and Erie began to fall instead of rise, Work, Schell and their fellow bulls got the shakes, for their long contracts would soon become due and they stood to lose heavily. Some operator was confounding them by bearing Erie. They began tracing shares they had bought through brokers, and discovered that almost all of them had come from Drew. The Great Bear had been up to his old tricks. He had betrayed the members of his own pool, bearing while they bulled, raking in profits with every rise and fall.

They descended on Drew with imprecations. He coolly told them not to use unchurchly language. To be sure, he had been bearing a mite, but he had done well at it, and he proceeded to split his winnings with his disgruntled partners. While they emerged as gainers, they were smarting at being duped in a hoax that had Wall Street in stitches for days. This was just the sort of hocus-pocus that would appeal to the fun-loving Fisk, who was deep in the Deacon's confidence and undoubtedly profited in the deal.

Vanderbilt was not amused. Yet he went ahead with a program indicating his belief that he was running the Erie board. Early in 1869 he raised the New York Central freight rates to Rochester, Syracuse and other cities where Erie competed, asking Erie to do likewise. At the same time he joined the Pennsylvania Railroad in a baldly monopolistic proposal that the three roads refrain from rate-cutting, gouge shippers to the utmost and pool their earnings from the New York City traffic, each road taking one-third.

The Commodore, who could swear magnificently even when discussing the weather, must have loosed sulphurous oaths when the Erie directors he thought a parcel of obedient clerks considered these proposals and *turned them down*. The rascally Drew, whom he had saved from expulsion, had cheated him. What was worse, Drew now had a majority of the directors on his side, having convinced them that if it came to battle he had the heaviest guns.

The Commodore declared war. He set out to take over Erie, to crush Drew, Fisk, Gould, Eldridge and all the rest of the traitors, as Charles Francis Adams later phrased it, "with the brute force of his millions."

5 *Who's Your Judge?*

EVER prone to live as if he were racing the clock, Fisk did not seem to regard his involvement with such contestants as Vanderbilt and Drew as a full-time job. Not long after he became a director of Erie, he acquired a new responsibility in Helen Josephine Mansfield, a woman one historian later dismissed with a line of crushing finality: "Perhaps a colder disgrace to her sex has never helped to ruin man since the world began."

Born in Boston *circa* 1840-42, the daughter of a newspaperman, convent-educated Josie moved with her family in 1852 to Stockton, California, where her father soon was killed in a duel arising from a political quarrel. At an early age she discovered there was something about her the boys liked. Described as "an incorrigible flirt," she was taken by her mother to San Francisco, where the widow Mansfield married a man named Warren. It was here that Josie caught the eye of a wealthy, middle-aged attorney named D. W. Perley, whose attentions to the young beauty precipitated a scandal about which the accounts of the time are delicately vague. It was said that Perley pursued her with such ardor that her stepfather Warren "on two occasions pointed a loaded pistol to his head, and forced him to take to his heels —once with very little clothing upon him."

Josie herself claimed that she was being used by her mother and stepfather as an innocent pawn in a blackmail plot. While her word was not invariably trustworthy, there is some evidence that her parents were indeed employing her as bait in squeezing hush-money out of the lecherous Perley.

She became acquainted with a strolling actor named Frank Lawlor who was playing at the San Francisco opera house at the time. As Lawlor later described it, she proposed that he marry her and rescue her from her stepfather, who was bent on ruining her reputation. "Finally I did marry her to save her from the evil influences of her own parents," he said.

In the young lady's defense it could be pointed out that her home life was less than inspirational and that she had wed an impecunious actor even though her beauty was so overpowering that, to quote Lawlor, "she might have married almost whom she pleased in San Francisco."

The young couple drifted east, living for a time in Washington and Philadelphia before going to New York in 1864. Lawlor described her as a virtuous wife for some two years, when, he said, "I found that she was going astray," whereupon they were divorced and Josie resumed her maiden name of Mansfield. Possibly she began to stray even before she met a former actress named Annie Wood, who lived on Thirty-fourth Street. While the newspapers of the day were squeamish about references to prostitution, they made no bones about referring to Miss Wood as "the notorious Annie Wood," and the inference is clear that her establishment was a fairly exclusive bordello. Josie's penniless condition at the time seems proof that she was not one of the attractions at this palace of pleasure. Yet her intimacy with Miss Wood and the way she employed it suggests that whatever purity still lingered with her she jettisoned in favor of subsistence. Fisk was an occasional caller at the Wood menage, and it seems that Miss Mansfield was present often enough to take notice of the free-spending Vermonter, digest the fact that his wife was in Boston, and conclude that herein lay opportunity.

According to Annie Wood's later account, which Josie denied only in part, Josie had failed to find employment as an actress and was in such poverty that she had only one passable dress to wear and could not pay her rent, which if true indicates a willingness to depart from virtue only on fairly regal terms. She asked Miss Wood to arrange a meeting with Fisk. One night in November of 1867 he arrived at the Wood menage with a few companions, one of them George Butler—a visit that would later prove embarrassing to Butler when he became United States Minister to Egypt. Josie was there, and Miss Wood obligingly introduced her to Fisk. Fisk was so delighted with her, and so moved by her genteel poverty, which to him meant at least an approximation of purity, that he paid her overdue rent at her barren Lexington Avenue flat, installed her in a suite at the American Club Hotel at Broadway and Seventeenth Street, and thenceforth saw that she had plenty to wear. There is no record that Josie thereafter sought work as an actress, an indication that what she had been seeking was security rather than employment. Fisk's friends noticed a significant change in him. His pale red mustache, which had hitherto wandered over both sides of his lip in brushy anarchy, was now narrowed and brought into submission by sharp waxing at the ends.

The Mansfield financial crisis must have seemed small potatoes to him in the winter of 1867-68 when he started to spend millions on another woman of dubious reputation. The war for Erie began officially on February 17, 1868, with Vanderbilt on the attack. The Commodore had no doubt of the power of his millions to defeat the stock-jobbing trickery of Drew, but he was always one for pushing to victory at the cheapest possible price. He had expressed irritated curiosity about Fisk, and on being told that he was a Drew man said, "Then we must kill him off. He's too sharp for a greenhorn and too bold for an old hand. I don't know what to make of him." He had learned that Drew, in addition to other holdings, still had the 58,000 shares of Erie stock he had received as security for his loan in 1866. This would be a weapon in Uncle Daniel's hands, and Vanderbilt resolved to deprive him of it.

The Erie board which Vanderbilt had believed his own property had so sadly defected to Drew that Nephew Frank Work was now the only director the Commodore could count on. He made Work live up to his name. On February 17, Work got an injunction from Supreme Court Judge George Gardner Barnard, sitting in Manhattan, restraining Erie from paying interest or principal on the money borrowed from Drew, and restraining Drew from using the 58,000 shares for speculation. This was followed two days later by an even more sweeping Vanderbilt-inspired injunction from Barnard that forbade Drew to have any transactions in Erie until he had returned to the company the 58,000 shares, forbade Erie to issue any more stock or convertible bonds, and finished by suspending Drew as a director pending a hearing. Since this was a battle for stock control, many outsiders believed that Drew was mortally hit before he even got into the fray—shorn of the stock he had and enjoined from issuing more. Vanderbilt meanwhile was buying Erie stock like mad. Even the *Herald's* financial editor was impressed, writing, "It is believed that he [Drew] is in what is generally called a fix, and that he will be sent to smithereens."

The Great Bear seemed unperturbed. He even saw advantage in a report submitted to the board by Hugh Riddle, general superintendent of Erie, portraying the condition of the road in terms so frightening that riding an Erie train seemed almost as risky a business as going over Niagara in a barrel. It read in part:

> We have passed through three months of unusually severe winter weather . . . with the road-bed frozen solid as a rock, the rails incased in snow and ice, so that it has been impossible to do much in the way of repairs; the iron rails have broken, laminated and worn out beyond all precedent,

until there is scarce a mile of your road . . . between Jersey
City and Salamanca or Buffalo, where it is safe to run a
train at the ordinary passenger-train speed, and many portions of the road can only be traversed safely by reducing
the speed of all trains to twelve or fifteen miles an hour,
solely on account of the rotten and worn-out condition of
the rails. Broken wheels, rails, engines, and trains off the
track, have been of daily, almost hourly, occurrence for the
last two months . . . The condition of the iron at the present
time is such as to give me much anxiety and apprehension
for the safety of trains . . . It has been only by the exercise of extreme caution that we have been able thus far to
escape serious accident.

Here, Drew said piously, was proof that Erie needed new
equipment, especially steel rails. On February 19 he held a
secret meeting of the board, with the traitorous Work excluded. He persuaded the directors to issue $10,000,000 in
convertible bonds on the old pretext—the need for steel
rails to replace shaky iron. Erie had needed steel rails for
years, but precious few had been laid or would be laid while
Drew was in charge. The efficiency or safety of the road
was a trivial consideration with the directors, who knew
that the $10,000,000 would be used not for steel rails but
for fighting Vanderbilt in his bid to seize Erie.

It was at this point that Judge Barnard's second injunction, restraining Erie from issuing new capital stock, fell
on them. Drew went right ahead with his plans, reinforced
by a battery of lawyers headed by the eminent David Dudley Field. Vanderbilt's brokers were buying every share of
Erie offered on the market, and Drew, a bear as always, was
selling. Under the Vanderbilt onslaught the price was rising,
so that the Commodore was paying more for every share
while Drew was profiting heavily on stock he had acquired
for a song. In defiance of court order he was already selling
limited blocks of his 58,000-share kitty. His strategy was to
create more stock and dump it on the market at the critical

moment so that Vanderbilt would be pouring money into a sieve as the price fell and would take terrible losses. Wall Street gazed in awe at this battle of titans, wondering if the Deacon was crazy to pit himself against the vast Vanderbilt resources.

Drew now sent Fisk, Gould and several sharpshooting lawyers up to Binghamton, a strong Erie town, where they appealed to Justice Ransom Balcom for redress. To Balcom, Fisk and Gould represented the Drew party as the defenders of Erie's independence against the monopolistic designs of Vanderbilt, while Frank Work was nothing more than a Vanderbilt spy. Judge Balcom obliged with an order staying all proceedings before Judge Barnard and suspending Work from the Erie board.

Returning triumphantly to New York, Fisk and Gould joined Drew in a stealthy visit to the cellar of the Erie office to meet with their most useful ally, a printing press. Some forty years earlier, when Drew was a drover, he was said to have invented the process of watering stock. Bringing a large herd of cattle into New York, he would feed them salt until their tongues were hanging out with thirst, but deny them water until shortly before they were weighed for sale. The cattle would drink water by the gallon, which buyers paid for as beef. Uncle Daniel had long since adapted this ruse to corporate stock. The press was soon clacking merrily, turning blank paper into Erie convertible bonds which would be worth easily sixty dollars each on the market.

"If this printing press don't break down," Fisk chuckled, "I'll be damned if I don't give the old hog [Vanderbilt] all he wants of Erie."

The press did not break down, turning out $10,000,000 in new bonds without a hitch. Drew immediately converted them into 100,000 shares of Erie stock, negotiable in the market, keeping 50,000 himself and giving the other 50,000 to Fisk, which each of them distributed with great secrecy to their brokers "much as ammunition might be issued before a general engagement," as one historian described it.

Vanderbilt was likewise ready with some paper bullets of his own—more injunctions from the agreeable Judge Barnard, who applied himself to corruption so whole-heartedly as to bring it near brilliance. The judiciary, with some exceptions, was so venal that persons going to the law often "retained" judges much as they hired attorneys, but no judge could equal Barnard in cynical knavery. Laboring for the Vanderbilt cause as diligently as if he had a large financial interest in it—as the Drew party said he did—he fulminated a new order. He set aside the ruling of Judge Balcom, forbade the Erie board to meet without the presence of Frank Work, and once more warned the Drew partisans not to issue any more stock—something they had already done.

". . . it is surprising," the *Herald* remarked, "to see the facility with which judges can be found who will do the things wanted at the proper moment."

This was one result of a new state legal code which was largely the work of the same David Dudley Field, Erie's courtroom generalissimo. By its provisions, thirty-three justices sitting in thirty-three courts scattered over New York had equal jurisdiction in certain equity actions throughout the state. Thus, one judge could nullify an order of another judge, and could in turn find his own order set aside—a spectacle the code's designers had never contemplated. Attorney Field, who deplored this perversion of the law he had helped frame, was quick to resort to the same device. To counter Barnard's latest order, a body of Erie stalwarts marched over to Judge J. W. Gilbert's court in Brooklyn, peppered him with the same argument that Vanderbilt was out to swallow Erie and added a new one: that Judge Barnard himself was speculating in Erie stock on the Commodore's side and therefore was not a truly disinterested arbiter. Judge Gilbert complied with an injunction forbidding Work to act as a director and ordering the Erie board to issue such stock as was felt necessary.

Five contradictory injunctions had now been issued to the two sides. Judge Barnard ordered Erie to *refrain*, while Judge Gilbert ordered Erie to *refrain from refraining*. If the directors issued new stock, they were violating Barnard's injunction. If they failed to issue new stock, they were flouting Gilbert's order. Finding himself in contempt of court regardless of what he did, Drew naturally obeyed the judge who was on his side. Under the steady Vanderbilt buying, Erie shares had risen steadily until on February 29 the quotation was 68 ¾. Feeling that the decisive moment had come, Drew ordered his brokers to dump his newly-printed stock on the market—a flood that washed the price down to 65. The Great Bear beamed. Every point that Erie sank meant the loss of a small fortune to Vanderbilt.

"It'll git to 60 afore long," Drew predicted, "and I'm not afeard to venture that it'll go as low as 55 afore the day's over."

He was wrong. The Stock Exchange was in a turmoil as the new stock poured in, but Vanderbilt's brokers bought it up with such speed that after its momentary slump Erie pushed steadily upward, reaching 73 by the day's end. By March 10 it had risen to 83, and Drew was beginning to sweat. Were Vanderbilt's resources inexhaustible? Opinion on the Street now was general that the Commodore had cornered control of Erie, and friends were pumping his hand.

On that same day Fisk took the field and threw his 50,000 shares on the market. The Vanderbilt brokers, still buying, tumbled to the awful truth when they noted that these new shares were dated only a few days earlier. Drew had violated Barnard's injunction—he had issued more stock. How much more? There was no telling. The price dove to 71, ruining dozens of speculators. A frantic broker hurried to Vanderbilt and asked if he should sell and salvage what he could out of the debacle.

"Sell, you fool!" the Commodore thundered. "No! Buy every share offered!"

He knew that Drew had beaten him by methods as piratical as his own. He would seek legal redress later, but the law could not help him now, when minutes and millions were the only things that counted. Vanderbilt truly had a bear by the tail. He had no choice but to hang on, keep buying, soak up all this pretty new paper with good money. Many of his henchmen, appalled at the turn of events, had abandoned him in a *sauve qui peut* rout and were selling, throwing more shares on the market that Vanderbilt had to buy or be inundated. Unless he kept buying, the bottom would drop out of Erie, the panic would strike the stock of his own three railroads, and the end would be ruin for him and hundreds of others. In the midst of the crisis his cash resources were exhausted. He sent his lieutenant, Richard Schell, to negotiate for credit with a group of bankers. Schell encountered a situation unheard of. The Commodore's credit was not good—not with Erie stock as collateral.

"We can't lend on Erie," the bankers told him. "There is an illegal issue of stock, and Erie isn't worth anything."

"What will you lend on?" Schell demanded.

"Central—that's good."

Schell did some quick thinking. He knew that almost all bankers had brokers' loans on which they had taken New York Central stock as security.

"Very well, gentlemen!" he snapped. "If you don't lend the Commodore half a million on Erie at 50, and do it at once, he will put Central at 50 tomorrow and break half the houses on the Street!"

Vanderbilt got his credit. Deserted by many friends, he stood like a rock, showing no outward perturbation, and kept buying. Virtually alone, a splendid example of ruthless courage, he stemmed the Erie decline at 71 and even managed to push it up a few points. When the Exchange closed that afternoon of March 10, the battle was over. The Commodore had lost his corner on Erie but saved his hide. He had bought some 150,000 shares without gaining control of the road. Of these, the newly-printed 100,000 shares were useless to him, for the Stock Exchange stepped in and declared them illegally issued and valueless. Vanderbilt had lost eight million dollars. Worst of all, he had lost it to Daniel Drew.

6 *The Siege of Fort Taylor*

ON THE merry morning of March 11, Fisk, Gould, Drew, Eldridge and other less notorious Erie directors gathered at the company offices to perform a joyous chore—count the millions gouged from the Commodore. Aware that their maneuvers were open to legal question, they had snatched their loot out of the banks lest it be attached. They had also planted a spy at Judge Barnard's chambers to learn what was in the wind.

These transportation moguls, some of whom had never boarded an Erie train, were busy tieing greenbacks in stacks when their sentinel hurried in. Judge Barnard, he said, was preparing writs for the arrest of the whole Erie board, including "the body of James Fisk, Jr.," for contempt of court. Drew, the church pillar, was appalled at the thought of going to jail. Fisk, who never favored losing control of his body, suggested moving across the Hudson to Jersey City, out of Barnard's jurisdiction.

"Up in Brattleboro in my kid days," he said, "I used to see people avoid interviews with the sheriff by crossing the bridge over the Connecticut, and once there they would let the Vermont sheriff whistle for them. I always did like the air of Jersey."

Drew was reluctant to leave his home and family, but anything was better than the Ludlow Street jail. It was recalled that Taylor's Hotel, hard by the Erie terminal and dock in Jersey City, was a comfortable place. Reservations were made there by telegraph for a whole block of rooms.

The plan was to move the entire Erie office staff, books and records, and operate the railroad from Jersey City—which was its eastern terminus anyway—until some program could be perfected to counter the contempt action. Packets of Vanderbilt money totaling some $8,000,000 were tossed into a trunk, Drew also taking his personal winnings. Drew, Eldridge and a half-dozen other directors left in a hurry along with a few clerks carrying trunks of money and records. They saw three policemen chatting on the opposite corner—a sight so chilling that they broke into an undignified run to the nearby ferry, reaching it in a breathless condition and not feeling easy until the vessel made midstream. Other lesser employes followed on later ferries, all of them carrying ledgers, account books or office equipment.

Fisk and Gould, feeling it would take some time before the writs could be acted on, stayed at the office all day, supervising the removal of equipment, ready to flee at the sight of a deputy sheriff. ". . . a regular stampede took place . . . among the [Erie] officials," the *Herald* noted, adding that "so complete a clearing out has not taken place since the Fenians fled from Dublin on the night of the suspension of the habeas corpus."

Fisk and Gould even felt reckless enough to dine that night at Delmonico's, nearby at Broadway and Chambers Street. While they were over the meat course a tipster warned them that the law was moving. Fearing that the ferries would be watched, they jumped into a carriage and rode to the foot of Canal Street, where they dickered with an officer of the steamer *St. John*, offering him a gratuity. A boat was lowered for them, manned by two deckhands, and they headed across the river in a dense fog. "Mr. Fisk directed the men to head up the river, to keep out of the track of the ferry-boats," *Harper's Weekly* recorded, "but the fog was so thick that they lost their reckoning and rowed for some time in a circle. They were at one time nearly run down, only saving themselves by the vigorous use of their lungs. Once they escaped from one ferry-boat only to see another bearing down upon them." Hopelessly lost in mid-river, they hailed another ferry but could not make themselves heard. "They made a clutch at the supports of the guard, and were drawn so near the wheel as to nearly wash the whole party out of the boat. They however saved her from swamping, and climbed on board, arriving shortly after at Jersey City, safe and sound, but thoroughly drenched."

Two directors who did not choose to run were arrested and released on bail. Wall Street, Judge Barnard and all of New York were exercised over the flight of a whole railroad headquarters to New Jersey. The claims and counterclaims of the opposing sides, and the flood of writs now so labyrinthine that not even a Blackstone could pick his way through them, made mere laymen throw up their hands and conclude that none of the contenders were blameless. Certainly the Drew crowd's hurried exodus did not betoken a clear conscience. Newspapermen, knowing the rascality of Drew and the ruthlessness of Vanderbilt, were hard put to choose between them. It had to be admitted that the Commodore ran his railroads efficiently and could rescue Erie from the junk heap if anyone could, but the thought of allowing him a monopoly in the New York-to-Buffalo heartland appalled shippers already aroused by his rate-boosting. The question seemed to be whether the road should remain in the hands of Drew, to sink into even worse decrepitude, or be handed over to Vanderbilt, giving him a stranglehold on the state's commerce.

The Commodore was in a parlous condition, stuck with 100,000 worthless shares and still forced to support Erie in the market lest he lose on his 50,000 valid shares. While he privately swore vengeance, he managed to keep an unruffled mien, playing whist and talking horses as usual, inspiring confidence among his badly shaken followers. Judge Barnard, who may have taken a speculative licking himself, made out to be outraged solely on the score of wounded justice, vowing that if he could get his hands on the Erie culprits he would hold each of them in $500,000 bail. He was agreeable to anything the Vanderbilt lawyers suggested. At their urging, he appointed George A. Osgood receiver for the money taken by Drew & Company in the sale of 100,000 tainted shares—hardly a display of judicial impartiality, since Osgood was his own close friend and a son-in-law of Vanderbilt. When the Erie lawyers replied with an injunction against the Osgood appointment, Barnard junked Osgood and appointed Peter B. Sweeny, the sidekick of Boss Tweed, as receiver. All this was purely rhetorical, since the money was safely in Jersey where neither Osgood nor Sweeny could touch it. The next move was up to the Erie exiles, unless they wanted to stay in New Jersey permanently.

Newspapermen who rushed over to Jersey City to view something new in their experience, an absconded corporation, found to their surprise that it was neither Treasurer Drew nor President Eldridge who was doing the talking for Erie. Pudgy, jovial James Fisk Jr. was handling that end as if he had been born and raised on the line. He had already put in a supply of liquor and cigars for reporters and anyone else whose good-will was desirable. He waved a Park & Tilford perfecto as he regaled newsmen with stories that Erie had simply been following Horace Greeley's advice about going west and expanding with the country. But he was careful to leaven his nonsense with a ringing reminder that Erie was fighting a holy war deserving the support of every honest man.

". . . this struggle," he said piously, "is in the interest of the poorer classes especially."

Knowing that the flight of the directors had a smell of guilt about it, he insisted that it would be the greatest of errors to surmise that they had fled justice. On the contrary, he said, they had circumvented the illegal plotting of the villainous Vanderbilt, a man who set his freight rates so high that New York's poor were starving for want of grain, and was using the corrupt Judge Barnard as a well-paid tool. Erie, said Mr. Fisk, was the defender of the people—and won't you have another drink?

"We were satisfied," he went on, "that the Judge was under their [Vanderbilt's] influence, and that we stood no show of justice. Mr. Drew's opponents would have taken him by the neck and said, 'Fork over that $8,000,000 or go to jail.' In that case we should have been down on our knees at once, and the Erie road would have passed into the hands of a monopoly."

"Suppose you don't get justice in New York?" the *Tribune* man asked.

"Then," Fisk replied firmly, "we shall stay here until we rot. This is a battle between right and wrong, and we have no fears as to which will win."

While there might be some doubt that the decamped directors were selfless martyrs to the public weal, it was evident that Fisk had whipped together an efficient standby organization on the second floor at Taylor's Hotel. Superintendents and clerks were functioning as usual so that Erie trains were running with hardly more than customary insult to schedules. The directors took quick steps to woo the state of New Jersey as an ally against tyrannical New York. The legislature at Trenton, happy to snatch a tax-paying railroad, hurried through a bill giving Erie the benefits of Jersey incorporation—a move menacing to Vanderbilt, since Erie could now issue more watered stock at its pleasure. To show how warmly they had the public interest at heart, the directors with great fanfare lowered by one-third the Erie passenger and freight rates to Buffalo, Rochester and other points also served by the New York Central. This meant they were running at a loss, but they could afford to do it on their winnings from Vanderbilt. They loosed a fusillade of publicity about the rate reduction, picturing it as one of the glories of free competition and pointing out with some truth that if the Commodore owned both roads he would be boosting rates, not lowering them.

Director Fisk, feeling lonely, battened down for what might be a long exile by sending a clerk across the river to fetch Josie Mansfield. Until then, her status as his mistress was not a matter of notoriety, but she seemed unafraid to publicize it, arriving by ferry to be escorted to a hotel room adjoining Fisk's. Drew, whose transgressions were mostly in the field of larceny, disapproved of this sinful arrangement, as did Gould, a faithful husband whatever his other derelictions. Uncle Daniel, in fact, was unhappy about the move to Jersey. He had taken it only as an alternative to jail, in the belief that the stay would be short. He felt that Vanderbilt, being in straits himself, could be persuaded to compromise —a strategy Fisk and Gould violently opposed—and his feelings were hurt because these two striplings seemed to think they were dictating Erie policy.

On March 16 Drew got a shock. Groups of hard-faced characters from New York's Five Points began drifting over by ferry until about fifty of them were loitering around the hotel. The rumor spread that Vanderbilt had offered $50,-000 to anyone who would kidnap Drew and spirit him into New York jurisdiction, and that these worthies were out for the prize. Fisk flew into action, ordering Hugh Masterson, head of the Erie detectives, to gather a defense force from the local shops. Jersey City's Police Chief Nick Fowler arrived with a platoon of bluecoats to safeguard the city's distinguished guests. Several of the roughs, when questioned, admitted they had come to seize Drew.

Seeing themselves outnumbered, they gave up their mission and retired across the river, but Fisk declared that this was only a scouting party sent out by the Vanderbilt camp, to be followed by heavy assault. He spoke gravely to Chief Fowler, who agreed to post a twenty-four-hour guard around the hotel as long as the crisis lasted. The demands on the police force were so great that twenty extra men were sworn in for emergency duty. It was arranged that in case of a Vanderbilt night attack, rockets would be fired from the hotel windows to summon policemen on beats elsewhere in the city. Erie clerks were mustered in as sailors, handed muskets and ordered to patrol the Jersey shore in rowboats after nightfall, while three twelve-pound cannon were mounted on the dock and the state militia and Hudson County artillery were alerted to be ready for instant call. It appeared almost as if a new War Between the States was brewing. Miss Mansfield nervously locked herself in her room with a sentinel at the door. Daniel Drew found himself shorn of privacy, guarded like a queen bee.

"The head of the stairs was duly guarded," the *Times* noted, "a body guard of half a dozen men occupied Mr. Drew's room, to prevent his being spirited out of the window, and a reserve force ready for immediate action occupied an adjoining room."

Fisk now christened Taylor's Hotel "Fort Taylor," announcing that the defenders would sooner be annihilated en masse than surrender to the Vanderbilt legions. "The excitement of the situation was rather enjoyed . . . by Mr. Fisk," another scribe observed, "who now bustled about with a most determined looking visage, mounted his guard, issued orders, puffed away at his cigar, kept up a constant discharge of puns [and] vowed he would never be taken alive. . . ."

No attack came that night, but two days later another rumor of imminent action kept the defenders on the *qui vive.* Except for the night vigil involved, the city police and the Erie shock troops took pleasure in their assignments because of Fisk's generosity with liquors, and it was said that some of the defenders were not always strictly sober. To reporters covering the siege, Fisk described the kidnap plot as another evidence of Vanderbilt criminality and terrorism. Not until later did some shrewd observers surmise—probably correctly—that Vanderbilt had nothing to do with it at all and that Fisk himself had hired the toughs and cooked up the whole crisis. It made good propaganda in two ways. It painted Vanderbilt as a thug, and was calculated to convince Drew, whose devotion to a last-ditch fight against the Commodore was weakening fast, that he had better stick tight in Jersey City and rely on Fisk and Gould for protection.

If so, it failed to rally Drew. The Great Bear missed his home and family, but most of all he missed the Wall Street chicanery that was meat and drink to him. The founder of the Drew Theological Seminary, surrounded by liquor, threats of violence and sin in the pretty shape of Miss Mansfield, felt like a parson in a gin mill.

"I want to go home," he said.

7 The Black Horse Cavalry

IT HAD already occurred to the Erie high command that since Judge Barnard could not be budged from his stand that what they had done was illegal, the thing to do was to have a law passed that would *make* it legal. The New York state legislature had expressed concern over the railroad collision in Wall Street and appointed a five-man committee headed by Senator A. C. Mattoon to investigate. The legislature was a glittering example of the carefree rapacity that could be found in officialdom almost everywhere during the postwar years. Its honest members were in such a minority as to be almost negligible. Legislators were paid $300 a year, and many of them scarcely bothered to conceal their conviction that it was only right for their labors in Albany to be rewarded by those who sought their votes.

Senator Mattoon carried this philosophy to the point of religion. "A man more thoroughly, shamefacedly contemptible and corrupt," wrote Charles Francis Adams, "—a more perfect specimen of a legislator on sale haggling for his own price, could not well exist." Arriving in New York to give the railroad crisis his on-the-spot scrutiny, Mattoon interviewed Drew before the exodus to Jersey City. Drew got the impression that the merits of the controversy, if they counted at all, came second to money with the senator. He later visited the directors in Jersey City, letting them know he was likewise conferring with Vanderbilt, so the opinion existed that he was bidding one side against the other, much like an auctioneer. There is no outright record that a roll of

Erie currency was thrust into his hand, and perhaps it would be more correct to say that if this was not done a miracle came to pass, for when he left for Albany the directors had no doubt that he and his vote were with them.

Still, there were other senators and representatives besides Mattoon, and it was well known that Vanderbilt liberality had kept the legislature favorable to him for several years. To make success sure, the Erie leaders decided to send an emissary to Albany to mix with the legislators and apply persuasion. Several Erie attorneys had already gone to the capital and whipped up a bill legalizing the watered stock and forbidding the New York Central and Erie roads to be controlled by the same financiers. If this bill were passed, the Erie moguls could keep the millions they had won via the printing press. None of the directors were inclined to go to Albany, where Judge Barnard's arrest warrant would be waiting when they set foot inside New York State. Instead, they sent a lawyer named John E. Develin to the capital, armed with funds and instructions to push the bill through.

But the directors misjudged the temper of the legislators. According to common report, Develin offered only $1000 a vote to win over the Black Horse Cavalry, as the corrupt section of the Assembly was called. They felt this was niggardly when such a large issue was involved. On March 27, partly to teach Develin and his employers a lesson in the amenities of bribery, the Assembly defeated the Erie bill by the heavy majority of 83 to 32.

Everybody understood that this was only a preliminary skirmish. All Erie had to do was draft a new bill containing the same key stipulations with minor falsework changes and try again, with a better understanding of the cost of votes. Erie's lawyers framed the new bill, while the directors in Jersey City selected Jay Gould to supplant Develin as vote-buyer. To make this plan feasible, steps were taken to keep Gould from being clapped into jail when he appeared in

Albany. Erie's legal helmsman in New York, David Dudley Field, arranged a truce with Sheriff James O'Brien whereby Gould agreed to appear before Judge Barnard April 4 and would be immune to arrest before then. Just the same, the directors spread a fake report that Gould was off for a survey of the western lines when he left for Albany carrying a dozen checkbooks and a suitcase said to contain $500,000 in cash.

Albany was already teeming with Vanderbilt lobbyists fighting the Erie efforts. The small, bearded Gould, an easy man to recognize, had hardly poked his nose into the Delavan House in the capital when he was arrested, proving that Sheriff O'Brien's attitude had been hardened by exposure to the Vanderbilt partisans. Indignant at the betrayal, Gould won temporary freedom by posting $500,000 bail, which was furnished by his friend Erastus Corning, Gould having other needs for his money. Surveying the scene, he found that Senator Mattoon, whom he thought Erie's friend, had gone over to the other side.

Mattoon had returned to Albany to learn that of the four members of his committee, two were in favor of absolving Erie in the over-issue of stock while the other two were for punishing the directors with the full force of the law. Mattoon held the deciding vote, which increased his obligation to view the matter correctly. Before committing himself, he did still more fieldwork in Albany that made him see virtues in the Vanderbilt arguments that had escaped him before. The *Tribune* said the argument that most impressed him was $20,000 in Vanderbilt cash. He voted against Erie, so that the majority report of his committee held the stock-watering directors to be outlaws—a development that must have made Gould wonder whether his suitcase was large enough.

Meanwhile, Fisk spent his thirty-third birthday on April 1 in command at Fort Taylor, with Drew in a funk and President Eldridge demoralized by railroad maneuvers unknown in Boston. The directors had made a great show of affection for Jersey City, representing themselves as happy to stay there eternally, and this fellow-feeling along with the free liquor won them many concessions. Police Chief Fowler was acting like an Erie employe, his men still guarding the hotel. Truthfully, the exiles were heartily sick of Jersey City—even Fisk, who missed the Manhattan fleshpots—and were taking advantage of a New York statute forbidding arrests in civil suits on Sunday. On Saturday night they streamed out in a body to catch the New York-bound ferry at the stroke of midnight, Fisk with Josie on his arm, Drew to rejoin his family and pass the plate at St. Paul's Church on Sunday. The Vanderbilt-Barnard minions sullenly watched this exploitation of the Sabbath armistice, determined that anyone overstaying the twenty-four hours of grace would suffer. Director Henry Thompson made that error, arriving in New York before midnight Saturday, and was arrested at the Astor House.

For all their outward accord in the struggle with Vanderbilt, the solidarity of the Erie leaders was shaky. They were men of some prominence and wealth whose flight to Jersey had not only deprived them of freedom and domestic comforts but had also put them in disrepute. Substantial newspapers like the *Times* and *Tribune* were calling them outlaws. Their position was vulnerable and embarrassing. Each of them knew the others too well to be certain of undying loyalty, and underneath the superficial cheer among the fort's garrison were sharp glances of suspicion. With millions at stake, the knowledge that Vanderbilt was hard pressed and undoubtedly ready to compromise might make it profitable for any group of the directors to defect to the Commodore's side, and ruinous to the rest. Fisk and Gould, who had worked hand in glove almost from the start, were agreed that the war must be carried on from Jersey City and Albany until Vanderbilt was crushed. Fisk did not have the same faith in President Eldridge, who had flirted with Vanderbilt before. As for the mercurial Drew, no one in his right mind would trust him.

Fisk was even making a joke that flattered their common enemy at Drew's expense, saying, "Vander built, but Dan just *drew*." He mistrusted his old mentor as an incurable turncoat who might attempt some traitorous negotiation with Vanderbilt. Drew, an inveterate Scripture-spouter, never seemed to take to heart the part about money being the root of all evil.

Fisk's suspicions were justified. Vanderbilt, aware of Drew's homesickness and his love of secret deals without regard for anyone but Drew, was working on him. The Commodore, it was said, sent an agent across to Jersey City in the guise of a commercial traveler. The spy managed to bribe a waiter at Taylor's Hotel, who passed a note to the Deacon reading, "Drew: I'm sick of the whole damned business. Come and see me. —Van Derbilt." Fisk stayed in Jersey City one Sunday and detailed an Erie detective to shadow Drew in New York. The sleuth followed the old man from his Union Square home to the Vanderbilt mansion on Washington Place, where he rang the bell and was admitted—clear evidence of treason that the detective telegraphed to Fisk.

The fat man was already in a towering wrath. He had discovered that Drew had quietly removed the Erie funds, doubtless taking them across the river with him. Since the money was precisely what they were fighting for, and what was keeping them alive and aggressive in Jersey City, no greater disaster could have occurred. Fisk, thinking fast, recalled that Drew had deposited his personal fortune in a Jersey City bank to save it from being seized in New York. He wheedled a local judge into putting an attachment on Drew's money until he returned the Erie millions. Still, it was a question whether he would come back at all, since with all that capital he could easily work out some agreement with Vanderbilt. The other directors were relieved when the Great Bear returned late that night.

"How did you leave the Commodore?" Fisk purred.

Drew started, gazing at him warily.

"And what have you done with our money, you damned old hypocrite?" Fisk went on.

"Why Jeems," Drew protested, "ain't I Treasurer of the Company?"

He explained that he had felt the money unsafe at the hotel and had banked it in New York. Fisk, twirling his mustache and enjoying the situation, replied that he had likewise felt Drew's money unsafe and had had it attached. The old trickster's jaw dropped. Seeing himself outwitted by his own pupil, he suggested a parley which ended in a compromise: Drew returned the Erie funds in return for the removal of the attachment on his own. Tranquility was restored, but thereafter he was eyed as a renegade.

The anxious Fisk, with Josie Mansfield at his side, was hanging on the telegraph wire from Albany to learn what progress Gould was making. According to Josie's later account, Fisk put the outcome of the struggle in blunt terms: "It was either a Fisk palace in New York or a stone palace at Sing Sing." If he went to Sing Sing, he urged her to take a cottage nearby, saying that her presence would make his "rusty irons garlands of roses" and would make the stones easier to crack.

In Albany, Gould had no such sweet delirium to spur him on, although money was causing a delirium of its own. Legislators were looking to the Vanderbilt-Erie quarrel as a bonanza. The amount of corruption was less astonishing than the openness with which it was practiced and commented on. The Erie bill, said the *Herald*, was "a godsend to the hungry legislators and lobbymen, who have had up to this time such a beggarly session that their board bills and whiskey bills are all in arrears." Rumor had it that Erie was willing to pay $2,000,000 for passage of the bill, while Vanderbilt might go higher to defeat it. Legislators were debating the tariff they should place on their votes, some declaring $3000 a fair price, others refusing to consider a penny less than $5000. One honest man, Representative E. M. Glenn of Wayne County, was so outraged and lonely that he got up in the Assembly to say that he had been offered money for his vote, charging widespread bribery and demanding an investigation. The House promptly appointed an investigating committee, one of whose members was Representative Alexander Frear. Glenn said this was patently ridiculous, since Frear was the one who had offered him money. Mr. Glenn was entirely mistaken, said Frear. The committee went on to censure Glenn and whitewash the House members, causing Glenn to resign in disgust.

Jay Gould was installed in Parlor 57 of the Delavan House, where liquor and other inducements were handed out to legislators who strolled in for advice. "In this room," said the *Herald*, ". . . is a trunk literally stuffed with thousand dollar bills which are to be used for some mysterious purpose in connection with legislation." On the floor directly above, the Vanderbilt forces were gathered in the magnificent seven-room suite of William Marcy Tweed, boss of New York City but now appearing in his role as state senator. It was said that six bars were set up in Tweed's rooms for the benefit of thirsty solons, and Tweed later recalled that he had spent $180,000 in buying votes for Vanderbilt. Amid cigar smoke and the fumes of alcohol, the bidding and counter-bidding reached something close to frenzy. Some legislators frankly shuttled from Tweed to Gould and back to Tweed again, to make certain they were getting the top price. Some were so bereft of principle as to accept money from both sides. According to one authority, a lobbyist arrived in town with $100,000 to spend for Vanderbilt votes, and was given $70,000 by Gould to disappear with the money, which he did, "and thereafter became a gentleman of elegant leisure."

Few of these lobbyists and legislators thought of the Erie road as anything but a vast paper contrivance of dollars, stock certificates and legal briefs. On April 15 something occurred that should have demonstrated otherwise.

At 3:15 that morning the New York-bound Buffalo Express, nine cars long, was forty minutes late and trying not to lose more as it rounded a curve in the rugged country around Carr's Rock, thirteen miles northwest of Port Jervis, New York. Its thirty-miles-per-hour speed was too much for the streaks of rust beneath it. Conductor Jasper Judd was horrified to discover that he had lost the last four cars of his train, three of them sleeping coaches. The four cars had snapped their couplings, jumped the track and hurtled over a precipice to land with shattering impact in a ravine fifty feet below. One of the cars, heated with coal stoves, immediately caught fire. The darkness was illumined by the blazing coach as the screaming injured passengers roasted to death and those already dead were incinerated. It was hours before doctors could reach that remote spot, to find it more in need of undertakers. The final toll was forty dead, many of them unidentifiable, and seventy-five injured, some of whom would never fully recover. This disaster, Erie's worst, caused a wave of public horror that was succeeded by indignation when an inspection of the tracks next day disclosed them to be in deplorable condition.

Superintendent Riddle's March 3 report about the "rotten" condition of the rails and equipment had been published by Drew as propaganda to justify his over-issue of stock for "steel rails" which he never intended to get. Riddle's "apprehension for the safety of trains" was seen to be well founded as the public was handed gruesome proof that the Erie directors—notably Daniel Drew—were more preoccupied with Wall Street profits than with any responsibility toward passengers. There was a fusillade of outraged editorials against the Erie management.

"The Erie railroad has lately been playing all sorts of fantastic tricks before the multitude," snarled the New York *Times,* one voice among many. "Today it appears conspicuous in the role of public execution."

The Vanderbilt lobbyists in Albany pointed gleefully to the wreck as a demonstration of the righteousness of their cause against the homicidal Drew regime, while the Erie supporters gave out dark hints that saboteurs were deliberately wrecking trains. Yet the senators and representatives were less concerned about railroad disasters than about their own wallets. Gould, who was ordered to appear in New York City to answer contempt charges, evaded it with a physician's statement that he was too ill for the downriver trip. He could barely muster enough strength to keep his Delavan House liquor dispensary going and to confer with legislators who sought his counsel. "They all departed with smiling faces," one writer observed, "and Mr. Gould soon had little left of his check book except the stumps."

The Erie bill that came up in the Senate was essentially similar to the one previously defeated in the House. It legalized Drew's over-issue of stock and forbade any common ownership of Erie and New York Central. On April 18, while the burying was going on at Carr's Rock, the Senate passed the bill by 17 to 12. Senator Mattoon, who had first seen things Erie's way, then veered to the Vanderbilt side, executed another flip and voted for Erie. Without mentioning Mattoon by name, but making it clear they meant no one else, the newspapers said he had taken $15,000 from the Vanderbilt side and $20,000 from the Erie side, also asking an additional $1000 honorarium for his son, who acted as his secretary.

That left it up to the House, whose members were happily anticipating their innings. There was brisk bargaining for votes, until a paralyzing report struck Albany. Vanderbilt had withdrawn his opposition to the bill. *He would not bleed another dollar—had even closed the liquor dispensary.*

"The observer was reminded of the dark days of the war," wrote Charles Francis Adams, "when tidings came of some great defeat . . . In a moment the lobby was smitten with despair, and the cheeks of the legislators were blanched. . . ." Members rushed to Gould's rooms, hoping to salvage something from the wreck. Those who had been demanding $5000 were now willing to settle for as little as $100. Some did not even get that, for Gould knew he had enough votes. In a rage, the House on April 20 passed the Erie bill by the whopping vote of 101 to 6—a bill almost identical with the one they had rejected three weeks earlier by 83 to 32. So furious were they at Vanderbilt for cheating them that they began looking for other bills that would hurt him and his odious New York Central.

Fisk and Gould had won, at an estimated cost of $500,000 in stockholders' money. But their victory was not as complete as they thought, for Vanderbilt had meanwhile staged a coup of his own.

8

Thunderstruck and Dumfounded

CORNELIUS VANDERBILT had known all along that he held a weapon over the Erie exiles' heads in the shape of Judge Barnard, whose thinking tallied so perfectly with the Commodore's that onlookers were calling him "Vanderbilt's judge." While the legislature could legalize Erie's over-issue of stock, it could not lift Barnard's judicial curse. The directors had to perform some other magic to enable them to return to New York without facing heavy fines or even imprisonment for flouting Barnard's injunction. It was a safe bet that if Vanderbilt could be mollified, so could the judge, his mental counterpart. Drew knew it. Vanderbilt knew that Drew knew it. After talking with the Commodore, Drew knew that Vanderbilt knew that he knew it.

At their first meeting, Drew, who could spurt tears at will, wept as he protested it was a terrible thing for old friends like him and the Commodore to be at loggerheads.

"No one knows how my bowels yearn for you, Drew," Vanderbilt was said to have rejoined. "But as I understand it, this is a business interview. So if you'll wipe that tobacco juice off your chin and draw up here to the table, we'll talk."

The Erie battle, he said, had taught him it didn't pay to kick a skunk. He could have licked Drew hands down in Wall Street, but he couldn't lick that infernal printing press. The two had several secret meetings, at which Vanderbilt outlined the terms on which he would persuade Barnard to let the exiles return without fear of imprisonment. They reached agreement. Privately Drew communicated the terms to President Eldridge and his Boston coterie, who fell in with him. Not until Vanderbilt knew he had a majority of the Erie directors willing to compromise with him did he instruct his Albany agents to stop spending useless money to defeat the Erie bill.

It was while Fisk and Gould were rejoicing over their Albany victory that they got wind of this betrayal. They paid Vanderbilt an early-morning visit, Fisk with his usual cheek rushing into the Commodore's bedroom before he was fully dressed. Vanderbilt, pulling on his shoes, said bluntly that unless his 100,000 shares of watered stock were taken off his hands he would make the directors permanent outlaws in New York. Fisk, testifying in a later lawsuit against Vanderbilt, gave a vivid account of the talk:

"[Vanderbilt] said I must take the position of things as I found it, he would keep his bloodhounds [the law] on us, and pursue us until we took his stock off his hands; he would be damned if he would keep it. I told him I would be damned if we would take it off his hands, and that we would sell him stock as long as he would stand up and take it; upon this, he mellowed down, and said that we must get together to arrange the matter; I told him that we could not submit to a robbery of the road under any circumstances, and that I was thunderstruck and dumfounded that our directors, whom I had supposed respectable men, would have had anything to do with such proceedings."

Vanderbilt evidently formed a high opinion of the fat man's sagacity. After Fisk's death a few years later, Vanderbilt, a believer in the spirit world, occasionally urged his favorite medium to get through to Fisk in the Beyond and pump him for market tips. Now, however, Fisk and Gould saw that Drew had outmaneuvered them. They must go along with a majority of the directors in a settlement, to gain no more advantage than the miserable permission to return to New York as honest men not subject to arrest.

Their disgust at this turnabout arose less from their conviction of the sanctity of their cause than from their belief that they were on the verge of gaining absolution in New York without paying Vanderbilt a penny. Aware of Barnard's formidable teeth, they had taken steps to pull them. The Tammany judge was known as a faithful follower of Boss Tweed. Fisk and Gould had already had several conversations with Tweed, so pleasant in tone that friendship seemed in the offing. With Tweed about ready to accept inducements to shift from the Vanderbilt side to the Erie camp, Barnard would naturally do likewise, and all the Erie directors had to do was stand firm, man their guns at Fort Taylor for yet another campaign, and total victory would be theirs. Now Drew, in his sniveling anxiety to get back home, had spoiled all that. Fisk and Gould were disgruntled men when they attended a meeting a week later at the home of ex-Judge Edwards Pierrepont along with Vanderbilt, Drew, Eldridge, other interested parties and a covey of attorneys. Here a compromise settlement was ironed out with terms showing utter disregard for Erie's voiceless stockholders.

Vanderbilt was paid $3,750,000 for 50,000 of his "worthless" shares of Erie stock, and in addition was given a cash bonus of $1,000,000. His two lieutenants, Frank Work and Richard Schell, got $429,250 to repay their losses in speculating in Erie stock the previous winter, although as one observer commented, these private losses as well as Vanderbilt's were no more Erie's responsibility than were their butcher bills.

Eldridge and his Boston group came out of it very well. They got $4,000,000 in cash for $5,000,000 in the dubious bonds of their Boston, Hartford & Erie Railway—the road that was supposed to link up with Erie and give it a rich stream of New England traffic. Since the road was never completed to its junction with Erie, the latter road paid for a promise never to be fulfilled.

Daniel Drew was rightly considered to have got his. He was allowed to keep his speculative winnings by paying Erie $540,000 in discharge of all claims against him.

Tweed's henchman Peter B. Sweeny, who had been appointed Erie receiver by Barnard, had nothing to receive and therefore did nothing, was given a $150,000 fee (paid for by Erie) for what he did not do.

Erie's lawyers, headed by Field & Shearman and including a dozen others, drew fees running into the hundreds of thousands.

Counting the estimated $500,000 which Gould had distributed among the Albany legislators, it cost Erie close to $10,000,000 to have all lawsuits called off so the company could set up shop again in New York. Vanderbilt had lost both money and prestige. Erie had suffered so heavily that it would be impoverished for years, the burden being dumped into the laps of its stockholders. The only apparent gainers were Drew, Sweeny, the attorneys, and Eldridge and his Boston brethren, who walked off with $4,000,000 in exchange for some B., H. & E. bonds no one else wanted anyway.

Yet Fisk and Gould, who had borne the brunt of the battle and now seemed forgotten at the peace table, actually carried away the choicest prize of all. While they protested strongly against the settlement, they went along with it on being granted certain concessions. One of them was the retirement from the Erie board of Daniel Drew, for whom both had developed a lasting mistrust. Surprisingly, Drew agreed to get out, feeling that all the juice had been squeezed from the Erie plum.

"There ain't nothin' in Airy no more, C'neel," he said privately to Vanderbilt.

"Don't you believe it!" growled Vanderbilt.

The Commodore was right. Late in April the flag at Fort Taylor was struck and its garrison crossed the Hudson to reopen the old offices on West Street, leaving a void in

Jersey City that would never be filled. Fisk and Josie, all thoughts of Sing Sing behind them, entrained for Boston, where they separated, Josie to visit relatives, Fisk to pay a call on his wife, who had been utterly confused by newspaper accounts of the Erie-Vanderbilt war. Fisk also took the opportunity to visit his family in Brattleboro, not forgetting his demented father. Though his sins were as the sands of the sea, his love for kin and friends would never change. Brattleborans would come to read many bloodcurdling things about James Fisk Jr., many of them true, but would continue to regard him as their most famous semi-native son as well as the most incredible character outside of Dickens.

Returning to New York, he resumed residence at the Fifth Avenue Hotel and gave some thought to a proper establishment for his mistress. From all accounts he was smitten by her in an exuberant Fiskian way that did not visibly alter his esteem for his wife. There is no record of discord between Lucy and Fisk. He continued to support her in luxury and treat her with consideration and courtliness despite the distance and the woman between them. To Lucy he wrote frequent affectionate letters. He bought her a villa at Newport. It was with Lucy that he spent Christmas and such other holidays as he could spare. When she made one of her occasional trips to New York, he squired her around to the shops and theaters while Josie gnawed her nails in temporary eclipse. Friends who pondered this paradox speculated that Lucy, for all her sweet attraction, was very likely frigid—a condition that was not believed to afflict Miss Mansfield. Yet Fisk seemed to have such reserves of affection that he could spread it out over two women and possibly more without skimping on any of them.

"She is no hair-lifting beauty, my Lucy," he once said, "just a plump, wholesome, big-hearted, commonplace woman, such as a man meets once in a lifetime." Again, when a friend boasted of his wife, he rejoined, "Bring your wives along, I ain't afraid to measure my Lucy with 'em. For, look here, you mustn't judge Lucy by her James!"

In New York he put Josie up at the Clarendon Hotel for a time, moved her to the Sherman House, then found just the thing for her—a comfortable house at 18 West Twenty-fourth Street, right around the corner from his hotel. While it was said that he spent so much time at the Twenty-fourth Street house that he got little value out of his hotel suite, he maintained separate quarters and continued to do so until he entered Commodore Vanderbilt's spirit world.

Meanwhile, Judge Barnard had made such a huff-and-puff about the retribution he would visit on the Erie directors that he had to save face by exacting some punishment for their contempt. After long thought, he fined the lesser directors ten dollars each. The transgressions of the ringleaders, however—Drew, Fisk and Gould—were so heinous that their penalty required more deliberation. The judge thought that over so long that he eventually forgot about it entirely.

On July 2, 1868, the Erie board of directors met to make official the settlement with Vanderbilt. Drew announced his resignation, and so did President Eldridge. Gould was promptly elected president *and* treasurer pro tem, while Fisk stepped up alongside his crony as comptroller and managing director.

The sudden rise of these two back-country upstarts to leadership of a great railroad was so astonishing that no one on the outside could understand it at the time. Not until later, in one of Erie's interminable lawsuits, was an explanation made that remained unofficial but still convincing. According to this version, Fisk and Gould, having arranged the exit of Drew, had only to get rid of Eldridge to take command of a feeble board of directors. Knowing that Eldridge had entered Erie in the first place only to succor

the B., H. & E., and that he could get a $3,000,000 grant from
the state of Massachusetts if he put up a like amount, they
gave him a $4,000,000 ticket back to Boston at Erie's ex-
pense. The way the other directors danced to the Fisk-
Gould tune makes it plain that the pair convinced them it
would be to their advantage, for the new president and
comptroller immediately did away with the old board of
auditors and concentrated all the power in their own hands.
They found the treasury depleted, the road's equipment in
ghastly shape, and the reputation of its management in bad
odor.

There was little they could do about the odor, nor indeed
were they greatly concerned about that. But they *had* to
do something about the treasury and equipment. Much as
they may have disliked to squander money on prosaic rolling stock and rails when Wall Street beckoned with such
allure, one Carr's Rock disaster was enough. Erie was a
goose that laid golden eggs, but needed a little corn at in-
tervals. Uncle Daniel had left a legacy of ruin. The mending
would take capital. "We needed more engines, more cars,
and the track was in bad order," as Fisk later put it. ". . . As
we went on, our need for money became more pressing. I
did not stop to run and ask my mother how I should get it
—the first thing was to get it—get it. . . ."

Getting money without asking mother was something at
which this pair became proficient. Feeling out their new
property, they saw that Erie had an agreement with the
United States Express Company. When they told the
express officials that their annual rent to Erie would be
increased by $500,000, the officials protested that they could
pay no such outlandish charge. Very well, said Fisk and
Gould, you may get out and we will form our own express
company. News of this reverse made United States Express
stock dive from 60 to 16, and the two Erie leaders bought
heavily at 16. Then they did a fast turnabout, signed a new
contract with the express company at the old rate, and

cleaned up an estimated $3,000,000 when the stock climbed as a result.

They managed to sell the 50,000 shares of stock they had taken back from Vanderbilt at about 70, bringing some $3,500,000 into the coffers. Then they repaired to the Erie basement and put the printing press to such use as it had never known before, making Drew's previous stock-watering efforts pale by comparison. Within fifteen weeks after their accession to power, and without asking a by-your-leave from the board of directors, Fisk and Gould secretly issued 235,000 shares of new stock, raising the railroad's capital stock from $34,265,300 to $57,766,300, an increase of $23,501,000. Loosing such a flood of stock on the market even piecemeal would obviously lower the price—a drop which only they and a few friends in on the deal could predict. Thus they were betting on a sure thing when they unloaded their new stock, sold Erie short in anticipation of the drop, and reaped millions when it plummeted below 40.

Some made the mistake of thinking that when Fisk and Gould grew richer, this would have the effect of lifting their railroad out of poverty. If ever there was any visible connection between the financial condition of these entrepreneurs on one hand and Erie on the other, it was in inverse proportion. As long as they remained in charge they were millionaires whose road wallowed in such a morass of debt that the prospect of Erie ever paying a dividend became the sourest of jokes in Wall Street. It was this apparent discrepancy between the wealth of the operators and the destitution of the road's treasury that would continue to puzzle and annoy the more naive of the stockholders until they tumbled to the fact that their road was not being run so much by railroad men as by stock market gamblers using the corporation as a handy tool for their manipulations.

Fisk and Gould, who had already disproved Drew's judgment that "There ain't nothin' in Airy no more," were hobnobbing frequently with Boss Tweed. Tweed, whose Duane Street office was only a stone's throw from the Erie building, was a busy man that summer. He was nominating District Attorney A. Oakey Hall, a jovial little fashion plate and sometime writer, for mayor of New York. He was nominating John T. Hoffman, the present mayor, for governor. He was nominating Horatio Seymour, a former governor, for President. Yet he was not too preoccupied to think of going into the railroad business. The two young Erie moguls were doing some nominating of their own, for full-year board members to be elected at the annual meeting scheduled for October 13. On August 19 Erie announced that its stock transfer books were closed to get ready for the election. This was a fast trick in violation of company rules, which said the books should be closed only a month before the election. It meant that Erie stock would be voted according to its ownership as of August 19, at which time Fisk, Gould and their friends knew they held a majority. Thus they had almost two months' grace during which they could speculate with their shares, dispose of them advantageously, and still vote themselves back into power with other peoples' stock.

This they did at the annual meeting on October 13, 1868.

Jay Gould was reelected director and president.

James Fisk Jr. was reelected director and comptroller.

William Tweed was elected a director, as was his Tammany colleague, Peter B. Sweeny.

When these men climbed into the Erie cab, they pulled the throttle wide open, let the whistle shriek and forgot all about the brakes.

9 *The Big Fix*

THE love affair between wispy Jay Gould and fat Jim Fisk has been called a puzzle because of their many visible differences. The two were alike only in shrewdness and freedom from any hampering sense of business ethics. Gould was quiet, nervous, shy, conservative in dress, a family man who liked to raise orchids but found his greatest joy in compounding schemes for making money. Although he was pained by Fisk's diamond-studded vulgarity, the Vermonter's good cheer brought warmth into his otherwise dollar-haunted life. Fisk loved money too, and a sprinkling of dollar signs on his velvet vest would have made him the archetype for the caricature soon to be adopted by cartoonists to represent bloated capital, but he loved money in a wide-eyed country-boy way—for the show he could make with it, the things he could buy, the fun he could have. The two men realized that they complemented each other to make an efficient team. Gould, a genius at long-range strategy, was a poor tactician, awkward at handling subordinates, a downright liability in public relations. Fisk, who could be deficient in the long view, was an executive of unusual ability who kept employes happy and got things done, and when it came to opening the sideboard and entertaining the press, he had no peer.

But this was not entirely a marriage of convenience. Both men had emerged from a battle in which the double-cross had so prevailed that they trusted no one but each other. They saw eye to eye business-wise. They would be inseparable partners, attached by interest and affection for four years, and if Gould's loyalty would eventually waver it was because Fisk became so hopelessly enmeshed in scandal that no corporation could afford to own him as a director.

Both were honor graduates of the Drew school of financial flimflam who had studied their mentor's tactics and spotted the fatal flaw. Drew was stock-foxy, to be sure, but when he came at odds with the law he had been caught miserably in the net. Fisk and Gould had taken steps to remove this threat so that they could operate illegally while appearing to observe the forms of the law. They were not the first, but they were the largest and most thoroughgoing practitioners of the corrupt alliance between business and politics: the big fix. When they took Tweed and Sweeny into the Erie board, it was an amalgamation of the Erie Ring with the Tweed Ring, a sign that all of Tammany—which included Judge Barnard—had ushered them into the wigwam to smoke peace pipes.

It was Fisk who had conducted much of the negotiation with Tweed and had developed a liking for the massive, big-nosed Boss and the sinister-looking Sweeny. On the day of the Erie election, Fisk was so delighted at the limitless prospects ahead that he gave Josie an opportunity to play hostess to New York's emperor and other notables.

"My Dear Josie," he wrote her, "James McHenry, the partner of Sir Morton Peto, the largest railway builder in the world, Mr. Tweed and Mr. Lane will dine with us at half-past six o'clock. I want you to provide as nice a dinner as possible. Everything went off elegantly [at the election]. We are *all* safe. Will see you at six o'clock."

They were indeed all safe with Tweed on the board. Fisk and Gould had been printing so much new stock, throwing the market into such a turmoil, that there were threats of investigations and lawsuits. A worried Stock Exchange committee called on Jay Gould to ask if he had indeed issued new stock. With Tweed on the board, Gould did not bother to fall back on the threadbare Drew alibi of the need for steel rails. He said yes, new stock had been issued for the improvement of the road, and he wouldn't be surprised if more might be necessary, which gave the gentlemen a chill. Now that Tweed was with them, Fisk and Gould were ready to spring a trap they had been setting in combination with Daniel Drew. For weeks they had been selling new Erie stock and systematically locking the money up, taking it out of circulation. By the end of October their bear movement had sunk Erie to 35, its lowest quotation in years. The market was in chaos, with brokers failing, caught not only by the drop in Erie but also by the shortage of currency. Drew, who had contributed $4,000,000 to the pool, made enormous profits until he disagreed with his two young partners in its operation. The Great Bear, always a bear, felt sure Erie was going down still more and saw an opportunity to make a killing on his own. He deserted Fisk and Gould, withdrew his money and continued selling Erie heavily short.

The two younger men, out of patience with him, decided to give him a taste of his own Wall Street medicine. On November 12 they unlocked $12,000,000 they had been holding, put it in circulation and began buying Erie at low prices. The sudden flood of money in addition to the buying spurt made Erie shoot from 35 to 54. A day earlier the bulls had been in anguish. Now it was the bears who were suffering, chief among them Drew. He had sold short some 70,000 shares of Erie at an average price of 38. If he fulfilled his commitments by delivering at 54, he stood to lose more than a million. The crafty churchman, well knowing it was Fisk and Gould who were applying the torture, looked around for succor. He thought he found it in August Belmont, another wounded bear.

Belmont, the wealthy, German-born New York agent of the Rothschilds, loathed Drew but welcomed any ally. Would Drew make an affidavit exposing the earlier Erie

misdeeds participated in by Fisk and Gould? Much as he
hated to confess his sins, the Deacon was even more reluctant to lose a million, and he allowed he would. Lawyers
were called in. With Drew's aid a long affidavit was made
out narrating the illegality of the settlement with Vanderbilt, alleging that Fisk and Gould had illegally bought the
resignation of Eldridge by paying him $4,000,000 of Erie
money so that they succeeded to the leadership, and that
since then they had issued millions in unauthorized stock and
committed many other frauds. In order to incriminate Fisk
and Gould, Drew had to admit that he was a willing party
to much of this knavery. It was Belmont's plan to take the
affidavit before a judge as grounds for the removal of Fisk
and Gould as directors, a ban on their further speculation,
and the appointment of a receiver for Erie. This would instantly send the Erie quotation downward and save the
bears.

This was on Saturday night, November 14. The court
action could not take place until Monday morning. Drew
told Belmont and several other bears in the deal that he
would take the affidavit home to read it more carefully
before signing it. He saw in the affidavit an opportunity to
play both ends against the middle. He could either sell out
Fisk and Gould, or Belmont and his allies—whichever was
most profitable to Drew.

After attending church on Sunday, Drew went to the
Erie building and found Fisk in his office, breaking the
Sabbath in gainful toil. Drew put on a woebegone expression and said pathetically that he was an old man. He
dwelled on their several years of friendship and mentioned
that he had been of considerable help in bringing both Fisk
and Gould to their present prominence. He was caught
badly short, he admitted. Would Fisk loan him 40,000 shares
or so to get him out of the hole?

Fisk grinned at him. "You're in and you can't get out,"
he chuckled, "bellow as much as you may."

"Then, if you put up this stock [keep raising the price of Erie], I am a ruined man," Drew wailed.

Fisk knew this was not true. Drew could lose a million or two and still have a dozen millions left. The Great Bear kept pleading for an hour, shedding a few ready tears. He went into Gould's office and implored him for a loan of "Airy sheers." Finding no compassion there, he returned to Fisk. At last, with both of them adamant, he brought out his secret weapon, the affidavit aimed at expelling Fisk and Gould from Erie.

"You know," he said, "during the whole of our fight I objected to ever giving my affidavit, but I swear I will do you all the harm I can do if you do not help me in this time of my great need!"

Now, he went on, he would betray Belmont, refuse to sign the affidavit, if he could only be loaned "them sheers." Although the Belmont move could be dangerous, Fisk was fed up with Drew's ingrained treachery and refused to make any deal with a man who might jump the other way the moment he was out of sight. He reminded Uncle Daniel how many times he had held others in precisely this same vise and squeezed them without mercy.

"You are the last man who should whine at any position you have put yourself in with regard to Erie," he said.

Drew left in despair. Yet, bearing in mind his standing as a churchman, he so cringed at the thought of publishing his own wickedness in the affidavit that he returned to Fisk's office that night with more pleas for stock. He groveled in vain. It was midnight before he gave up, clapped on his stovepipe hat with a pathetic effort at dignity, picked up the ancient umbrella he used as a cane, and said, "I will bid you good-night."

Fisk and Gould, forced to move fast against the Drew-Belmont threat, knew that the courts would not open until 10 Monday morning. Somewhat after 7 that morning, Fisk, along with the inevitable clutch of attorneys, got out of a carriage at Judge Barnard's residence on Twenty-first Street. This was the same Barnard branded only seven months earlier by the same Fisk as the corrupt tool of Vanderbilt—the same judge who had denounced Fisk and Gould as swindlers and fugitives from justice. Now that Tweed was on the board, the tall, elegant judge forgot all past unpleasantness and greeted Fisk genially, both of them being habitués of Delmonico's. Barnard, who had just got up and had not yet shaved, listened attentively to Fisk's story that the baleful Drew-Belmont combination was aiming to oust him and Gould simply to discredit Erie and manipulate the market in their favor. Barnard said that sort of thing could not be allowed. His solution showed that in the realm of legal witchcraft he was second to none.

He directed all parties bringing suit against Erie to desist. *He* appointed a receiver for Erie—Jay Gould. And he appointed a bondsman for Receiver Gould—Jim Fisk.

Unaware of all this, Drew, Belmont and companions appeared later before Judge Sutherland and presented the Drew affidavit, claiming that its disclosures proved the unfitness of Fisk and Gould to head the Erie corporation. Sutherland complied with an injunction forbidding the Gould party from exercising any authority in Erie affairs and directing them to show cause why a receiver should not be appointed.

The chagrin of these gentlemen was unalloyed when they discovered they had got up too late in the morning and that Gould had already been appointed his own receiver. Possibly Drew reflected that intrigue could sometimes boomerang. There was a continuing rattle of legal gunfire from both sides, but the Fisk-Gould forces had clearly stolen a march, and while the court orders ricocheted the real battle was going on in the market. Drew and his fellow bears, receiving no help from the law, had to fight it out with dollars. Drew, committed to deliver 70,000 shares at 38, was forced to buy them at any price or default. He must have been reminded unhappily of a couplet he had once invented:

> *He who sells what isn't his'n*
> *Must buy it back or go to prison.*

Drew was alternately weeping and praying as the price crept up to 62 and he was losing twenty-four dollars on every share he bought. Fisk and Gould were buying with everything they had, trying to back the old man into the same corner where he had mercilessly crushed so many others. They would have succeeded had not the high price lured hundreds of small shareholders into the market to sell and take their profits. Fisk and Gould tried at heavy cost to absorb these new offerings, but the desperate Drew managed to buy enough to cover himself. When the struggle ended on November 24, Drew had saved his skin at a cost of $1,-500,000, while Fisk and Gould had lost almost all they had won in their previous bear movement. For once, Erie's mistreated small stockholders had profited at the expense of the big manipulators.

Although the Erie partners had a few wounds of their own, they had given the Great Bear the soundest licking he ever took, something Wall Street viewed without sorrow. Broker W. W. Fowler voiced amazement at the dash of Fisk's operations.

"Boldness! Boldness! twice, thrice and four times," he wrote of Fisk. "Impudence! cheek! brass! unparalleled, unapproachable, sublime!"

Veteran speculators saw that in the two young Erie moguls they had a formidable new force to contend with in the gambling arena. Within seven months they had made the nation's most powerful railroad operator, Vanderbilt, come to terms, and had whipped Drew, the nation's biggest railroad speculator. Uncle Daniel's humiliation was so complete that he became a laughingstock, a has-been who never recovered his touch, for thereafter his speculations were dogged by ill luck. Fisk and Gould merely had to parry a swarm of lawsuits—a routine matter. Before the dust settled, Fisk, who had never ceased to describe the settlement with Vanderbilt as "the Great Robbery," took his attorney, Thomas G. Shearman, and called on the Commodore.

"How are you, Commodore?" he said. "I've come on behalf of the stockholders of the Erie Railway Company to collect from you the four millions and a half of dollars which they were forced to pay over to you last July to have these suits discontinued." He opened his bag. "Here are 50,000 shares of Erie, which you made us take off your hands at 70, which, I calculate, is $3,500,000. We want you to take this stock, and draw your check immediately, with interest from July 11; and furthermore, we want another million from you, which was paid for no consideration; and please to make out your check for that amount also, with interest from the same date."

Vanderbilt, aghast at the fat man's nerve, reddened. "I ain't sold no stock to the Erie Company, nor received any million bonus," he said untruthfully and ungrammatically, "so I shan't pay the money."

"Well, Commodore," Fisk grinned, "we have come to make you a formal tender of the securities . . . If you won't pay up, why, we shall have to sue you. Good-day."

"Good-day, Jim," Vanderbilt roared. "You can sue and be damned."

Shearman promptly brought suit against him for $4,500,-000. Suit was also instituted against Work and Schell for the $429,250 paid them in the same transaction, while still another action was brought against Drew for $1,000,000, charging him with defrauding Erie while a director.

The air was so thick with lawsuits that Fisk donned a disguise "as of a man going to a masquerade" when he left his office at midnight of November 28 with two attorneys. He also disguised his voice as he ordered a cabman in loud tones to take them to the Fifth Avenue Hotel, rerouting him to the Cortland Street ferry after they got under way. Nevertheless, a suspicious process server followed in another hansom and presented him with a summons at the ferry house. He uttered mild imprecations, then crossed to Jersey City, where he and his companions were seen hurriedly boarding a train which had been waiting there for them and which departed immediately. Weighing these stealthy movements, and recalling that Fisk carried a large bag, reporters jumped to hasty conclusions. Next day the *Tribune, Herald* and several other papers published a rumor that Fisk had fled to Canada with millions in Erie funds to escape prosecution for his illegalities.

Actually he had only gone to Binghamton to confer with his old friend Judge Ransom Balcom about an injunction against the Drew-Belmont foe. On his way back, he stopped at Port Jervis and wrote a letter to the newspapers poking fun at them for suggesting that he was anything but the soul of honesty. He was impervious to ordinary insult involving mere reflections on his integrity, and indeed seemed to enjoy such attacks for their notoriety value. But when he returned to New York he executed a quick switch. It was an editorial in the Springfield *Republican*, edited by the eminent Samuel Bowles, that changed his mind. Charging that the canards had injured his good name and caused Erie stock to drop four percent, he filed suit against Bowles for $50,000.

". . . Fisk has probably destroyed the credit of the [Erie] railroad, while piling up a fortune for himself," Bowles wrote in his November 28 issue in an editorial headed "The New Hero of Wall Street," continuing: "The multiplication of its stock has been fearful . . . The issue of new shares seems to have been wanton, and to no purpose in great part but to gamble in Wall Street with. Nothing so audacious, nothing more gigantic in the way of swindling has ever been perpetrated in this country, and yet it may be that Mr. Fisk and his associates have done nothing that they cannot legally justify, at least in New York courts, several of which they seem wholly to own . . . Many even of his friends predict for him the state prison or the lunatic asylum; his father is already in the latter."

Bowles went on to describe Fisk as a one-time peddler of "silks, poplins and velvets by the yard," adding:

"He is almost as broad as he is high, and so round that he rolls rather than walks. But his nervous energy is stimulated rather than deadened by his fat, which gives, indeed, a momentum to his mental movement and his personal influence."

Had the Massachusetts editor called him a swindler and let it go at that, doubtless Fisk would have overlooked it just as he had already laughed off scores of New York newspaper aspersions on his character. While it was true that Bowles owned some textile properties and was fighting Fisk's suits in favor of the Goulding patent, Fisk never let a trifling lawsuit cause rancor. What incensed him was Bowles' descent to personalities, his derision of Fisk's dimensions and the malicious editorial sneer about his father's insanity—two sensitive spots in his otherwise invulnerable hide.

Undisturbed by the suit, Bowles visited New York with his wife late in December, putting up at Fisk's own hostelry, the Fifth Avenue Hotel. Having first brought suit against Bowles in Massachusetts, Fisk dropped that action and to gain jurisdiction brought a new one in New York. On the evening of December 22 he had but to whisper into the ear of Judge John H. McCunn, a Tammany jurist, to cause him to hold a special after-hours session as a favor and issue a warrant for Bowles' arrest. A brief tête-à-tête with Sheriff James O'Brien, another Tammany official who was now a bosom friend, and the stage was set. Fisk and O'Brien then left to join Tweed and other Tammany sachems at the Fifth Avenue home of Augustus Brown, where a reception was being held to honor A. Oakey Hall, the pleasant quipster whom Tweed had just elected mayor by virtue of thousands of fraudulent votes.

About 9 o'clock that evening, Samuel Bowles was chatting in the lobby of the Fifth Avenue Hotel with Murat Halstead when two sheriff's officers entered, flashed the warrant in the editor's face, then propelled him swiftly out the door to a waiting carriage. Almost before Bowles knew it, he was in a cell at the Ludlow Street jail. Not until then was he allowed to read the warrant charging him with criminal libel of James Fisk Jr. As jails went, the Ludlow Street institution was a comfortable one, being largely for prisoners involved in civil suits. Yet Bowles did not want to stay there all night. He was anxious about his wife, who was an invalid and would be alarmed at his mysterious disappearance. He demanded that he be freed on bail. Not a chance, said the jailer—there was no one around empowered to accept bail. Bowles soon realized that he was the victim of a Fisk plot to keep him immured overnight. Halstead and others of his friends were busy during the dark hours trying to find someone to liberate him. Sheriff O'Brien, when located at the Tammany celebration, said it was after hours and besides, he had no authority to interfere. Those who did have authority seemed to have gone into hiding. The upshot was that Bowles remained imprisoned until morning, when he was released on $50,000 bail.

Fisk had his revenge, and did not pursue the lawsuit further, but he lost rather than gained by his spite. Bowles, one of the nation's most influential editors, had plenty of newspaper friends who denounced the proceeding as petty and contemptible, which it was despite the offensive remarks that caused it. This was one of the few instances when Fisk's good humor gave way to a malice normally foreign to him. In a letter he wrote to the Boston *Evening Gazette* in an effort to justify his move, he showed a remarkable unawareness that he might have violated any principle of decency.

Bowles, he complained, had published an editorial "devoted to a bitter, abusive, untruthful and unprovoked attack on my origin, vocation, habits, personal appearance and family afflictions," and went on:

"Culpable as I am in selling 'silks, poplins and velvets by the yard,' the generous nature of Samuel Bowles, Esq., of Springfield, Massachusetts, is not finally and utterly turned against me until he has ascertained that I am guilty of having a father who is unhappily an inmate of a lunatic asylum . . . and he prophetically consigns me to a 'mad-house or state prison.' Under the circumstances, Messrs. Editors, don't you think I had cause to feel vexed. . . ?"

Truly he had cause to feel vexed. It did not seem to occur to him that the point at issue was the fitness of such a shabby revenge. Fisk sometimes had moral myopia. His letter was written from Boston, where the intermittent husband was spending the Christmas holidays with his wife Lucy.

10
The Sky Is the Limit

THE student of the sinful Sixties is apt to throw up his hands and reflect that had Diogenes been extant then, he would have tossed away his lantern and given up all hope of finding an honest man. There were honest men, to be sure, for Horace Greeley was living, but few of them seemed to be heard. The upheaval caused by the war, the quick boom in railroads and industry at its end, and the vast opportunities for wealth offered by an expanding people, made the nation suddenly outgrow rules that formerly had sufficed to keep illegality somewhere within bounds. Self-sacrificial patriotism was out of style. The profit motive went on a glorious spree. With busy minds like those of Jim Fisk and Boss Tweed figuring angles never figured before, the moral atmosphere became noxious. Almost before upright citizens knew about it, the stock market was a place of barrelhouse, bare-knuckled combat, Albany was a legislative Sodom and New York City was Tweedville.

The ponderous Tweed, a former chairmaker of meager education but gifted with magnetism and a talent for organization, seized enormous power in the fall of 1868 with some financial help from Fisk and Gould. In addition to campaign funds, he was given, apparently gratis, a large block of Erie stock right off the press as well as a place on the board. He had elected his amiable lieutenant, the elegant Oakey Hall, as mayor of New York. He had elected the more prosaic John Hoffman governor. True, his candidate Seymour had lost out in the presidential canvass to General Grant—because of voting frauds, Tammany had the impudence to

claim—but Tweed was expecting to elect *his* President in
1872 and to become boss of the nation as he now was in
the Empire State.

In New York, many of his votes came from "repeaters"
at five dollars a vote, many from jocular election judges
who threw away legitimate ballots and simply handed in
fraudulent Tweed majorities, and quite a parcel through
the aid of his loyal Judges Barnard and McCunn. For a
fortnight before the election, Barnard gallantly sacrificed his
own leisure, keeping his chambers open from 6 P.M. until
midnight to naturalize 10,093 men, many of them from Ireland, who must have been puzzled at the way they were
herded into citizenship in batches of forty, then given closest
individual attention by fast-talking gentlemen who handed
them cigars and instructed them as good citizens to vote the
Tweed ticket. "It is rumored," snapped the *Tribune*, "that
Judge McCunn has issued an order naturalizing all the lower
counties of Ireland, beginning at Tipperary and running
down to Cork. Judge Barnard will arrange for the northern
counties at the next sitting of Chambers." Civic leaders
should have noted an arresting arithmetical anomaly—that
eight percent more votes were cast than the entire voting
population—but nothing was done about it.

What the Tweed Ring was in government, the Erie Ring
was in finance. Each paid lip service to legality, Tweed with
crooked votes, Erie with foxy lawyers and accommodating
judges. Each ring, in addition to full-blown rascals, numbered men who shaded off in varying degrees toward some
semblance of honesty. While Oakey Hall and John Hoffman, for example, well knew that the machine that elected
them was incredibly corrupt and were glad to collaborate
with it, it was never proved that they personally stole anything. As for Erie, it had in the firm of Field & Shearman
two of the most outwardly respectable lawyers of the time.
The tall, imperious David Dudley Field, son of a clergyman,
brother of Cyrus Field of Atlantic cable fame, was known

as a law reformer, enjoyed the highest social standing, and in professional prestige was second to none. Thomas Shearman, an undersized man who looked like a midget beside Field, was superintendent of the Sunday school at Mr. Beecher's church in Brooklyn and knew the Good Book almost as well as Daniel Drew. Shearman's services were in such demand that he had an office right in the Erie building. Although Field & Shearman had other clients, it was their labors for Erie that brought them into company not usually chosen by law reformers and Sunday school superintendents.

Field himself, in fact, had time to attend only to the most important of Erie's legal work, leaving other matters to a host of lesser attorneys. As one stockholder remarked bitterly, Erie must be an intensely law-abiding corporation since it had so many lawyers working in its behalf. In the year 1868 alone, the company paid out $330,510.70 to forty-one different attorneys, Field & Shearman collecting $48,-289.10 of this—only a fraction of what they would collect in 1869. In addition to its own suits against Vanderbilt, Drew, Work, Schell, Belmont and others, Erie was constantly a defendant in actions brought by stockholders and market losers as well as by dozens of the injured in the Carr's Rock wreck and relatives of the dead. Although the railroad was clearly culpable, most of the blame resting on the neglectful Drew, it was claiming that the train was deliberately derailed, even accusing a feeble-minded character named Bowen of the crime. On top of all this, Fisk had his occasional private lawsuits, not to mention the endless legal wrangling in several states over his Goulding textile patent, which would continue until his death. Litigation became such a part of his life that he employed a personal attorney, William H. Morgan, who served as a sort of legal dispatch bearer and liaison expert, coming in daily to keep him posted on what all the other lawyers were doing in various cases that dragged on for months or years.

"The lawyers lap up Erie money," Fisk observed, "like kittens lap up milk."

Actually, Erie's own lawsuits were a matter of deliberate policy on his part and Gould's, designed less to seek the protection of the law than to dodge it, circumvent it, find loopholes in it, on the theory that their ultimate gains would far exceed their legal fees. Although the attorneys bore the courtroom brunt of these actions, it took considerable time and concentration for Fisk and Gould to keep abreast of them and to appear as witnesses. Yet they were not too preoccupied to go shopping for new quarters and, in December of 1868, to astonish New York by the purchase of Pike's Opera House as the future offices of Erie. The old building was inadequate, they said, but critics who called the move corporate lunacy were not far from the mark. There *was* something preposterous about the amalgamation of a railroad with play-acting that must have made engineers and brakemen out on the Erie line wonder if they were in safe hands. Catch Commodore Vanderbilt allowing his New York Central offices to be invaded by a parcel of dancing girls!

The Opera House deal, by its very absurdity, was a sign that Fisk and Gould felt their power secure despite all the howls of minor stockholders. With Tweed on the board, the sky was the limit. It also was a sign that Fisk, nominally second in command to Gould, nevertheless had a strong voice in the direction. Although the two bought the building jointly, it was Fisk's special plaything, and the fact that he could win over the self-effacing Gould to such a gaudy project is a measure of his influence.

While workmen were refurbishing the Opera House, the Erie partners took steps to perpetuate their hold on the road, borrowing a page from the book of Tweed. To avoid being ousted at the next annual election, they aimed to control the election. Strangely, more than half of all Erie shares were owned by English stockholders who had naively expected good dividends and who rightly should have controlled the road by virtue of their majority. By this time most literate Americans with idle money understood perfectly that while Erie might be a passable stock for speculators with iron nerves, as an investment it was hopeless. The British, who had discovered this too late, were sending wrathful and futile messages across the Atlantic. So far, Fisk and Gould had managed by various legal subterfuges to keep most of them from voting their stock, but they could not depend on maintaining minority control forever. They took this problem to the pliable state legislature at Albany, where they introduced the Erie Classification Bill.

This humbug classified the road's board of directors into five groups so that only one-fifth of them would be elected annually, the first group to hold office for five years, the second group four, and so on. While the stated purpose of the bill was to prevent a wholesale housecleaning of the board each year and assure an efficient continuity of management, its real intent was to keep Gould and Fisk at the helm for a full five years.

Boss Tweed now doffed his mantle as Director Tweed of Erie and donned his toga as State Senator Tweed. He reopened several bars at his Delavan House suite and with the aid of free-spending Erie lobbyists cultivated the Black Horse Cavalry. The bill passed, causing Gould to utter a priceless quackery:

"[The act will] secure to the property a responsible, experienced and intelligent management, and be the means of preventing in the future the sudden changes in the policy of this magnificent railway, peculiar to it in the past while it was a mere creature of Wall Street speculation."

The classification bill was only part of the Gould-Fisk program to domesticate Erie, make it a more tractable creature for their Wall Street speculations. Another step was to place their relations with Judge Barnard in a condition of even firmer rapport. There was a slight embarrassment here, for during the Jersey City exile Fisk had caused Field & Shearman to bring charges of corruption against Barnard. The judge's term ended December 31, 1868, and Tweed thought it might look indecorous to re-elect him while such a shadow hung over him. Erie withdrew the charges, giving a statement to the newspapers informing the public what a grievous error it all had been:

". . . whereas the complaint in such action charges the said Barnard with corrupt and improper action and conduct in his official capacity as a Judge of said Court; and, whereas we have become convinced, after a most ample and complete investigation that there is no foundation whatever for such charges; therefore

"*Resolved*, That the said charges be and the same are hereby withdrawn as wholly groundless. . . ."

With that misunderstanding cleared up, the said Barnard was re-elected for another fourteen-year term in a Tweed landslide of votes both single and repetitive. Having all these matters to attend to, perhaps it was no wonder that Fisk and Gould scarcely had time to give the railroad itself the attention it badly needed. All-steel rails being so infernally expensive, an arrangement was made for the purchase of cheaper steel-capped iron rails from the Trenton Rolling Mills, but it would be many months before any were laid. Erie's connections with the Pennsylvania coalfields were improved. Some new locomotives and drawing-room coaches were being built, some wooden bridges replaced by iron. But Erie, crying for an all-out program of rehabilitation, was getting only a once-over-lightly treatment that nudged ruin back rather than defeating it. Instead of rescuing their own road from disrepair, its leaders were mapping a secret campaign to swallow another line, the Albany & Susquehanna.

11 *Nothing Is Lost*
Save Honor

ONE of the saving graces of the Tweed and Erie rings was their capacity to admit past error and to breathe love into relations formerly darkened by discord. Thus Tweed, who less than a year earlier had fought tooth and nail for Vanderbilt, now sat happily on the Erie board and was glad that Vanderbilt had lost the fight. Field and Shearman, who had screamed at Barnard as corrupt and sought to impeach him, had the scales removed from their eyes and saw him as a benevolent dispenser of purest justice. Barnard himself, so lately moved by passion to brand Fisk and Gould outlaws and swindlers, found them simply charming fellows when he got to know them. Fisk and Gould were so delighted at the new Erie-Barnard *entente cordiale* that they presented a batch of Erie stock to the judge they had mistakenly called a bandit. Barnard took to dropping in at Josie Mansfield's occasionally for poker and champagne with Fisk, Tweed and other cronies.

George G. Barnard, a merry fellow, brushed aside any scruples that his acceptance of stock might damage his impartiality in presiding over Erie litigation. A native of Poughkeepsie, this thirty-nine-year-old Yale graduate had married the daughter of a tobacco millionaire and yet had pride enough to seek independent wealth. Tall, foppish in dress, he was a strikingly handsome man with black hair sprinkled with gray and a jet-black mustache some believed to be dyed. He was a regular at Delmonico's, the Astor House and other fashionable resorts, sometimes getting home so late that he was noticeably sleepy on the bench next day. Every morning his court officer had a stick of soft pine ready for him, along with a sharp penknife. All day long as he listened to arguments, Barnard whittled steadily, now and then amusing the court with witty or off-color remarks. Every night there was a heap of shavings to be swept up after him. In 1869, on behalf of his Erie friends and possibly after coaching at poker sessions, Barnard began whittling away at something bigger—the Albany & Susquehanna Railway.

The A. & S. was a brand new road, born to such grief as few carriers ever experienced. It covered 142 miles of pleasant hill country between Albany and Binghamton, being only a small local line in comparison with the great Erie network. Indeed, it had been planned primarily to serve its own area, with no delusions of trunk-line grandeur. Its president was a determined Scot named Joseph H. Ramsey, who had persevered through seventeen years of toil and disappointment that would have whipped a lesser man before he saw his dream realized with the laying of the last twenty-two miles of track. On January 15, 1869, there was quite a celebration to mark the final linking of Albany and Binghamton by rail, but Ramsey knew his troubles were not over. His treasury was bare, he owed several contractors, bankruptcy stared him in the face, and his board of directors had split into two warring camps. On top of that, he became aware that Fisk and Gould, the Erie carnivores, were out to eat him up.

These two had been licking their chops in anticipation, for ownership of the A. & S. offered them several glorious opportunities. It connected with Erie at Binghamton and was built on the same broad six-foot gauge, allowing the transfer of trains from one line to another. It also connected with the Delaware & Hudson at Nineveh. But most important of all, it would give Erie its long-sought gateway to New England and the eastern seaboard via connecting

lines from Albany, opening a vast new market for Erie coal
and produce. Nor did Fisk and Gould ever forget that possession of the A. & S. would also enable them to steal much
of the through east-west freight now monopolized by Commodore Vanderbilt and his New York Central. In seizing the
new line they could at one stroke enrich Erie and bring
woe to Vanderbilt, whom they were suing for $4,500,000
as the author of the Great Robbery.

The internal struggle in the directorate seemed provi-
dentially designed for their purposes. The road's financial
crisis had bred dissension. Of the fourteen directors, seven
who were headed by one Walter S. Church were out to oust
Ramsey. The other seven, including Ramsey himself, were
fighting for his retention and for the expulsion of the Church
group. The quarrel became so bitter that Ramsey let it be
known that at the next directors' election in September
either he or his opponents must go, so that the road could
have a harmonious board. The election would therefore
hand complete control over to one side or the other. It was
said that in June the Church faction, fearing they could
not gain a majority of voting stock, "invited" Erie to aid
them—another way of saying they favored Erie control of
the road and Erie payment of its debts. It seems more likely
that Fisk and Gould maneuvered the invitation, seeing their
opportunity to divide and conquer, but at any rate they did
not have to be invited twice into the road's humble parlor.
They promptly sent agents carrying carpetbags stuffed with
Erie money along the line to buy up stock for voting purposes.

However, the carpetbaggers ran into a snag. There was
very little floating stock in A. & S., most of the shares having
been subscribed by towns along the route under an agreement that forbade town officers to sell it at less than par.
Since par value was $100, and the stock was now quoted at
only $20, the Erie treasury would be taking a quintuple
licking at that rate. The Erie moguls hit on a better plan.

They gave a number of the town officers free passes to New York, where they wined and dined them, then proposed a bargain: They would pay the towns par value for their stock *after* the election provided that at the election the town shares would be voted as Erie wished. The town officers, charmed by Fisk's jovial entertainment, evidently did not smell anything fishy in the proposal, and some of them agreed to it. They should have known that since they had no power to sell except for cash, the agreement was illegal and could not be enforced against Erie after the votes had been secured.

Joseph Ramsey got wind of this and knew he was in for the battle of his life unless he was willing to quit, step out of the road it had cost him seventeen hard years to bring into being. He also knew that he was a puny David to pit himself against two Goliaths like Fisk and Gould, who had beaten Vanderbilt, beaten Drew, and had all the resources of Erie behind them. But Ramsey was so infuriated at the invasion of his bailiwick by the New York Philistines that he resolved to fight even though his slingshot was small. By his order, on August 3 Treasurer William Phelps of A. & S. refused to transfer town-owned stock to Erie which he believed bought only by illegal bargain. The battle was on.

Erie immediately got an injunction from Judge Barnard ordering the transfer of the stock. Ramsey countered with an injunction from an Owego judge forbidding it. Lawyer Shearman, deserting his Brooklyn Sunday school to serve as Erie's chief of staff in this phase of the conflict, rushed up to Owego with more Barnard ammunition—an order removing Ramsey's injunction and going a lot farther than that. It suspended Ramsey as president and a director of the line and restrained him from issuing any more stock.

Ramsey, being well acquainted with the history of Fisk and Gould, must have reflected that an order inspired by these busy printers restraining him from issuing more stock was much like a drunkard denying liquor to anyone but himself. A hard-fisted fellow, he was not above resorting to bamboozlement when assailed by brigands. He was in real peril. Since the board of directors was equally divided, Barnard's order removing him gave the majority to his enemies and also put them in charge of the books so they could make stock transfers to their own liking. In a word, it gave them control of the road.

To prevent this, Ramsey took the stock transfer books from the company's offices in Albany and put them in the best hiding place he could think of—a mausoleum in a local cemetery. He had plenty of unsold shares that would help him vote-wise if he could unload them on sympathizers. Working fast, he disposed of 9,500 shares to friends, a move that took some doing since they did not have the money to buy them. He solved this by furnishing his friends not only with the stock but also with the funds to make the necessary ten percent down payment. He raised the money by appropriating $150,000 worth of bonds in his own road —a speedy piece of illegality worthy of Fisk and Gould at their slipperiest. Then, on August 6, he got an injunction from Judge Rufus Peckham, sitting in Albany, forbidding the Church-Erie party from acting as officers of the A. & S.

This left the road in a managerial vacuum, with no one at its head. Attorney Shearman, now back in New York, recognized the opportunity. He drew up a petition praying that receivers be appointed. It happened that Judge Barnard had hurried to Poughkeepsie, where his mother was dying. Although other judges were available, Shearman seemed to feel that this was a job no one else could perform with the Barnard finesse. A telegram was sent to the judge:

"Come to New York without fail to-night. Answer care 359 West Twenty-third Street.—James H. Coleman."

Coleman was a young lawyer who ran errands for Barnard, the latter in turn often referring legal work to him. The address given was interesting, being that of Josie Mansfield. Barnard left his ailing mother and caught a train to

New York with fireman urgency, but he later insisted he did not hold a special session of court at Josie's. One of Shearman's legal staff met him with the petition ready for his signature. The two men darted into Fisk's bachelor diggings, which Barnard solemnly swore he believed to be a real estate office. There he signed the papers appointing James Fisk Jr. and Charles Courter receivers for the A. & S.

Courter, a resident of Cobleskill, was one of the dissident directors belonging to the Church faction, but he was only a straw man. Fisk was ready, his bag packed, his five-carat diamond shining in his shirtfront like an Erie headlight. Aware of hostility in Albany, he had rounded up a dozen Erie roughnecks as bodyguards. Bearing the Barnard-signed papers, he and his crew caught the 11 P.M. Vanderbilt train to Albany, which would allow him a few hours' sleep at the Delavan House before assuming his new duties in the morning.

The state capital was already in a ferment over the affair. Being served by the A. & S. and the New York Central, Albany was strongly loyal to Ramsey and Vanderbilt. There was general indignation at Erie's attempt to muscle in on Ramsey's inoffensive little railroad, and also at the fusillade of scattergun injunctions fired by Judge Barnard, sitting more than 100 miles from any point of the A. & S. Vanderbilt, too, was eyeing the struggle as anything but an outsider. He well knew that "them blowers," as he characterized Fisk and Gould, were out to rook him of some of his most profitable traffic, and that Ramsey was fighting his fight. Ramsey was getting Vanderbilt's moral and financial support, but he was doing pretty well as it was. On the same evening that Barnard had made his fireman's journey to New York, Ramsey had gone to Judge Peckham in Albany and got an order naming Robert H. Pruyn of that city as receiver. This was blow for blow, since Pruyn, an A. & S. director, was stoutly behind Ramsey in his duel with the invaders. If time meant anything, Ramsey and Pruyn had the edge, for Judge Peckham had signed his papers almost an hour before Barnard, and on top of that Receiver Pruyn got up a bit earlier next morning than Receiver Fisk. By the time Fisk and his attorneys picked up co-Receiver Courter and reached the A. & S. offices on the Albany riverfront with his detachment of Erie halberdiers, Pruyn was already installed.

The Fisk party was met at the door by John W. Van Valkenburg, general superintendent of A. & S., a burly Ramsey man not easily intimidated. He admitted Courter, who was a director of the road and could scarcely be excluded, but told Fisk bluntly to stay out.

"This is my twenty-sixth raid," Fisk said, "and I'm going to take you fellows if it costs a million dollars."

"You'll have a good time doing it," Van Valkenburg snapped.

Fisk turned to his men. "Come on, boys," he said.

They advanced on the door. However, Van Valkenburg had a platoon of his own railroad mechanics ready. They resisted with spirit. There was a brisk struggle accompanied by hard language at the entrance before Fisk and his outnumbered forces were shoved ungently out the door, Fisk "with his spruce attire and toilet in a rather disordered condition." A pugnacious-looking man in civilian clothes who identified himself as a policeman strode up and arrested him. Fisk got all the way to the stationhouse with him before discovering that the man was no policeman at all, merely an A. & S. employe aiming to harass him.

One of Fisk's redeeming qualities was an ability to see humor in his own discomfiture. He returned to the railroad office, where Van Valkenburg still denied him entrance, and laughed uproariously at the absurdity of the situation. He even complimented the superintendent for his grit, saying he would like to have Van Valkenburg working for him.

"Get Ramsey out here," he suggested, "and I'll play a game of seven-up with him to see who runs this railroad."

Neither Ramsey nor Pruyn were agreeable to this mode of arbitration. Returning to his hotel, Fisk telegraphed Shearman in New York, who referred the problem to Judge Barnard. Barnard, incensed at the circumvention of his brand of law, granted a new injunction restraining everyone from interfering with Receivers Fisk and Courter. He bolstered this with a writ of assistance empowering sheriffs to impress posses to execute the injunction. He sent the orders by telegraph, something new in jurisprudence. Fisk, clad in new legal armor, went to the A. & S. offices once more, again getting no farther than the door. He waved the new Barnard injunction in Van Valkenburg's face and allowed that he would come in and take charge.

Van Valkenburg snickered at him. He brought out some papers of his own—an injunction from Judge Peckham restraining everybody from interfering with Receiver Pruyn. This was followed by another Peckham order enjoining all sheriffs from taking action on Barnard's writ of assistance.

No sooner was Fisk given a new weapon than the enemy contrived a defense against it. Indeed, so far the Ramsey forces had the upper hand, since they were in actual possession of the road and its office and could not be dislodged. At this point the law had reached such intricacy that mere laymen scarcely pretended to understand it. Yet it would get worse. According to Judge Barnard, Receiver Pruyn was illegal. According to Judge Peckham, who held the Albany view of things, Receivers Fisk and Courter were illegal. Sheriffs were ordered by one judge to depose Pruyn, while another judge commanded them to protect Pruyn against the Fisk-Courter aggressions. The New York Law Code was reaching a slapstick level similar to that during the Vanderbilt-Drew imbroglio the previous year.

Fisk retired to the Delavan House bar for refreshment and meditation. Balked on the legal front, he took recourse to propaganda, calling in newspapermen to tell them that the good people of Albany had the wrong idea of the question and were overlooking the great benefits of Erie control of A. & S.

"Look at the past," he urged. "Has not everything been done by the Central line to make you a mere local station, to ruin your shipping and wipe out your instruments of business. . . ?"

It was here that he was struck by an inspiration of the most limpid clarity, the kind that was said to have burst on Napoleon in his moments of omniscience. He had, he saw, made the mistake of attacking the enemy at his strongest point, which was Albany. How could he have forgotten that the A. & S. was 142 miles long, with its far end at Binghamton, a loyal Erie town? He decided, in the phrase of a later strategist, to assail the foe's soft underbelly at Binghamton, take possession there, then work up the line toward Albany.

He got on the telegraph wire to Erie General Superintendent L. D. Rucker, Riddle's successor in New York, ordering him to speed to Binghamton to take overall charge. He wired Erie's Division Superintendent H. D. V. Pratt in Binghamton, directing him to mobilize an assault force, capture the A. & S. terminal and all rolling stock in Binghamton, then move northeastward along the line. He likewise telegraphed Judge Barnard's writ of assistance to Sheriff Browne in Binghamton, commanding Browne to support the Fisk-Erie forces in their flanking movement.

Superintendent Van Valkenburg, field leader of the Ramsey array, had not been blind to the possibility of some such maneuver. That same morning of August 8 he sent out a special train from Albany containing Lawyer Henry Smith of A. & S. along with almost 100 muscular railroad workers under Master Mechanic Blackall to strengthen his hand should need arise. This train was steaming toward Binghamton at a fast clip, stopping at stations along the route to

serve local officers with Judge Peckham's injunction in-
validating Judge Barnard's injunction.

At Binghamton, the Erie superintendent took possession
of the A. & S. terminal with the aid of Sheriff Browne, who
favored the Erie side of the quarrel. There were four A. &
S. locomotives at Binghamton, three of which the sheriff
captured in the name of Judge Barnard and Receiver Fisk.
The engineer of the fourth, a loyal Ramsey man, sniffed foul
play and was off in his iron steed before he could be seized,
making good time toward Albany. The Erie party now
made up a small special train, manned by an Erie engineer
and conductor, having Sheriff Browne as its chief passenger
along with a group of Erie employes. They set out eastward
that afternoon, stopping at each station to carry out the
orders of Receiver Fisk—that is, to discharge the A. & S.
station agents and other help and replace them with Erie
personnel. The sheriff was so enthusiastic in the cause that
he forgot that his jurisdiction was confined to Broome
County. The train kept right on to Afton, in Chenango
County some thirty miles from Binghamton, where the
A. & S. employes were likewise fired and replaced by Erie
men.

The telegraph meanwhile was sputtering. Van Valkenburg in Albany knew that the tail-end of his railroad was
in enemy hands. At Afton, Sheriff Browne and his party got
a telegram from Van Valkenburg warning them that they
were breaking the law and that any further advance would
be at their own peril. Browne, uncertain of his ground, wired
to Fisk in Albany for instructions. Fisk was delighted at the
success of his strategy, which had already won him possession of thirty miles of the road, and was impatient only because there was no way he could reach the scene of action
and take command in person. He telegraphed Browne, ordering him peremptorily to continue the advance and re-
minding him it was his sworn duty to carry out the mandate

of Judge Barnard. Browne and his dwindling forces pressed on.

Although small, this war employed the most advanced of tactics, the opposing forces being entirely motorized and receiving their instructions from the two rival generals, Fisk and Van Valkenburg, by telegraph. Van Valkenburg, seeing that a clash was inevitable, began to worry about innocent A. & S. passengers riding the regular trains. He telegraphed a blanket order that all trains except those bearing the military be stopped on the nearest siding. All along the line wayfarers were marooned, many of them miles from their destination, as traffic halted.

Late that afternoon, the Ramsey train carrying Lawyer Smith and his men reached Bainbridge, thirty-six miles from Binghamton, where Smith was informed that a train bearing Erie minions was coming at them. Deciding it was best to wait developments, Smith had his train backed into a siding. His men had with them a patent frog used for getting cars back on the track, which was equally effective for derailing cars. They fastened the device on the main line and waited. It was growing dark when the Erie train pulled into Bainbridge, traveling at low speed because of possible tampering with the rails. The engineer did not see the frog. The Ramsey men, watching from the siding, cheered lustily as the locomotive hit the frog and bumped off the track. Attorney Smith walked over and handed Sheriff Browne a copy of Judge Peckham's injunction warning all officers not to obey Judge Barnard's order.

The sheriff was nonplused. One judge said Gee, the other Haw. No matter which one he obeyed, he was illegal in the other's view. As he pondered, Smith pulled out of the siding with his train and headed toward Binghamton, leaving Browne and his men prisoners cut off from their base. As the Smith party traveled westward, they stopped at each station, ejected the Erie employes Browne had installed and

reinstated the original ones. From Bainbridge, Browne telegraphed news of his predicament both to Albany and Binghamton.

In Albany, this tidings must have afflicted Fisk with a
sense of disaster similar to Lincoln's on the news of Bull
Run. Yet, according to one historian, "During all the intense excitement of this remarkable period, Jim Fisk was the
same easy, jolly, rollicking creature of impulse that he ever
was, and his jokes and champagne were lavishly distributed
to the crowd of visitors who thronged his parlors at the
Delavan House. Here he had a corps of clerks, hard at work,
and [an] army of messengers rushing in and out all day
long. . . ." Jolly or not, he knew that the thirty-six miles of
track he had captured was dwindling by the minute. He
wired urgent instructions to Binghamton to organize a massive assault party and retake the lost ground.

As luck would have it, Binghamton had only a small railroad yard manned by a handful of workers, so Superintendent Rucker and Division Superintendent Pratt were going
sleepless and unshaven while they strove to gather an army.
They sent a special train to the town of Susquehanna, some
twenty-three miles southeast of Binghamton, which brought
back a load of recruits from the Erie shops there, and also
some coal miners. Another train rolled in with several companies of skirmishers from the Erie yards at Owego, a similar distance west of Binghamton. The logistical task of organizing, arming and provisioning these raw soldiers was
enough to drive Rucker and Pratt almost insane, what with
frequent peevish telegrams from Fisk urging speed, but they
persevered in a complex of troop movements almost as in-
tricate as those preceding Second Manassas. Not until next
morning, August 10, was the mobilization complete. Several
hundred men, armed with shovels, wrenches, clubs and
flasks of liquor crowded into a train and headed east for the
front, shouting defiance although few understood what the
quarrel was about. "They took a good supply of flour and

beef with them," a *Tribune* reporter noted, reflecting that this seemed to presage a full-scale campaign.

The oncoming A. & S. troop train meanwhile had lingered during the night at Afton and other stations, awaiting daylight to make sure the track was intact. The two opposing hosts approached each other at the Long Tunnel, a 2200-foot hole through a hill fifteen miles east of Binghamton. Each side appeared to regard the tunnel with misgivings, not knowing what dangers might lurk in its depths. Each stopped at its own end of the tunnel, sending out reconaissance parties over the hill who discovered the enemy at the other end.

Although there were uncomplimentary shouts, neither side seemed eager to come to blows. Hours passed in this stalemate, the A. & S. men seeing they were outnumbered at least two to one, the Erie men lacking a field officer with sufficient mettle to organize a charge. Superintendents Rucker and Pratt, who were in command, may have been too exhausted by their efforts to organize their unit to lead it effectively into battle. In fact, the Erie army was an undisciplined mob, regarding the affair more as a holiday from routine toil than as a chance to smite the wicked hip and thigh. Sitting down under trees, they recalled the liquor they had brought, and as the day wore on there was unsoldierly drunkenness in the ranks. Colonel Rucker had brought a telegraph instrument with him, but some stealthy Ramsey zealots sneaked around and cut the wires both ways, leaving him bereft of communication with General Fisk for a time. Van Valkenburg had hurriedly sent another train from Albany with reinforcements that swelled the A. & S. army to some 300, a few of them carrying rifles or pistols. To this was added perhaps 100 residents of the area who were irate at the attempt of city-slicker guerillas to capture their railroad. The Erie army, much closer to its base, was reinforced several times during the day so that by late afternoon it was estimated at 800. The mayor of Binghamton, fearing dreadful carnage, wired the state capital at Albany imploring that the militia be sent to the scene.

"The Two Armies In Position," headlined the New York *Times,* adding with admirable restraint, "The situation at the tunnel at 2 o'clock today was very interesting."

In Albany, Fisk was as puzzled and impatient at the delay as Lee had been at Gettysburg, waiting for Longstreet to charge. He sent imperative orders to advance if the enemy had to be scattered over the track. But it was nearing 7 P.M. before some 250 of the more sober Erie stalwarts piled into their train and headed slowly through the tunnel. Reaching the eastern end, they stopped to replace a rail removed by the Ramsey men. They had no sooner got started again than they saw the Ramsey train puffing up the curved grade toward them as if it meant to crash into them, which indeed was its intention.

Here was a circumstance of awesome suspense, the sort of thing a railroad man might experience in a nightmare. There was also an element of pride and personal courage involved, since the engineer who first applied his brakes might be accused of cowardice. The gap between the two trains narrowed. Both engineers took to their whistles, setting up a piercing din. An observer noted that the Erie conductor leaned out and "gesticulated like a madman" as the Ramsey train kept coming with deadly inevitability.

The Erie engineer's nerve snapped. He set his brakes. The wheels threw sparks, but he had a heavy load pushing him downgrade. He and his fireman jumped for their lives just before the two juggernauts collided head-on with considerable impact. The front wheels of the Ramsey locomotive jumped the track. The Erie locomotive remained on the rails, its cowcatcher, headlight and smokestack wrecked, a bullet through its cab. One of the whistles jammed in an endless shriek. Men swarmed off both trains with fierce yells and the Battle of the Tunnel began.

Clubs and fists swung as the struggle developed into individual hand-to-hand encounters attended by railroad expletives. The Erie warriors, who had left two-thirds of their force behind them, were militarily in deplorable shape. Some of them were intoxicated, they had no effective leadership, and they lacked the *esprit de corps* that a worthy cause might have given them. The Ramsey men, on the contrary, were imbued with a spirit of righteous crusade, as of men defending their homes. On top of that, they had a few firearms. When they essayed a charge, the Erie forces faltered, broke and fled ignominiously over the hill. Not until they reached the other end of the tunnel, where the reserves waited, did their leaders manage to stem the rout and regroup them to face their pursuers. Here the battle resumed again, punctuated by curses, occasional shots and groans as clubs descended on skulls. "Threats, cries and horrid oaths were intermingled," wrote the *Tribune* scribe, "so as to be quite unintelligible except as to their hideousness and profanity." The fight was growing bloody when the combatants heard a sound familiar to those who had participated in the late War Between the States. It was the throbbing of drums. The militia was coming.

The fighting ended by common consent as both sides picked up their wounded and decamped. While exact casualty statistics are lacking, no one was killed. Two Erie men had bullet wounds and there were a number of broken limbs and severe concussions, but the greater part of the injuries consisted of bloody noses and bruises. The Ramsey men got their locomotive back on the track and fell back to Harpursville for the night, firing a few bridges as they went. On the day of the battle, Fisk left the telegraph when he received another injunction from Barnard and took a carriage to the A. & S. offices. He hailed Van Valkenburg, who was grinning at him from a window, and pointed to the papers in his pocket.

"Here's an order and writ of assistance from friend Barnard," he said, "fresh up from New York. It tells me to take possession."

Van Valkenburg just kept smiling, for he had summoned the police, several of whom were waiting. They arrested Fisk on a warrant from Judge Jacob Clute charging him with disturbing the peace. That made the fat man goggle, since he had made not so much as a threatening gesture, but he took it philosophically as one of the concomitants of strife in hostile Albany.

"All right! Git in here!" he said to the policemen, indicating his carriage. "Proceed, driver. Goodbye, Van Valkenburg."

They trotted off to the station, where he gave bail and was released. Returning to the Delavan House, he learned by telegraph that his military campaign had been broken up at the tunnel by the Forty-fourth Regiment of the National Guard. The railroad crisis had so frightened state officials that they called Governor Hoffman to Albany from his vacation at West Point. Although the governor was a Tweed man, he was annoyed at having his holiday interrupted and also impressed by the universal howl of protest from citizens along the A. & S. at the violence done to their railroad. Seeing that the two sides in the quarrel were hopelessly deadlocked, Hoffman ordered the National Guard to operate the road until the courts could settle the matter—an eventuality that seemed distant indeed, for Judges Barnard, Peckham and Clute were still sunk in a saturnalia of writs.

Judge Peckham had set aside Barnard's order of the day before, to which Barnard replied with writs for the arrest of Ramsey, Pruyn and Van Valkenburg for contempt. When the trio were rounded up by a reluctant sheriff, Fisk laid elaborate plans to transport them to New York. He chartered the private steamer *Erastus Corning Jr.* to take them downriver into Barnard's clutches. Like any resourceful commander he was quick to react to changes in the situation. His military offensive had come to naught, but with Ramsey, Pruyn and Van Valkenburg in Barnard's hands the head and front of the anti-Erie forces would be *hors de combat,* the enemy bereft of its leaders. Here again his strategy was foiled, this time by the alert Judge Clute, who saved the three A. & S. officials with a writ of habeas corpus. To add to Fisk's chagrin, he learned that same evening while dining at his hotel that an order had been issued for *his* arrest for contempt.

Fisk, who by this time must have cultivated a habit of selecting a table near the door, fled sans dessert, boarded the *Corning* and escaped to New York on the vessel reserved for his prisoners. Pruyn, Ramsey and Van Valkenburg were even more cautious. They hurried over the state line into Vermont until the smoke cleared away.

Observers who thought this legal low comedy could descend no lower were soon proven wrong. Ramsey at last exhumed the transfer books from the grave. At the A. & S. board election held on September 7—by which time there were twenty-one lawsuits pending—more injunctions flew along with occasional fisticuffs as the Ramsey and Church factions split in twain, each declaring the other illegal. One side elected Ramsey president, the other side Church. The issue was in doubt until the case came up before Judge Darwin Smith in Rochester. Judge Smith pronounced the Erie invasion unwarranted. He handed the railroad over to Ramsey. Ramsey, knowing that Judge Barnard still had many writs left in his quiver, hurriedly leased the A. & S. in perpetuity to the Delaware & Hudson Canal Company, taking it out of Erie's reach forever.

Fisk's twenty-sixth raid ended in total defeat. Yet he had enjoyed the fight and he girded himself for his twenty-seventh without bitterness.

"Nothing is lost save honor!" he chuckled.

12

Orgies Unspeakable

"The Erie Railroad ought to be regularly earning and paying fair dividends to its stockholders, and it is a burning shame to *somebody* that it isn't."—HORACE GREELEY

EARLY in 1869, Fisk, the lubberliest of landsmen, suddenly discovered a passion for the sea. He bought a controlling interest in the Narragansett Steamship Company, becoming the owner of two handsome vessels, the *Providence* and the *Bristol*, sailing between New York and Fall River. Undiscouraged by the fact that the line had been unprofitable for its previous owner, he refurbished the ships with new carpets, plush upholstery, gilt decoration, bronze statues and brass spittoons. He bought 250 canaries, installing a bird in each stateroom, naming many of them after friends and national figures—Jay Gould, William Tweed, Jeff Davis, General Grant and others. A lover of sounding brasses, he furnished each boat with a band to regale passengers as they sailed the Sound, an innovation regarded as sensational.

Alive to the dignity conferred on him by this new property, he had his tailor, an artisan named Bell who had turned out dozens of uninhibited civilian suits for him, fashion a blue naval uniform with gold buttons and three gold bands on the sleeves surmounted by gold stars. It was identical with the dress uniform of a United States admiral except for the Narragansett monogram on lapels and buttons. Fascinated by his new toy, he paid a jeweler $2,500 for a music box topped by a scale model of the *Providence* in solid gold and silver. He formed a habit of driving to the Chambers Street wharf a half-hour before his afternoon boat sailed. There he would pop into the steamship company office and emerge resplendent in his uniform, which still featured the non-nautical shirtfront diamond. "In this attire, which was quite becoming to him," relates a scribe of the day, "he took his place at the gangway, where he must be seen by all who entered." Although he did not know a compass from a capstan, he would stand there, arms folded, an expression of vigilant authority on his face as he watched the preparations for departure, giving the impression that the success of the embarkation depended on him alone.

One afternoon as he was thus engaged, a shambling, quaintly-dressed man walked up to the gangplank. Fisk immediately recognized him as Horace Greeley. Although Greeley had been assailing him in the *Tribune*, the admiral seized the editor's carpetbag and greeted him with cordiality.

"Mr. Greeley, I am happy to see you; you are welcome. Come right on board. We shall be off directly."

Greeley, taken aback, clung to his carpetbag as though he feared it might be stolen.

"My name is Fisk," the admiral explained. "You have probably heard of me before, Mr. Greeley?"

The philosopher of the *Tribune* pondered, then nodded. "Oh, yes; I remember you now. You were an ensign in the North Atlantic blockading squadron in 1864? I remember you very well. I had occasion to use your name while compiling 'The American Conflict.'"

Fisk drew back in astonishment, then laughed heartily. "You are much mistaken, Mr. Greeley," he said. "I am James Fisk, Jr., of the Erie Railroad; you should certainly know me, for I have been indebted to you for several compliments in the *Tribune* on the conduct of that road."

Greeley eyed him near-sightedly through spectacles as one might scrutinize a revolting museum curiosity. "Yes; it has been my opinion that the Erie road has been mismanaged. I am, and always have been a friend of the Erie. I urged the building of the road; I sank $10,000 in aid of it. The road should pay; there is no reason in the world why its stockholders should not receive a handsome yearly dividend. It runs through an agricultural section of country, and the milk-trains alone—"

Fisk interrupted the tirade by escorting his guest into the grand saloon, where he had the band play "Hail to the Chief" in his honor. Not even this hospitality could turn Greeley from his frequent editorial refrains: Erie should pay.

One of the many reasons why Erie did not pay was embodied in several hundred skilled artisans working at that same time on the Grand Opera House. After some six months of labor the renovation was completed so that the Erie staff moved in at the end of August, 1869, just as the A. & S. war was reaching its climax. The architectural taste of the time tended toward the baroque, and the Erie castle was baroque at its heaviest. Purists sneered at it as a structural extension of Fisk's diamond-and-checkerboard style of dress, but plain newspaper reporters were overwhelmed.

". . . there are but few palaces wherein so rich a *coup d'oeil* could be presented as that of the main offices of the Erie Railway Company," one of them wrote. "The carved woodwork, the stained and cut glass of the partitions, the gilded balustrades, the splendid gas fixtures, and, above all, the artistic frescoes upon the walls and ceilings, create astonishment and admiration at such a blending of the splendid and practical . . . Mr. Fisk, who planned and has superintended the arrangement . . . has certainly reason to be proud of the result, there being nowhere in this country or in Europe anything of the kind to compare with these splendid rooms."

The reporter must have had tongue in cheek when he added a significant line:

"There are in the basement very large and complete printing offices. . . ."

At the same time, Josie moved into her house a half-block away at 359 West Twenty-third. Fisk, pampering her taste for luxury, had remodeled the place and commissioned decorators to run amuck with furniture, rugs and objets d'art said to cost $65,000. Gould, who heavily disapproved of her and particularly of having her so uncomfortably near the Erie offices, had joined other friends in urging him to discard her or at least keep her in distant privacy. As one commentator put it, ". . . they finally resolved to endure what they could not cure—[his] open attachment to Mrs. Mansfield." What puzzled them was his unimpaired admiration for his wife Lucy, for whom he was noisy in his praises. Doubtless it was because of her occasional visits that he maintained his own rooms at 313, which he seldom used otherwise. Once, in discussing a divorce case in which a wife had surprised her husband inopportunely, he said, ". . . that's not the kind of wife I have. Never, *never* does Lucy surprise me with a visit, God bless her! No, she always telegraphs me when she's coming, and I—I clean up and have a warm welcome for her."

The uptown office location brought in its train other refinements, among them a new Erie ferry plying between the railroad terminal in Jersey City and the foot of West Twenty-third Street in Manhattan. That summer two new 176-foot ferryboats were commissioned, the biggest and finest yet seen on the Hudson, one christened the *James Fisk Jr.*, the other the *Jay Gould*. The *Fisk* bore life-size portraits of her patron at either end of the grand saloon, the *Gould* doing similar honor to hers. Free omnibus service was offered from the ferry, passing the Opera House and ending at the Fifth Avenue Hotel. While Commodore Vanderbilt admittedly had an advantage in bringing his passengers into the metropolis by rail, Erie was nevertheless getting them there in style.

The Fisk and Gould portraits in the ferryboats seemed to bring particular offense to stockholders who did not regard the pair as heroic. There were complaints that the Erie improvements were largely confined to their personal comfort and glorification, that the marble palace in New York was a false front concealing a railroad fallen into ruin. There was some truth in this, although at Dunkirk, New York, a new locomotive was completed that was a thing of beauty. "It was the handsomest locomotive ever made up to that time," relates the Erie historian, Edward Harold Mott. "It was decorated by paintings in oil, on every spot where one could be placed, by the late Jasper F. Crapsey, the artist. There were fourteen coats of varnish on the boiler." This spectacular iron horse was named the "George G. Barnard," and bore a medallion of Erie's favorite judge between the drivers.

Fisk's childlike pride in his new palace brought him a nickname—Prince Erie—that delighted him even though it was often used satirically. While his reputation as an amiable profligate was already well established, it was not until he installed himself at the Opera House that rumor painted him as a debauchee sunk in abandoned revels with squealing women of the stage. The employment of a half-dozen doorkeepers under a muscular Erie employe named Tommy Lynch was intended primarily to protect Fisk and Gould from process servers, but there was suspicion that the guards were posted to give Fisk privacy in his wickedness. According to a book based on a fragmentary diary left by Daniel Drew, Fisk had numbers of "concubines" among his entertainers, two of them being identified as Nully Pieris and Bella Lane. The same source has it that when Drew remonstrated against his sinful ways, Fisk replied with a lesson in hedonistic philosophy:

"No, Uncle, there isn't any hope for Jim Fisk. I'm a gone goose . . . I am too fond of this world. If I've got to choose between the other world and this, I take this. Some people are born to be good, other people are born to be bad. I was born to be bad. As to the World, the Flesh and the Devil, I'm on good terms with all three. If God Almighty is going to damn us men because we love the women, then let him go ahead and do it. I'm having a good time now, and if I've got to pay for it hereafter, why, I suppose it's no more than fair shakes; and I'll take what's coming to me. As for the vain pomp and glory of the world, I have covetous desires of the same. So there you are . . . I don't make any bones of saying that I like these scarlet women—they're approachable. . . ."

George Templeton Strong called Fisk a "roué." Preachers all over the country used him as a horrible example in sermons, although Henry Ward Beecher waited until after his death to label him "shameless, vicious, criminal, abominable in his lusts." One of Fisk's biographers blames his licentiousness on the insidious influence of Victoria Woodhull, who was then shocking New York with her free-love pronunciamento: "I have an inalienable, constitutional, and natural right to love whom I may, to love as long or as short a period as I can, to change that love every day if I please!" A stockholder sued Fisk for harming Erie's good name by appearing in public with "females of bad repute." It was charged that General Superintendent Hugh Riddle, an Erie mainstay for twenty years, quit his job in disgust at Fisk's low character. Mott, the sober historian of Erie, said ominously of the Opera House, "Its inner history can never be written, but many were the strange and bizarre scenes enacted within the privacy of its splendid apartments. No drama ever represented on its boards approached the unspeakable realities of its off-stage life." About Fisk himself, Mott wrote, "He shocked the country by the enormity and number of his transgressions against propriety. He housed gay women in splendid apartments, furnished and decorated to their desire."

Under this black pall of smoke must have been some fire.

Yet a dispassionate observer may suspect that the hair-raising tales of the Fiskian revels were to a large extent conjecture and exaggeration. Since his affair with Josie Mansfield was unconcealed, it was easy to imagine others. The puritanical idea that play-acting was immoral and that women of the stage were necessarily promiscuous was strong. When Fisk, with his already gamy reputation, was closeted in the sinfully gaudy Opera House with a flock of actresses, the opportunities for excited speculation were boundless. Far from being concerned about the talk, he seemed to enjoy it as he enjoyed almost any notoriety, even going out of his way to foster rumor. He was the sort of man who, if he happened to have a showgirl on his knee, would not bother to remove her merely because a caller, whether he be reporter or clergyman, was entering his office. He delighted in flouting convention. But whatever his willingness to dally, his intrigues were limited by the hard fact that he had only twenty-four hours a day, he needed considerable sleep, and he could not be consorting with droves of females in continuous wassail at the same time as he was fighting Ramsey in Albany, playing admiral, buying real estate, supervising contractors, shouldering a dozen lawsuits, operating actively in Wall Street, attending the races, managing his three theaters and giving at least a modicum of attention to running his railroad.

Fisk worked as he played—hard. The liberality with which he dispensed liquor to callers nourished the misconception that he was a tosspot, a fat voluptuary who wallowed in champagne, so that to his sexual lapses was added the vice of drunkenness. Some upstanding folk, not entirely illogically, took the stand that he could not possibly dress and act the way he did if he were sober. Actually, while he enjoyed an occasional bracer, he was a moderate drinker. No record of Fisk in his cups comes to light. Three years later, when he was dead and Josie was inclined to do anything but defend him, she testified in court, "Mr. Fisk was not a drinking man; he never drank much. . . ." Living descendants of his half sister recall talk in the family that he was "an absolute teetotaller," but Josie must have known better. By this time he had become a living legend, a public property, a topic of conversation at a million dinner tables. His sins were so numerous and so prominently displayed that gossip embroidered them, ballooned them, multiplied them with endless fictions that would have infuriated an ordinary man but brought only amusement to him.

The Fisk-haters in general were people who knew him only through the newspapers, the conservative and family-conscious old-liners who considered him a vulgar parvenu, upright citizens who were shocked by his immorality, and Erie stockholders who wanted a dividend. But at the same time as New York was building a strong anti-Fisk clique, an opposite or pro-Fisk faction was forming. The hard core of this circle was made up of his hundreds of friends, the men who knew him, did business with him and were warmed by his good cheer, his infectious euphoria. Out beyond, he had a multitude of admirers among the masses. Some of them naively believed him their protector against cutthroat monopolists like Vanderbilt, but the chances are that most of them saw in Fisk the American dream come true. He had risen from rags to riches, from a log cabin to a marble palace, from obscurity to fame. Fisk was success in the flesh, blowing a steam whistle. Far from being ashamed of his humble origin, he bragged about it. He had the common touch, the quip, the turn of phrase that ordinary people could understand. Even the scholarly Henry Adams, who loathed him, admitted that Fisk's humor was "really American." Somehow, a trace of his magnetism reached out to touch and win over many who never saw him, many who knew he was not blameless. The essence of his personality was simple—a genuine, boyish liking for people and an ability to express that liking—but he possessed these qualities in a colossal degree. A *Herald* reporter tried to analyze the Fisk charm and gave up almost before he got started:

"He is generous, social, and warm-hearted, and has a sort of winning way in his general deportment which it is impossible to describe, and almost impossible to resist. . . ."

Fisk's sunny grin helped to make his loud, high tenor voice sound pleasant. His style of utterance offended formalists and delighted everybody else. His smooth flow of language included a surprising number of polysyllabic words, but he cheerfully committed grammatical outrage and interlarded his speech with colorful phrases picked up somewhere in Vermont or on the circus trail. "How's your old tin oven?" he would roar to a friend by way of asking how he felt. If a situation was highly confused, it was "like Bedlam in a breeze." A man in a tough spot was "forty miles down the Delaware." To indicate something that had vanished without trace, such as money in the stock market, he would say "It went where the woodbine twineth." He loved to scramble proverbs, saying "Honesty is worth two in the bush," and "Better to have lost and won than never to have played at all." When he became admiral of his own fleet he immediately invented nautical expletives to match his uniform, one of them being, "Well, shiver my mizzen-mast and rip my royal halyards!"

Even as the Fisk-haters were piling mythical sins atop his real ones, the Fisk-lovers were building a folklore of his goodness. At the same time as he was looting corporations and demolishing Wall Street speculators, he was so touched by individual misfortune that he indulged a constant spree of disorganized but well-meant charity. While some enemies described this as a salve for his conscience, there are indications that Fisk's conscience did not trouble him at all. He did not bring corruption to New York. He found it already well established, and in his amoral way he merely played the game according to the rules of sharpers who had preceded him, adding a few refinements of his own. He had no sense of responsibility toward anything so impersonal as a corporation, nor did he waste pity on losing speculators, who to his mind had no business in such a risky enterprise if they could not take a licking without crying, as he had done in 1865. Yet any case of visible want moved him. One of his biographers wrote:

"His personal expenses were, at a liberal estimate, not one-fifth as large as the amount which he spent in providing for persons . . . who had seen misfortune in life."

Noticing considerable poverty in the area around the Opera House, Fisk arranged through Captain Stephen Killalee of the local police precinct to send either a ton of coal or a barrel of flour to needy families—both, if they were in dire straits. "I want what I do in this way kept out of the newspapers," he told Killalee. When his good friend John Morse of Boston died of a broken neck after diving into shallow water in Lake Ponchartrain, he provided for the widow thereafter as well as for the education of the two young daughters—something that did not come out until his own death. He supported an entire family of blind persons "for some years." He contributed to a struggling Negro church on Eighth Avenue, telling the astonished pastor, "If there's anything I like to boost along, it's early piety—and it's damned hard to have too much of it." When members of the Brattleboro Baptist Church asked him for money to build a new fence around the graveyard, he guffawed.

"What in thunder do you want with a new fence?" he demanded. "Those that are in can't get out; and those that are out don't want to get in; so what's the use of it?" Having had his joke, he donated $500.

Fisk was forever giving free railroad passes and market tips to friends, loaning them money, doing them favors or getting them jobs. He loaded so many cronies on the Erie payroll that efficiency suffered. His half sister Mary Grace, now grown to a strikingly beautiful young woman, had

married George W. Hooker, a Brattleboran, after the war.
Unlike many of Fisk's friends, Hooker had fought throughout the conflict, been wounded five times and won a medal
and a colonelcy. He had settled with his bride in Washington, but Fisk, who doted on Mary Grace, brought
George to New York as a broker with his old partner, William Belden, and saw the Hookers established in a comfortable house on Thirtieth Street. For his stepmother, still
proprietress of the Revere House, he demonstrated unfailing fondness, and was paying the bills for his father's care at
the Brattleboro asylum. Pop Fisk, not at all violent, spent
much of his time writing harmless letters. One of his
delusions being that the Civil War was still in progress, he
occasionally wrote Lincoln to advise him on strategy,
not knowing that Lincoln was dead. Another of his fixed
ideas was that his son was in mortal danger, causing him
to write Jim warnings to exercise vigilance—one instance
in which a madman possessed clairvoyance.

Among the Erie staff he was accused of debauching, Fisk
was the visible and popular running head of the road, since
the pussyfooting Gould was seldom seen among the lower
echelons. "[Fisk] so dominated Erie affairs in the
public mind," says one account, "that his name invariably
was mentioned first in the combination. It was always 'Fisk
and Gould,' never 'Gould and Fisk.' " At his desk he was a
genial martinet. His private secretary was John Comer, an
able upstater from Goshen—a good Erie town—with whom
he was on terms of intimate understanding. In addition to
handling high-level office detail, Comer assisted in the
dispensation of charity. Fisk was paid a fifteen-dollar fee
for each directors' meeting, a sum he instructed the secretary to give to the next worthy applicant. "The Lord will
send somebody for it," he said, and the Lord always did.
Comer had orders to let callers with hard-luck stories into
his office if they seemed reasonably sincere. A procession
of these candidates for bounty paraded into the Opera

House—an annoyance to Gould, who thought Fisk a sucker for panhandlers and disliked having the Erie palace littered with grimy mendicants.

"There never was another just such character as James Fisk, Jr.," wrote the usually imperturbable Mott. ". . . The fact that half a score or more of needy families and hosts of unfortunate men and women, were pensioners on his unstinted bounty, he would have cut his hand off rather than to have made known."

This persistent depiction of Fisk as a secret donor blushing to have his benefactions known strains credulity to the breaking point. Yet, while he was flamboyant in all else, a virtual walking billboard, he was generally quiet about his charities. In his character, superficially so simple, there were startling complexities. But it was the simpler aspects of his makeup that struck the common people, built the Fisk legend, pictured him as a sort of corporate Robin Hood, and even inspired a ballad that appeared shortly after his death, reading in part:

> *We all know he loved both women and wine,*
> *But his heart it was right I am sure;*
> *He lived like a prince in his palace so fine,*
> *Yet he never went back on the poor.*

In the busy summer of 1869, Fisk made what proved to be a fatal error when he formed a business connection with Edward Stiles Stokes, a Wall Street acquaintance. Stokes was twenty-eight, six years younger than Fisk, a social butterfly, sportsman, man about town and a splendid fashion plate who wore even more diamonds than Fisk, though none were as large as the famous Fisk shirtfront sparkler. One difference was that Stokes had a lithe, athletic figure to set off his fine raiment, another being that his gems were occasionally in pawn. Middle-sized, erect, with jet-black hair and mustaches and classic features, he was so handsome it was almost painful. It was said that he spent two hours every day grooming himself. He was one of those to whom horse-racing was not so much a sport as an addiction. He followed the season from one track to another, flitting from Long Island to Saratoga to Narragansett and elsewhere, figuring the dope sheets with a dedication that did not prevent him from betting on slow horses.

A Philadelphian, he had moved to New York with his family in 1860, his father being a rich produce wholesaler. He had married Helen Southwick, daughter of an equally rich furniture tycoon, and had a six-year-old girl. To Ned Stokes the Civil War was a thing of newspaper headlines that could mean profit if a man was smart. He had prospered in the Produce Exhange, then made a killing in the oil boom. Aided by capital supplied by his mother, he built an oil refinery in the Greenpoint section of Brooklyn. After the war, the oil bubble burst, the refinery was damaged by fire, and he was forced into bankruptcy. Possibly he signed the refinery over to his mother to avoid losing it to creditors, for she thereafter held title to it. He borrowed heavily and was trying to rebuild the refinery and make a comeback— a process that might have been faster but for his commitments at the racetracks and the Broadway sporting saloons. The possession of both a father and father-in-law of means enabled him to continue living with his wife and child at the luxurious Worth House at Fifth Avenue and Twenty-sixth Street and to act like a man without financial cares.

Fisk, bearing in mind that an Erie branch line tapped the oil fields of northern Pennsylvania, saw possibilities for profit in the refinery. He formed a company with Stokes and several others, furnishing capital to refit the plant, which was leased from Stokes' mother for $12,000 a year. Stokes himself was paid a $27,000 annual rental plus a $6000 salary and thirty percent of the profits. The Brooklyn Oil Refinery Company, with Fisk as president and Stokes as treasurer, was successful from the start, enjoying a two-way benefit from its connection with Erie—special low transportation rates and the sale of much of its oil to the railroad. This lucrative arrangement should have wiped out Ned Stokes' fiscal difficulties, but he had a propensity for incurring new debts before settling the old.

For all Fisk's capacity for overlooking human frailty and seeing the good in people, he was ordinarily a sharp judge of character who could spot an impostor from afar. Yet he took a liking to Stokes, even naming a canary after him. The young man began hanging around the Opera House, which had a convenient bar on the main floor in connection with the theater. Fisk gave fate a push. He introduced Josie Mansfield to Ned Stokes. ". . . from that time," as a contemporary writer put it, "James Fisk was a doomed man."

13 *The Gould Plan for Prosperity*

It was early in 1869 that a minor miracle came to pass when little Jay Gould, of all persons, discovered in himself a civic conscience and began to worry about the good of the country—particularly the farmers, workmen and other humble folk whose existence he had heretofore all but forgotten. He took to talking in tones of far-sighted patriotism and public weal, much like a Congressman running for reelection.

This came about because of a new interest of his—gold as a commodity for speculation. Strangely, Gould's family name a few generations back had been Gold, and he had shortened his given name from Jason, the same as that of the fabled prince who had captured the Golden Fleece, so possibly his bent for bullion was written in the stars. During the war, the government had abandoned specie payment and printed so much shin-plaster currency that at one time it took $241 worth of paper money to buy $100 worth of gold. Now, four years after Appomattox, prosperity had engendered confidence. A hundred dollars in gold could be bought for only about $135 in currency, but the quotation was fluctuating and gamblers could bet on its rise and fall precisely as they speculated in stocks. That spring gold fell to 131, at which price Gould bought $7,000,000 worth. Thereafter, of course, it was to his advantage to have the price rise, but he made it perfectly plain that any selfish consideration was farthest from his mind and he was think-

ing only of the broader good in preaching an economic dis-
covery he had made:

A rise in the price would benefit the whole nation.

While Fisk and Gould were as one in Erie activities, they
maintained autonomy in some of their other operations. Just
as Gould had no interest in Fisk's theatrical ventures, Fisk
did not immediately join Gould in the gold speculation.
Gould wanted him to enlist in this financial crusade for the
betterment of mankind, but the noisy Fisk in some respects
was more conservative than his quiet colleague. Although
their alliance with Tweed made them what Henry Adams
called "a combination more powerful than any that has
been controlled by mere private citizens in America," virtually untouchable in New York, the federal government still
stood above them. There were only about $15,000,000 of
gold in circulation in New York, so that offhand it would
appear possible for a bold operator to manipulate the metal
and even to corner it. But the government was keeping
something near $100,000,000 in the vaults, occasionally
selling a few millions as needed for trade. Thus the administration was in a position to control the price. If it
dumped more gold into the market, the price would drop.
If it kept the gold locked up, the price would hold or rise.
Since there was no telling what the administration would
do, Fisk regarded gold as too unpredictable an article to
play with.

Here was where the long-headed Gould was far ahead
of him. Gould's aim showed his colossal nerve. It was his
intention to dictate the government's gold policy, if possible by manipulating President Grant himself. Through
Tweed, the Erie Ring had bought immunity in New York.
Now Gould essayed the biggest fix of all—an understanding with the White House.

His medium of approach was a sixty-seven-year-old
scalawag named Abel Rathbone Corbin, who a year earlier
had married the President's middle-aged sister Jenny. Corbin

had had a checkered career as a lawyer, editor, speculator and lobbyist, his activities in the latter field having once been shady enough to raise the ire of a Congressional committee in Washington. Like Daniel Drew, he was a pious Methodist churchman, and although he perhaps could not quote as many of the Scriptures as the Great Bear, he was Drew's equal in his ability to keep religion strictly out of his secular activities. While he had accumulated a comfortable fortune and was technically retired, there was one thing he would never retire from—a chance to make easy money. The Corbin couple lived in a handsome mansion on West Twenty-seventh Street in Manhattan. They occasionally visited their distinguished relative in Washington, who had taken office on March 4 and was still new at his job. Corbin, who was a fluent speaker, liked to give the impression that he and Grant were on the warmest of terms and that the President, in fact, had great respect for his opinions on matters of policy.

Fisk and Gould had become acquainted with Corbin when they bought a piece of land from him in New Jersey for railroad purposes. Gould now improved the acquaintance, cultivating him with the same intensity the Chinese devote to rice lands. When he dropped a hint that there was money to be made in gold, the old man's antennae were instantly vibrating for further signals from the foxiest operator in Wall Street. Soon Gould was filling him with his new economic philosophy which so wonderfully combined profit with patriotism.

There was money to be made, Gould qualified, *if* the government did not commit the fatal error of selling gold and thus lowering the price. The crop outlook was excellent, and if gold was kept dear the farmers would get high prices that would stimulate the whole economy. Grain would be shipped by the millions of bushels, the railroads would be bustling with long freight trains loaded with produce, the working people would profit, industry would be enkindled, and in addition there would be a tremendous export of breadstuffs to Europe that would bring another rich harvest in foreign exchange. It was as simple as A-B-C, according to Gould's theory, that all this would create an era of prosperity such as the nation had never before witnessed. It was equally clear that the reverse was true. If Grant—heaven forbid!—sold gold, purchasing power would shrink, the wheels of industry would stop and privation would stalk the land.

Gould, who could be very persuasive in his insinuating way, made that even stronger. Such a disastrous course, he was convinced, might very well end in *revolution.*

Corbin, appalled at the possibility of such a dreadful thing happening to his brother-in-law, became a convert to the Gould Plan. It was cheering to him also that the course of national well-being in this instance could simultaneously enrich him personally through speculation in gold. Late in May, the Corbins went to Washington, where the old man advised Grant strongly against selling gold. Early in June the Presidential couple went to West Point for the commencement, dropping the Corbins off in New York on the way. Gould, further impressed by these signs of intimacy between Corbin and Grant, hovered about the old man and treated him with flattering cordiality. He learned that Grant was coming back to Corbin's briefly before leaving for Boston to attend the Peace Jubilee there. This seemed to open a wonderful opportunity. What could be better than for Grant to make the Boston trip in one of Fisk's fine steamers—personally escorted by Gould and the admiral?

Corbin thought it a splendid idea. The President, unaware of all this maneuvering in his behalf, arrived at Corbin's on June 15. He was there only a few hours, so there was no time for a full-scale gathering, but he did meet Jay Gould, whom he knew by reputation. Gould probably did not mention the subject of gold to him then, knowing he would shortly have the President as a captive audience.

Grant, undoubtedly looking forward to a pleasant voyage up the Sound, did not suspect that he was letting himself in for a propaganda campaign. The peerless military leader was surprisingly innocent when it came to financial matters, nor did he have a touchy sense of the dignity of his office. He had an ingenuous admiration for wealth, and it apparently never occurred to him that a good many sensitive citizens in New York and all over the nation would be pained at the spectacle of the President of the United States consorting with the likes of Fisk and Gould—especially the fat man who openly broke so many of the Commandments.

That afternoon Grant, accompanied by Gould, Treasury Secretary George Boutwell, Cyrus Field, the Atlantic cable genius, and other prominent personages, received a military escort to the Chambers Street pier where Fisk's *Providence* was tied. The boat was festooned with pennants, her decks scrubbed clean and brasswork polished. Dodworth's band, the best in town, was playing a rousing march. Admiral Fisk, clad in full uniform and lavender kid gloves, was waiting at the gangplank to welcome his guests. This was his first meeting with the Chief Executive—one the latter would come to rue.

"His [Fisk's] mustache had paid a recent visit to his inimitable barber," said an account of the time. "His gold-trimmed uniform shone with extraordinary brilliancy, and his big diamond sparkled brighter than Venus on a frosty night. The Admiral received the party with that careless ease which always characterized him."

Grant shook hands with him and strode aboard, the warbling of the *Providence*'s 125 canaries doubtless lost on him in the din of the band and the booming of a cannon mounted on the wharf. In the saloon, cigars, champagne and other liquors were ready as the vessel slid away from the pier at 5 P. M. It may be that Fisk and Gould, recalling tales of the general's occasional tippling during the war, were not above hoping that his tongue might be loosened about government policy. If so, they were disappointed. Gould made short work of the necessary introductory conversational trivia, then steered into gold. The honored guest, never loquacious, seemed perfectly content to puff at his cigar and listen to the others without saying a word.

"The President was a listener," Gould later testified before a Congressional committee. "The other gentlemen were discussing. Some were in favor of [Secretary of the Treasury] Boutwell's selling gold, and some were opposed to it. After they had all interchanged their views, some one asked the President what his opinion was."

Henry Adams, in a later essay, declared that the "some one" was of course Fisk, "who alone had the impudence to put such an inquiry." Grant's reply was like a dash of cold water.

"There is a certain amount of fictitiousness about the prosperity of the country," he said, "and the bubble might as well be tapped in one way as another."

Although this was a fairly guarded utterance, possibly containing a hint that the President suspected he was being pumped, Fisk and Gould took it to mean the worst—that he was in favor of dumping government gold, reducing its price, perhaps even returning to eventual specie payment. Gould, never mentioning his own private speculative interest in gold, protested that such a course would be ruinous to farmers, railroads and prosperity in general.

"I gave it as my opinion," he later said, "that if that policy were carried out it would produce great distress, and almost lead to civil war; it would produce strikes among the workmen, and the workshops, to a great extent, would have to be closed . . . I took the ground that the government ought to let gold alone, and let it find its commercial level; that, as a matter of fact, it ought to facilitate an upward movement of gold in the fall. . . ."

The conversation continued until after midnight, but never once did the taciturn President indicate that he favored the Gould Plan. By the time the party turned in, Gould must have been reflecting that his gold venture was beset by unexpected risks, while Fisk could congratulate himself for his own sagacity in standing clear. Next day he took a prominent place in Grant's retinue, entering Boston's Coliseum with the President and other notables to witness a great musical festival, one of the events of the Peace Jubilee. Lucy Fisk was among the admiring spectators who set up a thunder of applause as Grant, with the splendidly uniformed Fisk close beside him, marched down the grand aisle.

"While he [Grant] reservedly acknowledged the cordial greeting," an observer noted, "Admiral Fisk, in the most gracious and unaffected manner, acknowledged such portions of the applause as he deemed intended for him, and his easy and profuse style left no doubt that he thought a large share of the plaudits meant for him." Some of the spectators, mistaking Fisk for the President, wondered who the unassuming man next to him was. Prince Erie's freedom from false modesty at the Jubilee won him a new nickname —Jubilee Jim—that stuck to him the rest of his short life.

Fisk and Gould had not given up hope of disabusing the President of his faulty economic notions and swinging him around to the Gould blueprint for prosperity. Old Corbin was with them too, confident that Grant would see the light if given time and persuasion. When the President returned to New York on June 18, he was met there by his wife and daughter, and they put up once more at the Corbins'. One would have thought that after his experience aboard the *Providence* he would have viewed the Erie moguls with suspicion and dodged any further fraternization with them, but Grant could be marvelously obtuse. That night he went with his wife and daughter to Fisk's Fifth Avenue Theater, where they occupied Fisk's proscenium box in company with Fisk, Gould and the Corbins to hear Irma and Desclauzas sing and watch the cancan in a performance of *La Périchole*.

Doubtless there were those in the audience who gazed in nervous fascination to see if the unspeakable Fisk could possibly be so gross as to bring in his mistress to meet the President and First Lady. Their fears were unnecessary. Fisk's perceptions were not so blunt that he did not know that what might be appropriate for Boss Tweed or Judge Barnard would not do for his guests this evening. Josie Mansfield was there, gorgeously attired but at a safe distance, experiencing another demonstration of the double standard of morality and the occasional mortifications a fallen woman must accept as an occupational hazard. She sat in a box on the opposite side, watching Fisk play host to the Presidential party, watching Grant and his wife chatting pleasantly with him, watching with hundreds of others in the audience the social interplay between Fisk and the highest political dignitary in the land, and possibly feeling some rage at the illogical proprieties that barred her. At the later impeachment trial of Judge Barnard, she appeared as a witness and was asked if she had been received by the President.

"No," she replied. ". . . I contented myself by remaining opposite." And in reply to a question as to whether Grant treated Fisk with "hospitality and deference," she replied, "Well, I thought he was very cordial."

At this same time occurred one of those fortuitous events that sometimes play into the hands of mischief-makers. H. H. Van Dyke resigned as Assistant United States Treasurer in New York, the highest Treasury post in the city, whose holder kept in constant communication with Washington on matters concerning gold. Gould, seeing what an advantage it would be to have an ally in this critical office, spoke to Abel Corbin about it. Did Corbin have enough influence with Grant to get him to name a friendly Assistant Treasurer? Corbin was confident that he did.

The man he hit on for the post was his stepson-in-law, Robert B. Catherwood. Catherwood thought he would like the job until he found there were certain strings attached to it. "I went the next day to have a conversation with Mr. Gould and Mr. Corbin," he later testified, "and I found that the remark was simply this: that the parties could operate in a legitimate way and make a great deal of money . . . I satisfied myself that I could not fill the bill . . . It was understood that if I took the position, Gould, Corbin, myself and others, would go into some operations such as the purchase of gold and stocks, and that we would share and share alike."

Not even Gould and Corbin's arguments about the immense national prosperity certain to accompany their gold speculations could budge Catherwood. They gave up on him and turned to another candidate—dapper General Daniel Butterfield, a man whose considerable abilities were marred by a weakness for intrigue. Butterfield had fought well in the late war until he joined a nasty little plot to discredit General Meade, after which his star had dimmed. Since he satisfied Gould and Corbin, perhaps the general was not plagued by the persnickety considerations of probity that bothered Catherwood—or possibly he saw the larger good and was willing against his will to profit so long as the whole nation would likewise benefit. In any case, he wanted the job. Corbin, the cunning old lobbyist, went to Washington and pulled some strings. Butterfield seemed an ideal candidate in another respect, for he had headed a fund-raising campaign to buy General Grant a home in Washington, an effort that was appreciated even though Grant sold the house soon after his inauguration.

Sure enough, Butterfield got the appointment, beginning his duties as Assistant Treasurer on July 1. Here was a development of the first importance to Gould, removing some of his misgivings about Grant and elevating Corbin several notches in his esteem. If Corbin could take the train to Washington and come back with the Assistant Treasurer in his pocket, did not that prove his power at the White House? Was it not reasonable to suppose that he could steer the President away from his erroneous opinions about gold? Corbin himself said he could—in fact, that Grant's ideas already were changing in the right direction. For a sharper, Gould showed some naiveté in putting any stock in the claims of that slippery old fraud. Until then he had been hesitating. Now he went ahead full speed with the Gould Plan.

Strangely, he did so without the financial support of his Erie partner. Fisk, for once a pillar of conservatism, viewed the whole project with suspicion, vowed that you could never tell which way a politician would jump, and kept clear. Gould, somewhat hurt at this attitude, formed a pool with two Wall Street brokers, Arthur Kimber and W. S. Woodward. The three quietly began buying gold. Although Fisk was not buying, he was willing to help with propaganda, ready to climb on the bandwagon should he eliminate the doubts in his own mind. In mid-August, Grant arrived in New York and boarded a steamer for Newport. At Gould's suggestion, Fisk visited the President on board before sailing time and once more peppered him with arguments picturing the national disaster that would result should the administration make the mistake of selling gold and thus lowering its price.

Bumper crops were maturing, far in excess of domestic needs, said Economist Fisk. If gold went higher, the farmers would get a good price and the nation would export grain instead of gold. Statistician Fisk doubtless waggled his finger as he warned that United States farmers were competing with cheap European labor, and that 300 sail of vessels were waiting in the Black and Mediterranean Seas, ready to supply the Liverpool market in the fall unless American grain got there first. Transportation Expert Fisk frankly admitted that as vice-president of Erie he was interested in filling his freight trains with grain, but wasn't it plain as a pikestaff that this would mean full employment and was only one facet of the prosperity that would spring up across the land from the grass roots?

Eloquent arguments, but Grant was a fellow who could listen, nod in an absent-minded way and never say yes or no. When Fisk ran out of breath and took his leave, he knew no more about the President's intentions than before. Grant himself later said that Fisk came "to ask that he would privately give them a little intimation as to what the administration was going to do on the financial question," to which he replied that giving such information would not be fair. Fisk's resolution to stay out of gold was strengthened, and he warned Gould that there might be breakers ahead.

Gould did not agree. He had entered his patriotic project with such enthusiasm that for the moment he forgot steel rails for Erie, the need for better freight facilities at Buffalo, and the fight that fellow Ramsey was putting up for his Susquehanna Railroad. As always with him, his interest in railroad operation came a poor second to the furtive thrill of manipulating, pulling wires, setting the stage for a vast gamble with the odds rigged in his favor. While he was thus preoccupied, another Erie disaster occurred that should have reminded him of his responsibilities as head of the road.

On the night of July 14, 1869, Engineer James Griffin pulled his Erie freight into a siding at Mast Hope, Pennsylvania, twenty-eight miles northwest of Port Jervis, to let westbound Express Train No. 3 pass on the main line. Griffin fell asleep in his cab, then awoke in some confusion, believing that the express had passed. He headed out into the main line just as the express rounded a curve and bore down on him at top speed. The collision was frightful, spinning one locomotive around, spilling coals from the firebox and setting the station and one crumpled passenger car ablaze. Nine persons were burned to death in the car, one of them the Rev. Benjamin Halleck of New York, who was uninjured by the crash but pinned by wreckage and held fast while rescuers vainly tried to save him. "He coolly gave directions as to the best way to extricate him," related a historian, "as the flames closed in about him, and he met his awful death without a murmur or groan." Ten passengers were injured, and among the dead were three burned beyond recognition.

"The long, dismal and bloody catalogue of disasters that marks the history of the Erie Railroad," said the New York *Herald*, "is made again to bear another burden of human slaughter. . . ."

14 *In Up to the Handle*

ANNOUNCED Vice President Fisk: "The accidents which have occurred are not attributable to want of care on the part of the company, but to the villainy of the man Bowen in the Carr's Rock disaster, and to the negligence of an engineer at Mast Hope." This was a weaseling subterfuge as to Carr's Rock, which was a clear case of rotten track, but Erie was determined to make a scapegoat of James Bowen, a man too feeble-minded to defend himself against the charge that he had wilfully derailed the train. It was true that the Mast Hope tragedy was not caused by decay but by human error. Yet a logical case could be made that this sort of human error was the natural end result of a management more interested in speculation and opera bouffe than in maintaining rigid operational standards.

While the unfortunate Rev. Halleck and his fellow victims were buried and a new crop of lawsuits loomed against Erie, Gould was not distracted from his Plan. He was now sending up a propaganda smokescreen. By subsidizing impecunious financial writers, he managed to plant stories in several of the minor newspapers to the effect that the Treasury would not sell gold. Minor newspapers, however, were not enough. He wanted to sneak a story into the respected New York *Times*, a paper that could not be bought, and the lengths to which he went to accomplish this fraud were typical of his genius at four-flushing.

Everybody knew that when Grant passed through New York early in August, John Bigelow, editor of the *Times*, had interviewed him. Following this, on August 6 and 7, two editorials appeared in the *Times* commenting on finance, and it was known that they represented Grant's views. Gould knew that the peripatetic President would again come through New York on his way back from Newport, as indeed he did on August 19. If another editorial could be smuggled into the *Times* shortly after this last visit, Gould reasoned, the psychology would be the same and the public would assume it to be genuine and official.

Gould got Abel Corbin busy with pen and ink. Corbin, a lucid fellow with words, wrote a long and careful editorial titled "Grant's Financial Policy," embodying in it the Gould economic theories and giving the clear impression that the administration would allow gold to rise and thereby assure prosperity. Corbin, who had no qualms about committing something near forgery in the name of his eminent brother-in-law, knew that the editorial—if it could be wormed into the *Times*—would serve a double purpose. New York speculators, accepting it as official, would rush to buy gold before it rose—a buying surge that would *make* it rise. The administration itself, assuming it to be the views of the *Times*, could not fail to be at least partially impressed by such an influential newspaper.

For a man with Gould's reputation to present the article in person would arouse instant suspicion. A stalking horse had to be found who could canter in with a minimum of clatter. Gould found him in his friend James McHenry, a British capitalist and stockholder in Erie, who was also president of the Atlantic & Great Western, a railroad in Ohio connecting with Erie. McHenry was a personal friend of Editor Bigelow. McHenry was willing to profit in gold himself, possibly on the theory that his Erie stock had never paid a dividend and he ought to get *some* good out of Gould. He called at the *Times* office and handed the editorial to Bigelow, telling him it was written by "one in the intimate confidence of the President."

Bigelow, who had served his country ably as wartime

Minister to France, seemed uncommonly naive for a newspaperman. He ordered the editorial printed in double-
leaded type. When he read it over in proof, however, it
struck him that the writer was singularly insistent that gold
should be allowed to climb in price, as if he had an axe
to grind. Instead of inquiring further into the source and
determining whether Grant knew anything about it, Bigelow handed it to C. C. Norvell, the *Times* financial editor,
and told him he had better soften it a bit. Norvell, not
knowing how far he should go, made only minor changes.
The editorial appeared in the *Times* August 25 retitled
"The Financial Policy of the Administration" and containing a few other modifications. Still, in at least two statements it expressed the very idea Gould wanted to spread.

". . . until the crops are moved," read one passage, "it is
not likely Treasury gold will be sold for currency to be
locked up." Another sentence made it stronger: ". . . the
President will not send gold into the market and sell it for
currency. . . ."

Jay Gould must have been delighted when he read that.
He acted like a man who had just read the newspaper when
he wrote to Treasury Secretary Boutwell to pat him on the
back, make sure he had read the editorial, and to fish for
his reaction:

"My Dear Sir,—If the New York *Times* correctly re-
flects your financial policy during the next three or four
months . . . then I think the country peculiarly fortunate in
having a financial head who can take a broad view of the
situation . . . It is only by making gold high and scarce
that . . . we are enabled to compete in the London and
Liverpool markets. . . ."

Secretary Boutwell, refusing to rise to the bait, sent only
a formal and noncommittal reply. Still, he did not disavow
the editorial, leaving Gould to reason by indirection that
the administration did take the necessary broad view of the
situation. The editorial created a stir in financial circles,

causing some buying of gold by those expecting a rise. Yet, contrary to Gould's expectations, after a short rise the price sagged a bit, due to a factor he had forgotten to consider— the influx of gold from elsewhere in the country. Frightened by this weakening, one of his associates in the pool, W. S. Woodward, lost his broad view of the situation. He quit and sold his holdings. Incensed at this betrayal, Gould had to buy some of Woodward's gold to sustain the price. Worse yet, his other crony, Kimber, was showing signs of fear.

Gould, who had many millions involved, was beginning to sweat. Yet he was confident that if he could weather the storm gold was bound to rise and he would emerge triumphant—always providing that the government would keep out. With the defection of Woodward, he badly needed financial help. Fisk knew this perfectly well, for his partner was abstractedly tearing paper into bits, an infallible sign of nervousness. Still, Fisk did not seem able to achieve a broad view of the situation, for he made no move to pitch in and help by buying gold. This was one of the few times when Gould was annoyed at his jovial partner, but it was the unjustified annoyance of a man in a tight spot. Fisk's attitude had been consistent throughout. He had been suspicious of gold in the first place, he had advised Gould against the speculation, and nothing since then had changed his mind.

Even then Gould could have sold his holdings and escaped with a sizeable but not crippling loss. Pride prevented him— pride and the gambler's hunch that courage during these critical days would swing the tide his way. He was disappointed in finding that General Butterfield was not quite as useful as he had hoped, for the Treasury Department in Washington was not confiding in Butterfield as to its gold policy. Nevertheless, should the Treasury abandon the broad view and sell gold in the New York market, it would be done through Butterfield, who would be the first person outside Washington to know it. His loyalty was therefore important, and Gould employed a familiar tactic to assure it—money. He afterward said he loaned the general $10,000 he happened to need and also bought $1,500,000 in gold for his benefit, meaning that Butterfield would collect whatever profits accrued from any rise in price.

Abel Corbin's influence with the President and editorial-writing abilities likewise merited reward. Gould, a bundle of nerves, was conferring with Corbin not merely daily but twice a day, discussing strategy and propaganda that could be aimed at Grant without arousing suspicion. This persistence seemed to pay off on September 2, when the President arrived in New York on his way to Saratoga and breakfasted with the Corbins.

Grant would have had to be blind and deaf had he not become aware by this time that Corbin and Gould were uncommonly interested in gold. Indeed, he had remarked to Mrs. Grant that Gould was "always trying to find something out." Presumably, while they breakfasted, Corbin sang his familiar refrain about national prosperity and high-priced gold. It was true that some sincere civic spokesmen had likewise been preaching the advantages of a good price for gold, and that as an economic theory it had some validity. In any case, while he was at Corbin's the President came to a decision, almost as if influenced by his brother-in-law. Then and there he wrote Secretary Boutwell instructing him not to sell any gold until further orders. And—here Grant made a sad error—he told Corbin about the letter.

Not all the events of that busy day are clear. It is known, however, that Jay Gould called at Corbin's and was admitted, although he did not see Grant. One gets a picture of Gould pussyfooting around like a gumshoe sleuth, holding a whispered conference with Corbin while the President was in another room, and learning from Corbin that Grant had written Boutwell not to sell gold.

Gould must have glowed. In addition to naming the Assistant Treasurer and seducing the New York *Times*, he could lay some claim to shaping the policy of the national government. More than that, he knew of that policy before Secretary Boutwell or any other government official did. He was so pleased that he offered to buy $1,500,000 in gold for Corbin's benefit. Corbin accepted, as he later put it, "for the sake of a lady, my wife," from which one must draw the conclusion that he never would have dreamed of taking it for himself. Gould bought the gold through his old brokerage firm of Smith, Gould & Martin so that Corbin's name did not appear in the transaction.

That same day, spurred by the President's unwitting tip, Gould began buying more heavily on his own account. Recalling that young General Horace Porter was Grant's good friend as well as his military secretary, and feeling that it might be well to have a gold interest right at the President's side, he wrote Porter, "Dear General—We have purchased half a million gold on your account." The price crept up. By September 6 it reached 137⅝. With the rise of every point, Abel Corbin—or more properly, *Mrs.* Corbin—was making a $15,000 paper profit. Gould paid him $25,000 on account. The outlook was rosy. The manipulators were congratulating each other until some gold holders began to sell and take their profits, believing the top had been reached, and a strong bear movement began to depress the price.

The spirits of Gould and Corbin sank with every drop in the quotation. Gould was frantic by September 10, when Grant once more arrived in New York to put up with the Corbins for three days. One can imagine that the smooth Corbin, with years of lobbying behind him, worked on the President with the greatest circumspection, not pressing his points too hard and yet making it very clear what awful hardship would be visited on the nation's farmers and workers should the administration falter in its determination not to sell gold. Grant was next going to western Pennsylvania for a few days, and Gould, in the midst of his panic, arrived at Corbin's to chat with the President and make arrangements to get him out of town in style. When Grant left on September 13, he rode in the luxurious Erie directors' car attached to a special Pennsylvania Central train.

Gold was still sinking. By mid-September it was down to 132, and Gould had lost a paper fortune on every point. Even in his extremity he was too proud to ask Fisk point-blank for help, but the wish was apparent.

"I could see by the way he would keep tearing up little pieces of paper," Fisk said later, "that he was in up to the handle. . . ."

Around September 15 the two talked it over. Fisk would have been happy to join the speculation but for his apprehension that the government would sell gold and collapse the market. Gould assured him earnestly that such misgivings were ridiculous. Why? Because, he said, *Grant was financially interested in pushing gold higher*. The President was implicated in the plot—or at least his wife was, which amounted to the same thing. Mrs. Grant, Gould declared, had a half million invested in gold through Corbin. Corbin had already sent her $25,000 as her profit in the recent rise. Even General Porter, Grant's sidekick, had sunk a half million in gold.

"This matter is all fixed up," Gould said. "Butterfield is all right; Corbin has got Butterfield all right; and Corbin has got Grant fixed all right."

Fisk was surprised. Even though this was their routine way of doing business with Tweed, he had not placed Grant in the Boss's class. Knowing Gould very well, Fisk was aware he was not a slave to the truth if the truth was a hindrance. Fisk hurried to Corbin's house to inquire into his partner's veracity.

"Mr. Gould has lost, as the thing stands now," he told

Corbin, "and it looks as if it might be a pretty serious business before getting it straight again. The whole success depends on whether the government will unload [gold] onto us or not."

"You need not have the least fear," the old fox replied. He assured Fisk that Porter was in the deal, that Mrs. Grant was likewise in it and had already collected $25,000. "I tell you it is all right," he insisted.

Someone was lying—either Gould or Corbin or both—for neither General Porter nor Mrs. Grant were involved in the gold movement, nor was the President himself anything but honest, however lacking he was in discretion. About that same time, Gould received a letter from Porter reflecting a most ungrateful attitude. It read bluntly: "I have not authorized any purchase of gold and request that none be made on my account. I am unable to enter into any speculation whatever."

Gould did not bother to inform Fisk of this letter. Fisk left Corbin's convinced that the President was secretly involved, that the government therefore would refrain from selling gold, and that gold would rise as certainly as the morrow's sun if given sufficient pressure.

He joined Gould in the movement, precipitating the nation's most fantastic financial hysteria as well as a first-class scandal. Yet he was still not quite at ease.

"Somehow or other," he said later, "when I was not with Corbin, I always felt shaky about the old rascal. I had my suspicions all the time, and yet when he talked to me I thought he was as innocent and guileless as a baby."

15

Collapse, and
Company

EVEN for Jim Fisk, who could outdo Caesar in the matter of juggling simultaneous enterprises, the summer and fall of 1869 were unusually busy. His ventures into gold were concurrent and intermixed with trips to Albany in the war against Ramsey, the marshalling of forces at Binghamton, the head-on crash of locomotives and more than twenty-one lawsuits. At the same time he was presenting opera bouffe in one theater and *East Lynne* in another, serving as admiral of his fleet, forming an oil company with Ned Stokes and sponsoring other sizeable enterprises. On August 24 he traveled to Newburgh to join Mayor Hall and Governor Hoffman in celebrating the opening of a shorter Erie branch to that city, responding with a speech to the second toast: "The Erie Railway." He attended the opening of Lucille Western in *Patrie* at his own Grand Opera House, causing the *Herald* drama critic to grow a little facetious: ". . . we observed many lovers of the drama itself, among whom we must mention the modern Hudson, the Erie king, the genuine man of the period, Fisk, Jr., the observed of all observers." Somehow he still found time to take the evening boat frequently with Miss Manfield to Long Branch, then one of the nation's most fashionable resorts, where Gould, Corbin and Judge Barnard also escaped the heat and President Grant had recently been presented with a cottage. Even granting Fisk the energy of a terrier and the perception of a chess wizard who defeats a dozen skilled opponents at once, he could not have indulged in drink and lechery to the extent rumor suggested, nor could he have given Erie the attention it needed. In fact, the fat man was spreading himself too thin, for in the gold movement he was hoaxed by his own playmates.

One point in the gold group's favor was that the President was now vacationing in remote Washington, Pennsylvania, southwest of Pittsburgh, at the home of W. W. Smith, Mrs. Grant's cousin. He was conveniently distant from Washington, D. C., as well as from telegraph facilities. He was separated from all his advisers and surely would make no drastic financial move until he returned to the capital. Yet Gould, who had told Fisk so confidently that "Corbin has got Grant fixed," was worrying about Grant and also about Treasury Secretary Boutwell. Boutwell was in New York to attend a dinner given in his honor at the Union League Club. Gould knew that the sponsors of the dinner were bears in gold—in favor of lower prices. The bears of course would fill Boutwell's ear with cheap-gold propaganda which might convince him, might make him send a message to Grant urging the sale of government gold.

Gould, now jumping at shadows, committed an enormous boner. He resolved to get word to Grant through the industrious Corbin to stand fast against all wicked bear blandishments. Fisk, who already had sunk at least $8,000,000 in gold, had no suspicions on September 17 when Gould proposed sending a letter by courier to Grant.

"Who is the most confidential man you have got?" he asked.

"I will give you Chapin," Fisk replied. He summoned W. O. Chapin, a trusted Erie employe, and told him to be ready at 6 o'clock in the morning to leave for Pennsylvania. Just to make sure he did not oversleep, Fisk had his brother-in-law, George Hooker, call at Chapin's lodgings next morning. The two drove to Corbin's house, where Corbin handed Chapin a letter for Grant. Chapin boarded the 8 o'clock Pennsylvania Central train, reaching Pittsburgh that evening. Hiring a horse, he rode all night as if the nation's fate rested on his shoulders. He arrived in Washington, twenty-eight miles distant, on the morning of September 19. He found President Grant and General Porter, two military men, playing a pacific game of croquet in the yard.

Grant took the letter, read it and said there was no reply. Chapin, following instructions, rode to the nearest telegraph station and wired Fisk, "Letter delivered all right." Perhaps because of a careless telegraph clerk, the message reached New York with a subtle change:

"Letter delivered. All right."

Never did a period, a small dot of ink, assume such importance. When Fisk and Gould read the telegram they immediately construed the "All right" as a reference to Grant's reception of the letter. Doubtless he had said, "All right," which meant that he agreed and everything was decidedly all right. They bought more gold with greater confidence.

While Corbin's letter to Grant was not preserved, it was of course a fortissimo rendition of Corbin's save-the-nation aria: *Do not sell government gold.* Grant was irked—a condition he had been a long time reaching. He must already have learned from Porter about the sly effort to buy gold for him. Grant spoke to his wife, who wrote Jenny Corbin in New York a brief note containing a significant sentence:

"Tell Mr. Corbin that the President is very much distressed by your speculations and you must close them as quick as you can."

But that was a Sunday, and it would take three days before the letter reached New York, during which time Fisk and Gould bought millions in gold. By Tuesday, Fisk's misgivings had returned. He paid another visit to the Corbins.

"If we should miss," he said, "if the government should sell this gold—it would certainly be a serious matter."

Corbin pooh-poohed such a thought, and his wife was as

confident. "I know there will be no gold sold by the government," she said according to Fisk's later testimony. "I am quite positive there will be no gold sold; for this is a chance of a life-time for us; you need have no uneasiness whatever."

This was the President's sister speaking. Fisk, reassured, continued buying through his brokers. Kimber, Gould's earlier partner, had taken fright and quit the pool the previous weekend. By Wednesday morning, September 22, gold had risen to 137, and later that day it shot up to 141. This sharp advance, contrary to all natural causes, made it apparent that a combination of buyers as yet unidentified was bulling the market. Many small bears were already ruined, and Horace Greeley was blasting the "Goldbugs" in the *Tribune,* demanding that the government take action. Stocks, which always moved in the opposite direction with any marked change in gold, were sinking. Fisk and Gould, their suit against Commodore Vanderbilt still pending, seized the opportunity to whipsaw their old enemy. They engineered a quick bear raid in New York Central, sending that stock into a twenty-two percent dive and cleaning up while the cursing Commodore took a heavy loss. This was enough to make Fisk wildly enthusiastic about the scheme he had mistrusted, unaware that on that same day Mrs. Corbin had received paralyzing tidings from Mrs. Grant.

Gould learned of it that night when he called at Corbin's home to find him in a swivet. He showed Gould the letter, with the ominous line: "Tell Mr. Corbin that the President is very much distressed by your speculations and you must close them as quick as you can."

It did not say *should*, but *must*. To Gould that word carried fearful connotations, implying that Corbin's speculations were not merely unwise but might be ruinous financially. It suggested that the government might step in— sell gold—and the phrase "as quick as you can" could mean that this would take place soon.

Corbin showed Gould another letter—one he had written
to Grant. In it this pious pettifogger assured the President
that there was some mistake, for he had not a dollar's interest in gold. He aimed to make this good. With peerless
effrontery he proposed that Gould take the $1,500,000 in
gold off his hands at once and pay him $100,000 as profits—
this after he had already received $25,000. Gould balked at
that. He knew that once he had paid Corbin any such sum,
his hold over him would be lost. The old man was running
for cover, trying to cash in before the expected crash. Yet
he held a weapon over Gould's head—the letter from Mrs.
Grant, which would send the gold price spinning if its
contents became known. The two larcenists, their mutual
esteem crumbling, still found it expedient to observe outward politeness.

"Mr. Corbin, I cannot give you anything if you will go
out," Gould said. "If you will remain in, and take the
chances of the market, I will give you my check [for
$100,000]."

"Mr. Gould, my wife says 'No!' " Corbin insisted.
"Ulysses thinks it wrong, and that it ought to end."

Gould eyed him mistrustfully. "Mr. Corbin," he said, "I
am undone if that letter gets out."

Corbin promised to keep it quiet. Gould left, saying he
would think over the matter of the $100,000, a sum he
never paid. He was running for cover too, but far from
looking for profit he was hoping only to avert disaster. It
was obvious now that Corbin's glib talk about his "influence" over the President was humbug. Gould, the sharper
who prided himself on covering all the angles, had made
an amateur's error—placed his faith in a fixer who could not
fix. He was carrying some $50,000,000 in gold on his
shoulders, bought on margin, and it would crush him unless
he jumped from under it fast. If he and Fisk dumped their
enormous holdings together, that of itself would break the
market and ruin them. He had to sell, but at the same time

he had to maintain a strong buying interest while he sold. Gould made a decision which on its face seemed the ultimate double-cross. He would keep the secret from Fisk, whom he had coaxed into the speculation against his better judgment. He would let Fisk be the catspaw—let Fisk buy while Gould sold.

On Thursday morning, when the two met at the Opera House, Gould said nothing to Fisk about the Corbin letter. Until now they had done their buying by wire from the Erie palace. Today, with great talk about a buying campaign in which only Fisk was sincere, they went down to the Street in person. Fisk began buying gold through his brokers, among them William Belden and Albert Speyers. Gould had forsaken the broad, patriotic view, the solicitude for farmers, wage-earners and general prosperity that had so long guided his economic thinking. He began to sell secretly, buying only enough openly to make it appear he was still a bull. Time was the vital factor. He was convinced that the miserably short-sighted administration was going to dump gold, but how soon? A day or two would give him time to unload. He kept several messengers breathless running back and forth to Butterfield's office to learn if there was word that Washington was selling.

Because of the specialized nature of gold transactions, they were not conducted in the Stock Exchange but in the adjacent Gold Room at Broad Street and Exchange Place, an amphitheater with a bronze cupid-and-dolphin fountain gurgling in the center and a mechanical indicator to tell the current price of gold. Normally it was an uncrowded place where brokers handled buying and selling for principals who attended to other affairs elsewhere. On Thursday, with gold starting at 141, it was packed with tense humanity. Speculators were no longer content to let brokers alone do the work. They were there in person, watching the indicator, ready with orders to their brokers to buy or sell. When Fisk arrived, beaming as usual, onlookers at once decided that he was the head and front of the bull brigade. Unlike his mousy partner, he leaned to the whoop-and-holler school of speculating, clapping acquaintances on the back as he told the world he was buying with everything he had and the bears had better watch out.

Despite Gould's secret selling, the Fisk boom was strong enough and noisy enough to push up the price. Men stared pop-eyed as the indicator climbed. It took capital to buy as Fisk was buying, even though it was done on margin—a problem he and Gould had solved by their recent purchase of a controlling interest in the Tenth National Bank, where they could get an endless stream of certified checks. The Gold Room was alive with rumors, the most persistent of them—spread by Fisk underlings—saying that the administration, including the President and Cabinet, were gambling on a further rise and aimed to make fortunes. Fisk himself exuded confidence.

"I'll bet any part of $50,000," he said, "that gold will go over 145."

There were no takers. Wild-eyed losers yelled curses at him. By now, all the small bears and some moderately large ones had gone under, either admitting bankruptcy or making disastrous settlements with the bulls. Everybody knew a financial crash was in the making. Stocks were skidding. Money was so scarce that domestic and foreign trade was hamstrung. The fever in New York was reflected in every other financial center in the country—even in Europe. Suffering bears were sending telegrams to Washington, pleading that the government sell gold to avert national collapse, never suggesting that such a move would also save those bears still faintly alive. When gold closed that afternoon at 144, Fisk left with a cigar jutting jauntily from under his waxed mustache, shrugging off the maledictions of scores of losers who united in execrating him as the cause of their destruction. Wilted speculators made a dash for Delmonico's, a few blocks up Broadway, where straight whiskey was the rule among men ordinarily temperate. Fisk and Gould met at the Opera House that night with Belden, Speyers and other colleagues. Gould was tearing paper, keeping his secret from Fisk, whom he could thank for supporting the market while he sold at a vast profit. Both knew that Grant was back in the capital, under terrific pressure from the bears.

The next morning, September 24, was bright and clear but would ever afterward be memorable as Black Friday. The *Times* that morning, still stung by the way it had been gulled the previous month, came out with an editorial describing the activities of "the inevitable and irrepressible Fisk, Jr.," and daring to mention the rumors of governmental complicity:

"His [Fisk's] presence in the gold-room was signalized by the rapid rise in gold . . . The other engineers of the movement were not idle . . . They had not only *bulled* gold with a will, but talked freely of the warrant which they had from Washington that the government would not interfere with them. The highest official in the land was quoted *as being with them,* and he, of course, controls the action of the Secretary of the Treasury and the New York Assistant Treasurer. Although this must have been known to be false, there were abundant rumors and suspicions insidiously spread around the street to create the belief or fear with good men that the administration would *not* interpose by further sales of gold from the Treasury . . . Among these rumors was one that the Gould-Fisk party were about to secure the services and influence of Mr. Corbin, (the brother-in-law of the President). . . ."

That rumor was a little late. Droves of bitter bears swore that the talk of governmental collusion must be true, not false—that Grant and his cronies were reaping crooked fortunes along with Fisk. More telegrams went to Washington, some angry, some pleading, some quoting the *Times* editorial on the theory that the administration would not dare refuse action in the face of such scandalous talk. One reason why the resentment was centered on Fisk was his air that all this was a glorious lark—an attitude that did not sit well with men who had lost everything, or even with the bulls who were holding their breaths for fear the market would break. That Friday morning, he arrived in the financial district in style, as one reporter noted:

"James Fisk, Jr., came driving down and turned into Broad Street with two richly attired actresses, one of them chiefly known to fame through her charms as displayed in 'Mazeppa' and 'The French Spy.'"

This day he did not go to the Gold Room, knowing he would very likely be mobbed if he appeared there in person. He went to William Heath's brokerage office on Broad Street and conducted his operations from there. Meanwhile Gould had a few whispered words with his chief broker, Henry Smith.

"Sell, sell, sell!" he told Smith. "Do nothing but sell—only don't sell to Fisk's brokers."

According to all contemporary accounts, the Gold Room that morning was less rational than any well-managed madhouse. When trading opened at 10, the indicator had already jumped to 150. The floor was jammed with 200 brokers and a throng of speculators—red-eyed, hoarse-voiced men, some of them intoxicated, others merely acting that way, "all wound up to a fearful pitch of excitement," one observer said, "yelling, screaming, jostling, crowding." Pickpockets took advantage of the crush, and some dealers were separated from their wallets in addition to their other losses. Little Albert Speyers looked clearly bereft as he shrieked offers to buy gold by the millions.

Business was paralyzed from Boston to San Francisco because of what was happening here. Stocks were still sinking because of what was happening here. The Union that had survived four years of bloody battle seemed shaken to its foundations by mere words spoken by a few determined gamblers in this grubby little room on Broad Street. Commodore Vanderbilt came down to his bank and with an imperturbability that must have masked inner rage at Fisk and Gould he spent a million shoring up his sagging New York Central shares and other holdings. In the ill-ventilated Gold Room the smell of sweat would have been unendurable had anyone been in a condition to notice such trivialities. Occasionally a speculator would slosh his fevered face at the fountain in the center. The disorder spilled out into the open, where hundreds milled around the outdoor gold indicator on New Street. One Major Bush, an officer of a National Guard detachment in Brooklyn, got telegraphed orders from Albany to hold his regiment in readiness to "quell the riot in Wall Street." Assistant Treasurer Butterfield was dutifully keeping Gould informed that there was no word from Washington. Butterfield was speculating himself, but now he was on the bear side in the belief that the price must fall. He sent a telegram to Secretary Boutwell in Washington, who was conferring anxiously with Grant about the crisis:

"Gold is 150: much feeling and accusations of government complicity."

Edmund C. Stedman, a young stockbroker with a flair for poetry, was observing antics he would soon set to verse, writing in part:

> *Zounds! how the price went flashing through*
> *Wall-street, William, Broad-street, New!*
> *All the specie in the land*
> *Held in one ring by a giant hand,—*
> *For millions more it was ready to pay,*
> *And throttle the Street on hangman's-day.*
> *Up from the Gold Pit's nether hell,*
> *While the innocent fountain rose and fell,*
> *Loud and higher the bidding rose,*

And the bulls, triumphant, faced their foes.
It seemed as if Satan himself were in it,
Lifting it,—one per cent a minute . . .

Everybody was certain that Speyers was buying for Fisk
and that Fisk alone held title to more gold than actually
existed in circulation—one of the paradoxes of speculation
beyond a mere layman's comprehension. Weeks later, in-
siders were convinced that by this time Gould had taken
Fisk into his confidence and the two were playing a sharp
game together. Now, on Black Friday, no one knew inner
motives and could only guess from what they saw. As the
morning wore on, with gold still climbing, fear rose to panic
with the suspicion that Fisk and Gould—with the administration's aid—had all but accomplished a corner in the metal.
Once achieved, this would mean that they could set their
own price. Those bears still solvent went pale at the thought.
As Fisk later explained it, ". . . there is no fright as great as
the fright in Wall street when the bears become panicky.
Burnt brandy won't save 'em, for the very reason that they
have sold what they have not got."

There was a throaty roar in the Gold Room around 11
A.M. when the indicator touched 155. When it reached 160
a half-hour later, some men were weeping while one fainted
dead away. A broker named Solomon Mahler went home
and shot himself dead. In his office in the Sub-Treasury,
Assistant Treasurer Butterfield received a fateful telegram
from Secretary Boutwell:

"Sell four millions gold tomorrow, and buy four millions
bonds."

Butterfield, the bear, knew he would make a handsome
profit. He took care to adjust his own investments, then
got the word to Gould some twenty-five minutes before it
became general knowledge. It was almost noon by the time
a messenger reached the Gold Room with the news. By then,
Gould's heavy selling was having its effect. The quotation,

which had risen to 164, teetered and dropped to 160. The tidings that the government was selling created bedlam among sweaty-faced operators who had become automatons rather than men. The government move meant that the ring was broken, the corner defeated, and the price would skid. It did. Within thirty minutes gold plummeted to 135. It was said that a half-dozen victims went temporarily mad. Albert Speyers was frantically offering to buy gold at 160 when it was selling at 135 a few yards away. Observers tried vainly to describe this drove of haunted creatures who had lost all resemblance to humankind save the sense of profit or loss. "The spectacle was one such as Dante might have seen in inferno," one of them wrote. Stedman, the Wall Street bard, tried to capture it in verse:

> *—but listen! hold!*
> *In screwing upward the price of gold*
> *To that dangerous, last, particular peg,*
> *They had killed the Goose with the Golden Egg!*
> *Just then the metal came pouring out,*
> *All ways at once, like a water-spout,*
> *Or a rushing, gushing, yellow flood,*
> *That drenched the bulls wherever they stood!*

Little Speyers wandered about, glassy-eyed. "I am Albert Speyers," he croaked. "Some persons have threatened to shoot me. I am here. Now, shoot, shoot!"

Black Friday was over, and half of Wall Street was ruined. Investment houses that had been bulwarks for years were caught in the riptide and went bankrupt. Arthur Kimber was bankrupt. William Belden was bankrupt. Jim Fisk —on paper—was bankrupt. Jay Gould had made eleven million dollars—real dollars. There was bitter anger against both of them—especially Fisk, who was believed the architect of the debacle. A mob of gamblers, many of them reduced from wealth to penury that same day, burst into the Heath brokerage office with the sincere purpose of murdering him if they could lay hands on him. Fisk and Gould had already made a strategic retreat through a side door and were on their way up town to the safety of the Opera House. Gould, the winner, looked like a loser, so haggard and hollow-eyed that Fisk described him with vivid verbal caricature:

"You won't see anything left of him but a pair of eyes and a suit of clothes."

According to his later testimony, Fisk immediately fixed on Abel Corbin as the villain of the piece, the man who had, as he put it, "run a saw right into us." He called on Corbin, telling him in small part, "I suspect that the whole thing was a damned trick from beginning to end . . . We are forty miles down the Delaware. . . ." Rumors swept the town that Fisk was assaulted, Fisk was murdered, Fisk had fled the city to save his life. The *Tribune* printed one of them, admitting it was unverified:

"Shortly after noon a carriage dashed rapidly down Twenty-third Street to the ferry house, and darting hastily through the gate the Admiral leaped upon the boat and shouted excitedly to the pilot, 'Cast off.' 'It lacks ten minutes of the time, Mr. Fisk,' 'Cast off, d—n you. Who is boss here?' Ting went the bell, and the boat started across the river. Mr. Fisk was in a tremendous state of excitement, ejaculating frequently, 'They are after me—going to hang me. . . .'"

Although there were plenty who wanted to hang him, he did not flee to New Jersey. He and Gould had taken refuge behind the marble walls of the Opera House. Even there, infuriated speculators howled at the door, which was guarded by a detail of policemen furnished through the intercedence of the kindly Boss Tweed. When a reporter from the New York *Sun* interviewed them, the statements of the two men were truly emblematic of their opposing characters:

Gould: " I regret very much this depression in financial

circles, but I predicted it long ago. I was in no way instrumental in producing the panic."

Fisk: "A fellow can't have a little innocent fun without everybody raising a halloo and going wild."

In Wall Street, a few gaunt survivors of the financial Bull Run were poking among the ruins. One of them noticed the shingle of a brokerage house named Coe, Lapsley & Co.

"A sign of the times," he muttered. "Collapse, & Co."

16
Propagandist Fisk

AFTER its Friday spree, Wall Street suffered a protracted hangover during which its denizens nursed aching heads and dyspeptic stomachs as they gathered in gloomy knots seeking to learn exactly what had happened while they were in their speculative cups. Strangely, gossip had it that Gould had lost his last dollar and that Fisk had made a fortune. Remarked the *Herald*: "It was curious to note how, here and there, wherever little groups of men were engaged in conversation, the name of 'Jim Fisk' was heard so frequently . . . It was the general opinion that he had made an immense 'pile' by the gold fever of Friday. . . ."

General Butterfield, who had gambled and won, said virtuously to a *Tribune* reporter, "No one has suffered but the gamblers."

The final score was not yet known because the gears of the Gold Exchange had been pushed to such a fearsome clip that the whole overburdened machine emitted smoke and flew apart. Trading had been so frenzied on Thursday and Friday, with something over $500,000,000 in gold bought and sold on Friday alone, that it would take the Exchange more than a week, using up dozens of clerks and hundreds of pencils, to compile and figure out the flood of transactions. During this time of confusion, many jittery speculators did not know whether they had lost or won—an uncertainty that dragged out the panic for days. Some who had won on paper eventually found themselves losers because their debtors had gone bankrupt. The Gold Room meanwhile was closed while mechanics tinkered with the works. This sort of suspense did not engender good cheer.

Since the Stock Exchange had suffered almost equal dis-
turbance, the cloud of woe that settled over the financial
district snuffed out almost everything but the imprecations
against Fisk as the cause of it all. Few paid heed to clergymen who preached that Sunday on the evils of avarice,
among them Henry Ward Beecher, whose text was from
Matthew VI: "Lay not up for yourselves treasures on earth."

Fisk was easily the "goat" of Black Friday. Men cheered
at a persistent rumor that he had been shot dead by John
Morrissey, the burly prizefighter-turned-Congressman who
was among the gold victims. Toasts were drunk to Morrissey
at Delmonico's, and the disappointment was general when
the report was exposed as a canard. Greeley's *Tribune*, commenting wonderingly on this approval of homicide by ordinarily law-abiding business men, laid it to—

". . . the feeling of the public that James Fisk is a man
whose hand is against every man's . . . that a man who made
sport of common honesty, of truth, of decency, in his own
life and in his dealings with men, in some sort satisfied the
claims of society upon him in dying the death of an outlaw."

Edmund Stedman, in his Black Friday burst of poesy,
rightly saw grave social implications in the disaster. Without troubling to name Fisk, he suggested that there was not
only something wrong with Fisk but also with a society
that gave him free rein, countenanced him and even admired him:

> *But it matters most, as it seems to me,*
> *That my countrymen, great and strong and free,*
> *So marvel at fellows who seem to win,*
> *That if even a clown can only begin*
> *By stealing a railroad, and use its purse*
> *For cornering stocks and gold, or—worse—*
> *For buying a Judge and a Legislature,*
> *And sinking still lower poor human nature,*
> *The gaping public, whatever befall,*
> *Will swallow him, tandem, harlots and all!*

Fisk, skeptical of the rumors of his own murder and careless of Stedman's opinion of his morality, was conferring behind locked doors at the Opera House with Gould and Shearman. The fruit of this talk was a batch of injunctions handed down by Tammany judges Barnard and Cardozo that even further manacled the helpless Gold Exchange. The Exchange was forbidden to pay out any money except as permitted by the court, and was restrained from imposing any penalties until the snarl was untangled. The wrath was unmitigated when Fisk repudiated most of his gold contracts, claiming that he had not been buying for himself but for William Belden and producing a note from Belden that seemed to prove it. Speyers, he said, had also been buying for Belden. Since Belden had failed to the extent of $50,-000,000, many who thought themselves Fisk's creditors wound up losers instead. Prince Erie had resorted to a dodge several times used by Daniel Drew, known in Wall Street argot as "squatting." He had renounced his own deals and taken refuge behind the law. A swarm of lawsuits were brought against him that would continue for years.

All this continued to make New York unsafe for him, a situation for which the Opera House was admirably contrived. He remained a virtual prisoner there for more than a fortnight, a recipient of threatening letters, keeping behind locked doors not only to escape assassins but to foil process servers waiting outside. Among the many complainants were the Messrs. Orlando Joslyn and John Bostwick, who had a writ of attachment against Fisk's Opera House for $117,450. He and Gould made use of the palace's excellent culinary facilities. The enclosed passageway to Fisk's house nearby also came in handy. Careful forethought against just such emergencies as this had equipped the bastion with everything but a moat and drawbridge. Fisk could even relax at theatrical performances within his own battlements, the annoying thing being that Lucille Western was still appearing in *Patrie*. He must have grown dreadfully tired of the Sardou drama by October 4, when Miss Western gave him something different by opening with *The Tempest*. All manner of luxury was within reach, including Josie Mansfield, yet his spirit rebelled at its cage.

In his disgruntlement he betrayed some of his less lovely traits. Fisk was a poor loser when his pride was hurt. Ordinarily careless of public opinion so long as his antics drew a fair share of applause from the galleries, he resented this universal opprobrium, seeing himself saddled with sole blame in an operation in which he felt he had been something of an innocent bystander, deceived by people he trusted. For four years he had trimmed Wall Street lambs and laughed uproariously while they bleated. Now that he had been tricked himself, he was getting ready for some stentorian bleating. Never did he blame his partner Gould. In his mind the double-crossers were Grant, whom he believed to have played false on a commitment to keep the government out of the gold market, and Corbin, who had miserably failed to deliver on his promise. He was aiming to nail their carcasses high on the night of September 29 when he summoned George Crouch, a *Herald* financial writer, and raised the portcullis to admit him. It was almost midnight when Crouch sat down under hissing gas lamps in the gilded Erie lair and poised his pencil for the most astonishing interview of his career.

"Everybody lays the blame on me," Fisk complained. "I've had the whole load to bear so far. I am threatened with assassination, I'm caged up here like a tiger in a menagerie, enjoy just about as much liberty; can't go out even at night, and that's just when I want to go about a little, without running pretty considerable risk of getting shot for the doings of other people. Now I've stood this just about long enough, and I'm determined not to stand it any longer; so I'm just going to make a clean breast of it and expose the parties who got up the 'corner.' I can make Rome howl at somebody else besides me—somebody you would never suspect of being connected with this affair. I have a most astounding revelation to make; but before I do so, you must promise that it shall be published. If the *Herald* won't publish it, I shall give it to one of the other papers. You saw the *Tribune* man waiting. I've got the other reporters here too. They'd publish anything, but then they represent parties, and people would think it an election dodge if they brought it out. Now the *Herald* being the leading paper, and the only one that is independent, I should prefer you publishing it—it would have more weight then."

Crouch noted that Prince Erie was seated in his specially-constructed walnut throne, with the monogram "E.R." impressed in the leather cushion.

"I do not deny that I was interested in the 'corner,' " Fisk went on. "Myself and my partner, Gould, were in the 'ring.' Now, then, we are speculators. I had nothing to do with the concoction of the 'corner'—it was all fixed before I was let into the secret. Now, do you or does anyone else imagine that we should have risked millions, as we did, unless we had positive assurances that the government would not interfere with our operations? Of course we should not. Anyone can see that. Well, then, I now tell you that we had something more than an assurance to that effect. Mere assurances would not have been sufficient. Members of the President's family were in with us. The President himself was interested with us in the 'corner.' That astonishes you, does it not?"

"Well," Crouch admitted, "I must confess it does, slightly."

"Slightly!" Fisk echoed. "Ah! you suspected it then? . . . I told you I could make Rome howl, didn't I? Well, won't that be sufficient to make Grant tremble in his boots?"

"We shall see," the reporter replied, according to the *Herald* account. "Do you mean to assert that President Grant was aware of the nature of your intended operations to bull gold?"

"Why, of course he was, and with him members of his family and parties holding high offices. And now I will tell you how it originated and who started it. It was planned by Jay Gould and Abel R. Corbin, President Grant's brother-in-law. Why, damn it! old Corbin married into Grant's family for the purpose of working the thing in that direction. That's all he married for this last time. Corbin's next move was to secure his son-in-law's appointment to the Sub-Treasury of New York. His son-in-law, R. B. Cath[er]-wood, you know. Ultimately Corbin got Cath[er]-wood to withdraw in favor of General Butterfield . . . Next the Tenth National Bank was bought, for a purpose which need not now be explained, it being a comparatively insignificant point. The first thing I did in the matter was to sound the President. I had several interviews with him on the subject, and finally, with Corbin's influence, everything was arranged and we set to work."

Why, Crouch asked, was he exposing his confederates?

"Because they went back on us and came near ruining us," Fisk said indignantly. "They would have ruined us had we not been smarter than chain-lightning and managed to turn when the log turned. We risked our millions on the assurance that the government would not interfere. Grant got scared, however, when the crisis came, and gave Boutwell instructions to sell. And now I'll tell you what scared Grant. Kimber, a man who was in the pool with us, backed out at the last moment. He sold out and got short. Discovering that he had deceived us, Gould 'put up gold' on him and broke him. Then Kimber leaked. Kimber's statement was telegraphed on to Grant, and the result was Boutwell's order to sell. Now, up to the time the government interfered with our operations I held in my hands the cards for fifteen millions, and should have made that had they let us alone that day. But the crash came before I had made nine millions even . . . As I said before, I've borne the entire load long enough, and now my life is in danger and I'm going to make them take their share of the responsibility. Another thing, I am a speculator. There's nothing wrong that I can see in my being connected with the 'ring,' but I don't know about Corbin, Grant and the rest of them. Guess they've been going a little out of their line, ain't they? Won't this statement make Rome howl, aye?"

Crouch had to agree on that. "So astounding a statement as this," he pointed out, "must be supported by proofs— something in the way of 'confirmation strong as holy writ,' Mr. Fisk. Can you show me anything in that line?"

Fisk told him to come back in the morning and he would have plenty of proof. When Crouch returned to his office that night, one can imagine the *Herald* city room convulsed by stop-press excitement. But the *Herald* was staffed by men much sharper than the sedate John Bigelow, and they did not stop the presses. They decided to play along with Fisk and see what developed. Crouch went back to the Opera House on the morning of September 30, picked his way through a group of men who were vainly trying to serve summonses on Fisk, and was admitted by the palace guard and escorted upstairs into the prince's chamber.

"You come with me," Fisk said, "and I will show you something."

The two men went down the grand staircase, walked through the empty theater and emerged at the stage entrance on Eighth Avenue, where a carriage was waiting in the care of Frederick Banfield, Gould's coachman. Fisk took a quick look around to make sure no sharpshooters or process servers were lurking here, then entered the carriage with Crouch. They drove to Corbin's home, a few doors west of Fifth Avenue on Twenty-seventh Street.

Instructing Crouch to wait and watch, Fisk went to the door and was admitted. While he was inside a reporter from the New York *Sun* arrived and was likewise admitted. About an hour later Fisk came out and was driven with Crouch back to the Opera House. The reporter was puzzled by all this rigmarole until he discovered that Fisk was simply trying to establish his close intimacy with Corbin. Fisk even called in a notary public and had Crouch make an affidavit swearing that he had seen him enter the Corbin house and remain there for some time, and also that he had seen the *Sun* man arrive.

Fisk had been involved in so many lawsuits and had consulted with so many lawyers that he had become something of a curbstone shyster himself, thinking illegally in terms of the law, often incorporating legal "to wits" and "hereinafters" in his ordinary conversation and showing a weakness for affidavits. He produced three more of them. One was from his good friend Charles McIntosh, superintendent of the Erie ferries, swearing that he met Corbin at the Erie offices on Black Friday, that Corbin acknowledged himself "deeply interested" and expressed the hope that Fisk and Gould "would come out all right." Another was from Coachman Banfield, swearing that Fisk was at Corbin's that day and that during the past three months he had repeatedly driven both Fisk and Gould to Corbin's. The third was from William O. Chapin, telling of his grueling journey to Pennsylvania to deliver a sealed message from Corbin to Grant at Fisk's behest.

With these in hand, Reporter Crouch next visited Gould, who had two items to add. Generals Butterfield and Porter were involved in the gold scheme, he said, along with "a number of prominent officials in this city." He also told of giving Corbin a $25,000 check for "securing government non-intervention" in the plot.

When Crouch returned to the *Herald* office, he gave his editors a mass of material that must have simultaneously electrified and frightened them. Still, it was apparent that Fisk, for all his talk and affidavits, had produced no real proof of anyone's complicity. It was also evident that Fisk's brain, in the portion normally devoted to ethical considerations, contained only a large vacuum. He actually regarded himself as a man with a legitimate grievance, deserving sympathy instead of condemnation because in winning only $9,000,000 instead of the $15,000,000 he had counted on he had incurred a $6,000,000 loss. "I am a speculator," he said, with the assumption that this gave him an unlimited license for fraud not enjoyed by others who were not speculators. He seemed perfectly unaware that in "exposing" his confederates he was in reality exposing his own moral shortcomings and that his tale of the trickery leading up to Black Friday only painted him as a greater rascal than had generally been known before.

Yet there had been rumors aplenty of governmental complicity. Grant had sailed in Fisk's boat, sat in Fisk's opera box, and his actions had been equivocal enough in other ways to arouse suspicion. The *Herald* was keen for a scoop if it could verify these suspicions, but it had a healthy fear of libel. Fisk had libeled President Grant, the President's family, Corbin, Mrs. Corbin and Catherwood, while Gould had libeled Butterfield and Porter. Any newspaper publishing all this without proof might as well shut up shop and let the lawyers take over. Very likely old James Gordon Bennett himself, now nearing the end of his career as the *Herald's* bitter genius, was called in to decide how to handle Fisk's package of dynamite.

It was determined to play it safe and hold the story over. Propagandist Fisk, watching for its appearance, was so irked at the *Herald's* unwillingness to help him make Rome howl that he handed the story over to the *Sun*. That journal likewise knew better than to publish unsupported charges against the President. It steered a safer course by ripping into Corbin, saying in part: "They [Fisk and Gould] found in Mr. A. R. Corbin, the brother-in-law of the President of the United States, one who would answer as a cat's-paw between the bull clique of Wall Street and Washington. [The assurances from Washington were] arranged by Mr. Corbin. . . ."

The canny *Herald*, seeing its opportunity to play one scoundrel against another, sent an emissary to interview Abel Corbin. The newsman found Corbin so prostrated by his woes that he had taken to his bed.

"Oh, yes," he groaned, "I have seen it [the *Sun* story] ... It is dreadful, but I can say nothing about it."

Surely, the reporter urged, he could at least make a formal denial of Fisk's charges. Corbin, who had made a good thing of his relationship to the President and was desperately hoping to wriggle out of the scandal, allowed that he could. He called God to witness that it was all a pack of lies, that he was a staunch Methodist and had no dealings with gamblers of the stamp of Fisk and Gould.

"I swear to you," he went on piously, raising his right hand, "that Fisk and Gould have never been to my house since Gould called last summer when the President was here. I have no connection with such men. When the President was here my house was open, and I received all who came to see him with open arms."

The reporter deftly laid a trap for the old rogue. "Then the statements published ... to the effect that Fisk was here on the 30th of September, last, are false?"

"False, every word," Corbin said firmly. "I will solemnly swear that Fisk was not in my house on that day, nor was his carriage at the door."

The *Herald*, now having ample proof that Corbin was a very monarch of mendacity, reached the conclusion that Fisk was lying too. On October 8 it published the Fisk interview, including the ticklish charges that "members of the President's family were in with us. The President himself was interested with us in the 'corner' ... old Corbin married into Grant's family for the purpose of working the thing in that direction." But the *Herald* was careful to make it plain that it did not believe any of this nonsense about Grant and was presenting the story simply as a great joke on a parcel of conspirators who had fallen out among themselves.

"The only thing the President had to do with the 'ring' was to defeat its ends," it said, adding that Corbin must have owed Fisk and Gould money as a result of the gold collapse, and "Fisk and Gould originated the slanders against the President in order to force Corbin to pay up." The *Herald* laughed heartily at its own cunning in out-witting "the great gorilla of Wall street, the gold-gobbling Gould; the amphibious what-is-it? or 'ring'-tailed financial orang-outang, otherwise known to naturalists and the world at large as the 'irrepressible Jim Fisk Junior,' and last but by no means least . . . that Methodistical monstrosity and per-plexing nondescript, that outrageous freak of nature, woolly horse Abel R. Corbin."

Gaily belaboring this menagerie of curiosities, the *Herald* went on: "Here, then, we have the explanation of the re-markable devotions paid to Mr. Boutwell by certain finan-ciers and lobby men on the occasion of his visit here a few weeks ago, and of the wonderful attentions of Fisk, Jr., and others to General Grant in his late summer excursions in these parts . . . Fisk may be an adept at manipulating gold stocks, shares and all that kind of thing, but he has a great deal to learn before he can manipulate the *Herald*."

Thus did Propagandist Fisk see the stench bomb he had so carefully aimed at President Grant, bounce back and ex-plode with horrid aroma in his own face. Yet even in his malodor he had the satisfaction of seeing Corbin thoroughly drenched and noting that some of the taint reached the President's coat-tails and clung there. For all the *Herald's* quips, the rumors of administration involvement in the gold plot were too thick and persistent to ignore. The Demo-cratic New York *World* called Fisk's fulminations "The gravest charges ever made against a President of the United States." New York was buzzing with gossip. Abel Corbin was sicker than ever under a weight of demonstrated false-hood that would embarrass him at two of his favorite places, his church and the White House. The unhappy Grant in

Washington found it necessary to issue a statement relating how Fisk had tried to pump him for information but had failed to get it. Congress, aware of an unsavory odor and outraged at the ability of a few gamblers in the Gold Room to create national panic, asked for an investigation by the Banking and Finance Committee under Representative James Garfield, who would himself be President one day.

In January, 1870, ring-tailed orang-outang Fisk, gold-gobbling gorilla Gould and woolly horse Corbin trooped off to Washington along with other unusual fauna to appear before the committee. The simians were no longer on nuzzling terms with the horse, taking every opportunity during the testimony to nip his rump. Fisk, who may have been sincere in his belief that the President and First Lady were linked with the gold ring, admitted that his only grounds for this conviction were Gould and Corbin's claims to that effect and the fact that Corbin had received a $25,000 check to be paid Mrs. Grant as her "profits." That check immediately became an object of nationwide curiosity. It was established that Mrs. Grant never got it at all. Corbin had cashed it himself, using the money to pay a debt. The check obviously was the one Gould paid to Corbin as *his* profit, and someone had been lying like thunder.

Possibly the falsehood was not restricted to one person, for it appeared that Gould as well as Corbin had deceived Fisk, nor was there any guarantee that purest truth sat upon the lips of Fisk himself. Fisk and Gould insisted they had never dreamed of gaining a corner on gold. On the contrary, their sense of civic duty had impelled them at great personal risk to strengthen the price of gold for the good of the Erie freight business and the country at large.

The President, Mrs. Grant and Mrs. Corbin were not asked to testify. Abel Corbin, a pathetic old ruin already thoroughly discredited, quavered that he had speculated a mite in gold—not for himself, mind you, only for his wife—but *never* had he used any improper influence on his distinguished brother-in-law Grant, or suggested to anyone that Grant had an interest. Gallantry was the rule, for while Daniel Butterfield admitted making a $35,000 profit in only one of his gold transactions and a good deal more in others, he likewise declared it was done not for himself but for Mrs. Butterfield.

Among this parcel of prevaricators, Garfield's committee found it impossible to achieve its goal, namely, the whole truth. The committee eventually threw up its hands and absolved Grant, who indeed seemed as innocent of guile as he had been of wisdom. It excoriated Fisk for his "singular depravity," blasted Gould as the plot's ringleader and Corbin as an example of "that worst form of hypocrisy which puts on the guise of religion and patriotism. . . ." But no penalty could be exacted because there was no law against buying gold or pressuring the President. Only Butterfield, despite his denial that he had accepted from Gould the profits from $500,000 in gold—which Gould swore he *had* accepted—received any punishment. He was allowed to resign as Assistant Treasurer.

Historians have had as much trouble as Representative Garfield in finding the truth in this gold-plated maze of deceit. Some have even marvelled that Fisk, "ruined" on Black Friday because of Gould's duplicity, should have remained his friend. Surely this is an exaggeration of Fisk's forgiving nature. For one thing, since he repudiated his contracts, he was not ruined, although he probably made nowhere near the $9,000,000 he claimed. For another, it is a safe bet that Gould and Fisk, after wiping out Fisk's vast debts by letting Belden go bankrupt, divided the $11,000,-000 profits and later remunerated Belden for his helpful insolvency—an old custom among Wall Street's faster gentry.

George Hooker, who was Belden's partner and Fisk's brother-in-law, must have seen enough in these transactions to make a Vermonter dizzy.

17 *Railroader Fisk*

ALTHOUGH Fisk soon was able to come out of hiding and roam abroad in comparative safety, he was still a leper to the righteous. He loved to spend an occasional day at Long Branch, only a two-hour boat trip away, a seaside resort of ornate hotels fronting on Ocean Avenue, parks strewn with flower beds and benches, broad drives where men of fashion could race their trotters, and a genteel gambling place, the Pennsylvania Club, operated by Fisk's good friend John Chamberlain. Chamberlain hailed from Pittsfield, Massachusetts, where Fisk had regularly sold tinware and silks a decade earlier, so they had much to josh about.

Fisk always put up at the glittering, 600-room Continental Hotel, run by another good friend, William Borrowes. After Black Friday, he was pained to note that when he arrived at the Continental, a goodly group of society people would immediately check out and move to the Stetson House, the Pavilion or some other hotel, letting it be known that they could not be happy under the same roof as Prince Erie. It was said that he scrupulously repaid Borrowes for every guest lost because of his contamination.

However, these viewers-with-repugnance were the upper crust, the people who had always loathed Fisk and who loathed him now more because he was the embodiment of vulgarity than because he was a symbol of something far more sinister and dangerous than mere vulgarity—corruption so strongly entrenched and brazen that it hardly bothered to conceal itself. Some of the linen-suited gentlemen who snubbed Fisk and enjoyed high social standing were reaping fortunes in corporate and financial piracy almost as larcenous as his but less publicized. Corruption was in the air, a national disease. Corruption reigned in New York, in Albany, across the land, even in Washington. Corruption was headlined in a thousand newspapers, deplored in a thousand pulpits. The smell of it spread to every hamlet and farm, so that humble citizens tended to become cynical and conclude that wealth, officialdom and rascality were synonymous. This was par excellence the Era of Avarice. Edmund Stedman's warning that Fisk was less an evil in himself than a symptom of social and political sickness fell on ears not attuned to hear such talk. It was no mere unfortunate coincidence that some of the sharp fellows of the day, among them Daniel Drew, Abel Corbin and Thomas Shearman, were pious pillars of the church. Wrongdoing seemed to arouse little public wrath so long as it was conducted with a reasonable amount of style. So the nabobs and brahmins continued to shun Fisk less because of his blunted ethics than because they thought him socially revolting, and they continued to pocket Boss Tweed and Judge Barnard, without whom Fisk might have approached some semblance of honesty, as honesty went at the time.

Possibly in part because of this almost unanimous rejection of Fisk by the elite, the less privileged classes were inclined to view him with forgiveness and even fondness. Obviously he was a rascal, but he was the *honestest* rascal in sight. The woods were so full of scoundrels subtle, scheming and sanctimonious that the hoi polloi had all it could stomach of that variety. Where else could you find a scoundrel as frank and merry about his misdeeds as Jim Fisk? It is a commentary on a time of copious fraudulence that Fisk won fame because he defined rascality in new terms, revolutionized it, infused it with a fresh originality and picturesqueness never before seen. Many humble citizens, sick of cant, thanked him because he beat rich impostors at their own game, carried on his larcenies without simultaneous resort to scriptures or hymns, and seemed comparatively free from one prevailing sin—hypocrisy. This socio-economic difference in attitude was reflected in the newspapers, the staid *Times* and *Tribune* always condemning him while the more earthy *Sun, Herald* and *World* as often as not found praiseworthy qualities in him.

Only a month after the *Herald* had ambushed Fisk in his own castle and labeled him "the ring-tailed orang-outang of finance," the same paper relented so far as to say, ". . . his acquaintance is sought by the very men who denounce him. His future career will be watched with great interest by the whole American people, and whether his life is spared for a longer or shorter period, he can make his exit with the proud satisfaction that he once made considerable stir in it." Since Fisk was then only thirty-four and almost indecently healthy, one has an eerie feeling that the *Herald* had a clairvoyant though dimly-perceived scoop on his coming violent death.

Far from expecting an early demise, he was scorning the advice of the Rev. Beecher and laying up for himself treasures on earth. On October 12, while the financial district was still reeling from Black Friday, a carefully selected portion of Erie's stockholders met at the Opera House to hold what was euphemistically called an election of directors. No one was surprised when Fisk, Gould and Tweed were re-elected along with fourteen hand-picked and obedient puppets. Among the directors, four were salaried employes of Erie thoroughly trained to the leash, a fifth being Commodore M. R. Simons, who managed Fisk's Narragansett Line and was equally docile in harness. A half-dozen of the directors were more substantial men, but they likewise tossed away any independence they might have felt when they signed a pledge to support Gould's policies or resign.

Here was where the Erie Classification Bill, bought at Albany the previous winter with Tweed's help, showed its worth. The directors "drew straws" to see who should hold the five-year terms provided by the law. With marvelous percipience Gould, Fisk and Tweed drew the longest straws. Barring a change in law, they could forget for five years the vexatious annual elections and devote their energies to printing and other cellar endeavors. These three, along with a strabismic lawyer named Frederick A. Lane, a Gould subaltern, formed the executive committee, and thereafter they guided the road to their taste, dispensing with the formality of calling board meetings.

"Indeed," one observer noted, "Messrs. Fisk and Gould have probably forgotten that there is such a thing as a board of directors of the Erie Railway, and practically there is none."

Despite his ignorance of railroading, Director Tweed's services were so valuable that he later estimated his profits from Erie for a three-month period as $650,000. The company had a unique system of bookkeeping in which bribes were listed under "legal expenses," better known by insiders as the India Rubber Account, but accountants later were able to piece together some astonishing figures. Between the time Fisk and Gould came into power and October 1, 1869 —about fifteen months—the printing press increased the capital stock of Erie by $53,425,700, according to one authority, who went on:

"The amount spent in equipping and improving the road during the same time was $6,297,067, leaving $47,128,633 wholly unaccounted for. No dividend was declared on any of the stock after the advent of Fisk and Gould; the debts of the corporation were largely increased, so that all the profits earned by the road, as well as the many millions received for new stock, remained unaccounted for. No one but Fisk and Gould knew anything about it."

This systematic plunder so exhausted the road's resources that it became the basis for a famous Wall Street axiom: "On the day Erie declares a dividend, icicles will freeze in hell."

With the waterlogged stock fluctuating dolefully between twenty and thirty percent of its par value, there were sour jokes about people starting fires or lighting cigars with it. One New Yorker, Frederick Van Wyck, recalled a stockholder walking into the Hoffman House bar and offering Joe, the bartender, "a certificate for 1 share of Erie railroad stock in payment for a drink . . . Incidentally, the offer was refused by Joe." While this sounds apocryphal, stockholders were doing what they always did—complaining and suing. One of them who sued to bring Fisk and Gould to account, found his suit switched to Judge Barnard's court in New York. Barnard issued an injunction forbidding him from taking further proceedings, then fined him $5000 for contempt when he tried to continue his suit— a discouragement to others so inclined. Railroader Fisk issued a long statement suggesting that the suits were inspired by Vanderbilt, who made a handy ogre to be blamed for everything, and showing that Erie was in good hands:

"We have never done anything . . . but there was somebody to find fault with it for the mere reason, as it seemed, that we had done or attempted to do it." Fisk, who may have been loose with his figures, declared that $14,000,000 had been spent in improvements, and went on: "These fourteen millions have been expended on the road, its equipment, its engines, its cars, its steel rails, its roadbeds, its connections, and in increasing its business convenience. This has been done notwithstanding the great plannings and plottings, mandamuses, and injunctions of our opponents. Mr. Gould has in all this been entitled to a great deal more credit than I. His head is long enough to control and carry out all the projects he undertakes; but it may be well enough, you know, to have a little assistance, and I have assisted him a little . . . The Erie is the greatest corporation on the American continent, and is as vital to the welfare of New York City as the Croton water is to her comfort and safety."

Despite this brave talk, Erie's treasury was bare—an anomaly that generally existed in this whimsical railroad, which could issue millions in stock and yet find it hard to meet current expenses. The wonder is that Fisk's popularity among the employes continued unimpaired although they were working on three-quarter time and even then their paychecks were slow in coming. In November, 1869, the brakemen in the Port Jervis area struck for this reason, causing a disastrous blockade of freight on the main line. Fisk hurried to Port Jervis with a gang of strikebreakers and special deputies who had orders to shoot anyone interfering with the movement of freight. The strikers were furious, says Mott, and "the peace of the community was greatly disturbed." Yet Fisk had the nerve to appear there in person, "and his very appearance was greeted with shouts and hearty cheers and expressions of delight from the very men he had ordered shot—such was the magnetism, the personal power, of this inexplicable man."

While Fisk always spent Christmas in Boston with his wife, New Year's was his own in New York. On New Year's Day, 1870, he and Josie entertained at an open-house reception at her Twenty-third Street house. ". . . There were hundreds of people there," Josie later testified. "I couldn't enumerate all of them." Among the hundreds were Judge Barnard, Judge McCunn, Boss Tweed, Edward S. Stokes, and "many bank and railroad presidents," guests she described as "some of the very best citizens of New York." Fisk, who had grown very fond of his oil partner, did not notice what some others did—that Stokes was hovering around Miss Mansfield with what seemed more than casual interest. In time his attentions caused the kind of talk accompanied by knowing winks; yet Fisk, his eye on the horizons of commerce and navigation, seemed unaware of any betrayal at his own hearth.

Although Judge Barnard had already been presented with some Erie stock and had a locomotive emblazoned with his name, his continuing friendliness won him other tokens of gratitude. Fisk waggishly sent him two stuffed owls to indicate how doubly wise he was. Gould "loaned" him $3000. Barnard took such a fancy to the walnut Erie office chairs with the tooléd monogram "E.R." that a whole set of such chairs turned up in his own dining room, identical except that they bore his monogram, "G.G.B." Although he later swore he had paid for them, there was no record of this and he was widely disbelieved. It was at this time that the Tweed Ring was building the New York County court-house, an edifice intended to be finished complete for $250,-000, but which had run into such "construction snags" that its cost already neared $10,000,000. A plastering contractor named Andrew J. Garvey had spread so many acres of plaster that his bill alone was nearly $3,000,000. According to Garvey, Judge Barnard met him one day outside of chambers and said, "I wish some work done at my house, and I can have any thing done I want. I have seen Mr. Tweed. . . ." A Garvey crew thereupon did $1000 worth of frescoing and painting at Barnard's Twenty-first Street house without charge, presumably adding this trivial item to the courthouse bill.

After Barnard's wife presented him with a son early in January, 1870, Fisk, Gould and many other notables were guests at the judge's home to see the baby christened John Charles Barnard. Fisk, embarrassed because others had brought gifts and he had not, later joined Gould in sending Mrs. Barnard a bankbook with a $1000 deposit for the son along with a formal note:

> "Dear Madam: A few days since we were much gratified at being present at the christening of your little son, and as a small memento of the pleasure we experienced on that occasion, we beg your acceptance, on his behalf, [of] the inclosed bank book.
>
> "With kindest regards, we remain, dear madam,
>
> > "Very truly yours,
> > "James Fisk, Jr.
> > "Jay Gould."

Josie Mansfield, who had come to think in large figures, mistakenly thought the gift was $10,000. She congratulated the judge, saying, "Your little boy has been in luck. It will be a pretty good sum when your boy becomes of age; it is $10,000, ain't it?"

"Not quite that," Barnard laughed. "Who told you so?"

"Never mind who told me so; I understand it is $10,000."

Barnard later showed her the bankbook to prove it was only $1000.

Although Josie was easily the best-kept kept woman in New York, and had been apparently content for more than two years, she was showing signs of dissatisfaction. Fisk had already tossed away a fortune on her, but knowing her propensity for spending, he was hard-headed enough to keep a mild check-rein on her expenditures. He maintained her in luxury and paid all her current bills, balking only at her suggestion that he give her a bank account from which she could draw at her pleasure—a wise provision in view of her weakness for diamonds and sables. She was forever in need of money. His letters show that he was constantly sending her sums of around $100 or $200, enough to tide her over but not enough to send her to Tiffany's. Possibly also he enjoyed these endless tokens of her dependence on him, for at times she was capable of a hauteur worthy of Mrs. Astor. To Josie, who forgot that she had come a long way financially in two years, these driblets were niggardly and humiliating. Far ahead of her time, she favored a social security or pension plan for kept women. As one commentator said, "she was continually importuning Fisk to settle something on her to make her independent."

She already regarded her four-story brownstone house as her very own, which technically it was. It was founded on a poker game at her previous house on Twenty-fourth Street, when Fisk and the other players had given her the night's winnings, some $2500. Fisk had invested the money for her in Erie, which he knew was then on the rise, and ran it up to $15,000. With this $15,000, plus $5000 he donated, she bought the brownstone in her own name, Fisk also carrying a considerable mortgage on it and spending some $65,000 for improvements and furnishings. Josie's blonde cousin from Boston, Marietta Williams, was living there with her as a companion and apparently also to lend an aura of respectability. Fisk probably paid her expenses as well.

Since Josie's yearning for independence coincided with her new interest in Ned Stokes, there is a plausible theory that she was preparing to throw Fisk over and was seeking to make hay while the sun shone. In Wall Street terms, Fisk was a solid investment for a foresighted young lady, while the spendthrift Stokes was the riskiest of gambles, and it seemed prudent to make one last killing in Fisk stock before taking a flyer on Stokes. Prince Erie, as yet unaware that he was being sold short by a secret Stokes-Mansfield pool, was wise enough in the tricks of the market to avoid any lump payment to Josie that would allow her to corner him. There were quarrels between the amorous speculators on this issue, with Josie using a familiar argumentative weapon, true only in reverse—Fisk was growing tired of her. Late in January she put her foot down. She was leaving him, she said, because he so heartlessly refused to remedy her financial insecurity. Fisk replied with a flowery farewell:

> Sunday Evening, Feb. 1, 1870
> My Dear Josie: I received your letter. The tenor does not surprise me much. You alone sought the issue, and the reward will belong to you. I cannot allow you to depart believing yourself what you write, and must say to you, which you know full well, that all the differences could have been settled by a kiss in the right spirits, and in after days I should feel very kindly toward you out of memory of the great love I have borne for you. I never was aware that you admitted a fault. I have many—God knows, too many—and that has brought me the trouble of the day . . .

I will give you no parting advice . . . A longer letter from me might be much of an advertisement of my weakness, and the only great idea I would impress on your mind is how wrong you are when you say that I have "grown tired of you." Wrong, wrong! Never excuse yourself on that in after years . . .

No more. Like the Arabs, we will fold our tents and quietly steal away, and when we spread them next we hope it will be where the "woodbine twineth," over the river Jordan, on the beautiful banks of Heaven. From yours, ever,

James

In the creation of billets-doux, Fisk was unique, combining in this one a spurious acceptance of the end of his affair with Josie along with the perfect assurance that he was aching to have her back. During the interim he retired to his diggings at 313 West Twenty-third along with his colored valet, John Marshall. It was of short duration. Josie, who knew him well, could see that her hold on him was still secure. Possibly she merely bided her time. In his next note, dated February 10, he unfolded his tent again:

My Dear Dolly: Will you see me this morning? If so, what hour? Yours truly, ever,

James

18 *Impresario Fisk*

FISK dove head-first into the theatrical business with a naive belief that it had bogged down under old-fogy leadership and needed only a clever young man with ideas—and circus experience—to breathe life into it. He found the water rather cold. His failure to win immediate success as the new colossus of stagecraft riled him, ruffled his poise. His critics declared that his interest in the stage was motivated purely, or impurely, by his desire to surround himself with lovely women in tights, but this was an injustice. While such a thought may not have been repugnant to him, he sincerely felt himself the savior of show business and worked at it with dedication.

In fact, he gave instructions and called the tune at rehearsals with such a bull-in-china-closet impetuosity that his managers came to cringe at his approach. He was impatient with nuances of technique he never knew existed. He wanted to make a splash. For a manager like John Brougham, who had grown up in the theater and could write a play, direct it and enact several characters therein, it was hard to see eye to eye with a man whose previous training had been largely with the hyenas and kangaroos in Van Amberg's menagerie. Fisk's tenure as proprietor of New York's three handsomest theaters was short-lived. After ten losing weeks he walked backstage at Brougham's Theater and quarreled with the manager. "You have been chipping away at my money long enough," he said, waving a black bamboo cane.

The Dublin-born Brougham, then appearing in *Pocahon-*

tas, was clad as the chief Powhatan and carried a tomahawk which he later admitted he was tempted to put to practical use. Instead, he quietly resigned and later went on tour. William Winter, drama critic for the *Tribune* and a good friend of Brougham's, believed that Fisk's motive was less to save money than to make the theater available for the opera bouffe troupe of Mlle. Irma, a French performer in whom he had grown interested. "A more obnoxious individual never imposed himself upon the stage," Winter said of Fisk.

The critic was incensed when Fisk's good friend George Butler offered him an easy way to make $2500 a year. Winter asked what he would have to do.

"Only to keep his [Fisk's] name before your readers," Butler said. ". . . anything pleasantly personal; anything that might do him good. There is no labor in it; all he wants is to have the good-will of the press."

"You can tell Mr. Fisk," Winter snapped, "that I have never been carried in anybody's pocket, and that I don't intend to begin."

Deficits dogged Fisk also at the huge Academy of Music, where he presented the opera *Lurline* to small houses. On the theory that the language difficulty was at fault, he tried having it sung on alternate nights in English and Italian, without noticeable improvement in receipts. After further unprofitable efforts with German and Italian opera, he allowed the Academy lease to lapse, taking a $20,000 loss.

But to his own Grand Opera House, one floor down from his Erie office, he devoted the constant and often exasperated attentions of a father on a refractory offspring. It was at this time that Jacques Offenbach's operas bouffes, the musical comedy of the day, were enjoying sensational success in Paris and had been tried in New York, one of them being on the boards at the Opera House when Fisk took over. While he liked the gay Offenbach operettas, he was smitten at the moment by serious art, like the clown who yearns to play *Hamlet*. When he sent C. W. Tayleure to Europe, Tayleure had instructions to seize the best Shakespearian players he could lay hands on. He was also to lure away other top European talent, the most glittering target being Christine Nilsson, the Swedish operatic soprano who was then the toast of the Continent. Undoubtedly Fisk hoped to astonish America by sponsoring Nilsson in a tour even more triumphant than Jenny Lind's nineteen years earlier. Excited rumors trickled back from Paris that Tayleure had signed Nilsson to a contract of staggering extravagance— "one thousand dollars in gold per night, with board, lodging, carriages, and all the *et ceteras*. . . ." But the deal fell through. Tayleure came back without Miss Nilsson, although he had other performers under contract.

Sending his "Grand Spectacular Opera Bouffe Company" to Brougham's Theater, now rechristened the Fifth Avenue, Impresario Fisk spent thousands in refurbishing the Opera House, then opened with *The Tempest* under Tayleure's direction, featuring a cast largely imported. The production had merit, even the snappish *Tribune* giving it a backhanded compliment: "Out of the Erie Railroad nest some good has come at last." Yet the impresario found hundreds of his 2600 seats empty. Since he was simultaneously losing money at the Fifth Avenue Theater, he gave up on that house, leasing it to Augustin Daly. That left him with only the Opera House on which to concentrate his ferocious attention. He closed *The Tempest* after a losing run, quarreling so bitterly with Tayleure that the director quit in a huff and found more congenial employment at the Brooklyn Academy of Music. Fisk's first theatrical season was artistically up to standard but so disastrous financially that no one not in possession of the Erie moneybags could have withstood it.

While he could afford the loss, he had a business man's dislike for red ink. It became a point of pride with him to make the Opera House a commercial success. He worked at this with enough diligence to offend stockholders who accused him of neglecting the railroad, one of them complaining in a lawsuit that Fisk advertised special trains for theatergoers "and [has] erected in conspicuous places in said city, at the expense of said Company, showy and costly lamp-posts, whereon are advertised, in elaborate glass panels, on the one side the location of the said 'Grand Opera House' . . . and on the opposite and less conspicuous side, the offices and business of the Erie Railway Company. . . ." The complaint further alleged "That said Opera House has free boxes and hospitality from its owners for their male and female friends. . . ."

Impervious to lawsuits, Fisk tried to lure crowds by lowering general admission from a dollar to fifty cents during the summer of 1869, when Lucille Western and her troupe presented a succession of melodramas. That meant he *had* to pack the house to make a profit. He was still in the red when fall came, still planning greater things. That winter he produced his first smash hit—*The Twelve Temptations*, a song-and-dance enormity that cost $75,000 to stage, boasted a cast of more than 200, a stage cataract with tons of real water, a rip-snorting cancan, and a truly Fiskian innovation one writer described with admiration: "A corps of beautiful blondes alternated with one of ravishing brunettes from night to night." Possibly later showmen like Ziegfeld and DeMille learned a few pointers from Prince Erie. One of the featured singers was a pretty, auburn-haired thing named Nully Pieris, said to be a special favorite of Fisk's. The impresario swelled with pride as *The Twelve Temptations* played to enthusiastic houses week after week. He racked his brain to keep it rolling, adding new dance sequences, bringing in an imported Spanish bal-

Before he met Josie, Jim Fisk allowed his red mustache to wander untrammeled.

Admiral Fisk, mustaches now tethered, sported gems even in nautical attire.

New-York Historical Society, New York City

Colonel Fisk somehow fell short of martial mien despite a $2000 livery.

New-York Historical Society, New York City

With an eye for gain, Josie Mansfield stirred passions that got out of hand.

Culver Service

New York gasped at the splendor of the Opera House which housed the Erie offices and also a bevy of women in tights. Right: Detail of one of the great doors carved with the monogram "E.R."

Both Photographs, Erie Railroad Co.

Handsome Ned Stokes—once Fisk's bosom friend, he became his bitterest enemy.
Brown Brothers

Commodore Vanderbilt came to respect Fisk as a redoubtable enemy.
New York Public Library—Prints Division

Horace Greeley beat the drum for airing the Fisk-Mansfield letters.
New York Public Library—Prints Division

Daniel Drew knew more Bible and less
pity than any operator in Wall Street.
New York Public Library—Prints Division

Judge George Barnard could twist the
law oddly in favor of Fisk and Gould.
New York Public Library—Prints Division

Jay Gould—he quailed at Fisk's glitter but
found him a perfect accomplice.
Erie Railroad Co.

Cartoonists had fun with Fisk. Above he appears in his four great roles, as Prince Erie "watering the stock" (note shirtfront diamond); as admiral; as *maitre de ballet* (note diamond); and as colonel of the Ninth. Below, Nast caricatures him as Falstaff, with wounded ankle bandaged after the Orange riot.

Both Cartoons New York Public Library—Prints Division; Nast Cartoon from Harper's Weekly

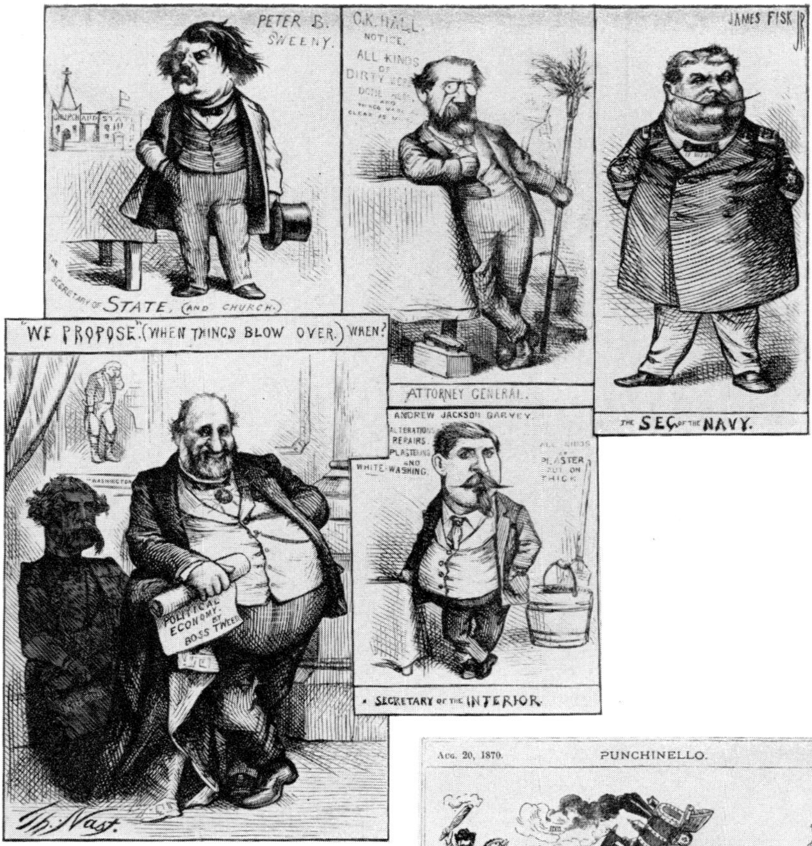

Satirist Nast proposed Tweed for President with a crew of fellow sharpers as his Cabinet. Above is Tweed, with Gov. Hoffman entirely in his shadow; then, reading clockwise, Cabinet Members Sweeny, Hall, Fisk (Secretary of the Navy), and Garvey (Secretary of the Interior). Right: Another artist pictures Fisk as a juggler balancing his varied enterprises.

Leslie's artist depicts the shooting of Fisk—an event as melodramatic as if he had staged it for his own theater. The fat man made an ideal target, and there was no escape.
New York Public Library—Prints Division

Nast shows Gould (with tall David D. Field, weeping Tweed, small Gov. Hoffman) indicating Fisk's grave: "All Erie's sins lie buried here." Justice: "I am not quite so blind."
New York Public Library—Prints Division, from Harper's Weekly

let troupe, increasing the army of leggy femininity from
seventy-five to a hundred. He advertised like mad:

THE DEMON CAN-CAN
Received Nightly with Wild Enthusiasm
TERPSICHOREAN AEROSTATICS
—The Mystery Sill Unsolved
THE EGYPTIAN BALLET
—The Most Novel of Novelties
THE GRAND
TRANSFORMATION SCENE
The Wonder of Wonders
100 BEAUTIFUL YOUNG LADIES
Contains Nothing Objectionable

Impresario Fisk was so delighted that he hardly even
winced at a nasty reminder of his railroad responsibilities.
On March 29, 1870, an ancient iron rail gave way near
Elmira, sending three Erie passenger cars catapulting off the
track and over an embankment. Not a soul was killed, only
fourteen people being badly injured—a casualty list that
seemed trivial after the previous massacres. Erie money
rightly should have been spent on steel rails rather than 100
Beautiful Young Ladies, but *The Twelve Temptations* clat-
tered on like a well-oiled locomotive for three months more
before it ran out of steam and closed.

Augustin Daly, now renting Fisk's Fifth Avenue Theater,
was a managerial autocrat fanatically opposed to outsiders
coming backstage—a privilege Fisk, as landlord, insisted
on. Although forced to allow him the freedom of the green-
room, Daly urged his players to have nothing to do with
him. This warning went unheeded, for the company found
him not only funnier than most stage comedians but also
gripped by a genuine passion for the theater. ". . . They
were all very fond of Jimmy Fisk," recalled Clara Morris,
a minor member of the cast. ". . . He never forgot them on

benefit night; whether the beneficiary was a man or woman there was always a gift ready from the 'Railroad Prince.' "

Miss Morris, who would later rise to stardom, at first obeyed Daly's dictum and shunned Fisk with such resolution that he said plaintively, "I'd like to offer her a word of welcome and congratulations, but she won't give a chap any margin." She soon fell under the Fisk spell and was friendly with him for the rest of his short life. "His blue eyes danced with fun," she said, "for he was one of nature's comedians . . . No one could talk five minutes with him without being moved to laughter."

She was fascinated by his atrociously showy clothing, his propensity for telling jokes on himself, his use of quaint rural phraseology. To her he seemed so much the soul of merriment that she could not believe the horrid stories about his immorality. Miss Morris was further impressed by his frequent praise of his wife, whom he pictured as a woman with a saintly ability to overlook his foibles. In illustrating this point, he told a story that was a mite risqué for the time.

On one occasion when Lucy visited him, he said, his valet was present when she noticed a hairpin on the sofa— a crinkled hairpin of a kind she never used but which were favored by showgirls. The valet rolled his eyes apprehensively.

"I saw myself in court fighting a divorce like the devil," Fisk went on. "And then, after an awful, perspiring silence, my Lucy says—she that has worn straight pins all her life: 'James, that *is* a lazy and careless woman that cares for your rooms. It's three weeks to-day since I left for home, and here is one of my hair-pins lying on the sofa ever since!' . . . Oh, I tell you, my Lucy can't be beat!"

No mere commercialist, Fisk enjoyed the glamour of show business, the organized confusion of rehearsals, the tantrums and jealousies of the stars, the novelty of seeing a new audience every night. It flattered his ego to be boss over a regiment of performers, stagehands and musicians, and he relished taking a bow under a spotlight with the cast after a final curtain. He never lost the beaming attitude of a country boy delighted but not surprised by his success in the city. It gave him immense satisfaction to sit in his great, red-curtained proscenium box, look down on the stage on one side and row upon row of spectators fading off to the rear, and reflect that all this was his. In the box directly above him was Miss Mansfield, whom he also believed to be his even though she was making as much fuss as a prima donna disgruntled with her salary. To him, every performance was a grand social occasion requiring his personal supervision to assure complete success. He liked to station himself in the lobby for a quarter-hour before the overture, greeting hundreds of friends like a jovial boniface as they entered—a hand-shaking ritual he continued between the acts, flitting from one box to another, with maybe a side trip to the bar.

Since most bluebloods shunned anything connected with Fisk on principle, the Grand Opera House could not be called a fashionable theater, but wealth and officialdom were there, wearing boiled shirts and pearls. Mayor Hall, himself a facile writer, occasionally was in the audience, as were Boss Tweed, Judge Barnard, Peter Sweeny, and a whole host of the Tammany faithful of great and small degree, including that record-breaking plasterer, Andrew J. Garvey. Ned Stokes, who had become a fast friend of Barnard, was often there. One of the town's best-publicized secrets was Josie Mansfield's status as Fisk's mistress, causing hundreds of necks to crane during intermissions to get a glimpse of the Twenty-third Street Cleopatra. Judge Barnard, a man with plenty of nerve, did not allow her notoriety to prevent him from going to Josie's box and chatting with her between the acts in full sight of the audience.

All this glitter was meat and drink to Social Lion Fisk, but Impresario Fisk was never far behind. During his first theatrical year he had ridden off in all directions, scattered his energies, tried everything from broadest farce to toniest opera. Now he reviewed the field and decided that opera bouffe offered the best combination of pleasant music and fun and that it could be presented successfully with a talented company despite some staid American opinion that it was wicked. Possibly his partiality came about, as some critics sniffed, because he was on opera-bouffe character himself. At any rate, he sent Max Maretzek across the Atlantic with instructions to wheedle away the brightest operetta stars of Paris—if possible to snag the great Offenbach himself.

One reason why Fisk had some trouble in attracting European talent was because he was known there as the *bête noire* of Erie, which had so grievously wronged European stockholders. He even turned for help to the State Department, seeking the influence of Secretary of State Hamilton Fish in bringing over a famous Belgian orchestra. He wrote General Daniel Sickles, an old Wall Street plunger who was now United States Minister in Madrid and a frequent visitor in Paris, asking Sickles to persuade Offenbach to come to New York under the Fisk banner. The irony of this was lost on Fisk, who was unaware that Sickles was then secretly organizing a movement sponsored by European stockholders and aimed at crushing Erie's Fisk-Gould leadership in a surprise attack.

Maretzek could not lure Offenbach, but he did bring back a group of skilled French performers, among them Mlles. Céline Montaland, Lea Silly and Marie Aimée. Aimée was the biggest catch, the second-best operetta diva in Europe, fetching both in voice and appearance as she strummed a guitar in the title role of *La Périchole*. Since this trio and others of the cast spoke little English, Fisk hired a multilingual Belgian named Georges Barbin as his full-time interpreter. It was said that he paid romantic attentions to Céline Montaland, which if true must have placed M. Barbin in an interesting middleman's position.

This far-flung search for expensive talent was a luxury Fisk could afford only because of his enormous stock winnings and the fact that unlike other impresarios he got his theater virtually free. Although the Grand Opera House had been bought with Erie money, the elastic Fisk-Gould bookkeeping system allowed them to collect $75,000 annual rent from Erie, at the same time drawing profitable rents from a row of ground-floor stores on the Twenty-third Street side. The corporation's stockholders were all too correct in assuming that they were supporting not only a debilitated railroad but also a flock of singers, dancers, musicians and scene-shifters, not to mention advertising lamp posts.

Operating the only endowed theater in New York, Fisk produced a series of operas-bouffes directed by Maretzek, but showed as much temperament as his stars. While there was an understanding that Maretzek would conduct at the Opera House during the 1870-71 season, Fisk hedged on signing a contract with him, thereby holding the Austrian at the mercy of his caprice. When the brothers Strakosch brought Christine Nilsson to New York that winter, Fisk sulked in his tent at the knowledge that others had succeeded where he had failed. Hearing that Maretzek had agreed to conduct at Nilsson's first concert at the Academy of Music, he exploded, sending him a peremptory note forbidding him to take part in a rival show. Maretzek, feeling himself free so long as no contract had been signed, ignored the command and conducted for Nilsson in full dress. At the next day's rehearsal at the Opera House, Fisk burst in with blood in his eye. He pointed a stubby finger at Maretzek.

"Swindler!" he roared. "Liar!"

"This was more than Max could endure," says a contemporary account, "and he immediately descended from his stand and levelled a powerful blow at Mr. Fisk's nose. The latter parried . . . and then the two closed in a fierce struggle and soon went down, Fisk coming on top. The *corps de ballet* and *prime donne* were screaming. Bystanders separated them. . . No great damage had been done beyond a serious soiling of Mr. Fisk's tidy toilet and the making of a slightly black eye for Maretzek."

Maretzek quit in a rage, threatening a lawsuit that never materialized. He was the last of Fisk's distinguished managers. Very possibly by that time Fisk thought he knew more than any manager anyway.

19 *Colonel Fisk*

EARLY in 1870, Fisk, the Civil War contractor, felt his martial spirit so stirred by the throb of peacetime drums that he could not resist the call to arms. This came about because the Ninth Regiment of the New York State National Guard had fallen into such a moribund state that without an infusion of new blood and capital it would have expired. Its membership had sunk below 250, its uniforms and equipment were in sorry shape, its band was sour and its morale so low that even some of its officers saw disbandment as a possibility.

Such a course was unthinkable to its commander, Colonel Charles H. Braine, who had fought with the Ninth during the war and cherished a fierce paternal pride in his outfit. It was going to take strong medicine, he saw, to save the Ninth. He dished it out with a steady hand. The thing to do, he said, was to elect Jim Fisk colonel if he would accept.

The picture of Fisk as a military leader must have occasioned a few snickers among the officers, but Braine was serious. It was pointed out that *he* was already colonel. Braine gave the next-to-last full measure of devotion. He stood ready to demote himself to lieutenant colonel if Fisk would take command. It is safe to say that Fisk's services were sought less as a leader than as a sponsor, or what today would be called an angel, and it is probable that some combat veterans of the Ninth quailed even then at the thought of taking on a man who had worn silk underwear and patent leather shoes throughout the late conflict. But combat veterans were in the minority, the regiment's condition was critical, and the bitter draught was swallowed. Colonel Braine led a committee of officers to the Opera House to sound out Fisk.

They found him refreshingly candid about his military inexperience. He admitted that while he liked to drive four- or six-in-hand, sitting a horse at the head of a regiment was not for one of his dimensions.

"I'm like one of our Erie locomotives," said the incurable punster. "I always have a tender behind. I never rode on horseback an hour in my life without having to take my meals from a mantelpiece for three days afterward."

Braine assured him that the occasions on which he would be required to sit a horse would be few. Fisk thought it over for a moment.

"You know I'm no military man," he said. "I've never trained a day in my life; never shot off a gun or pistol; and don't know even the A B C's of war, yet. Fact is, I doubt whether I could shoulder arms or file left, or make a re- connaissance in force, or do any of them things, to save my boots. And as for giving orders—why, I don't know any- thing about it. Elect me, though, and then we'll talk about it."

The election, held on April 7 at the Ninth Regiment Armory on West Twenty-sixth Street, only a few blocks from Castle Erie, was a mere formality. Of twenty officers present, only two—possibly Erie stockholders—failed to vote for Fisk. The new colonel, waiting in an anteroom, came out and was greeted with cheers by the soldiers. A *Herald* reporter, missing the solemnity of the occasion, referred to Fisk in his story as "the Mushroom Mars" and "Colonel Napoleon Fisk," going on: "The great god of war then mounted the dais and the trembling centurions were summoned before him. In a deep bass voice he then issued a pronunciamento, and to the obsequious satraps declared that there was a tide in the affairs of the militia which taken at the flood leads on to glory."

Punctuating his remarks with taps of his gold-headed cane, Fisk drew a laugh when he admitted that it would be impossible for a man of his shape to execute marching maneuvers in any but a large hall. He became properly serious, paying tribute to Lieutenant Colonel Braine as he observed that all the Ninth needed now was more men and more gumption, and he would do his best to help get both. He started off by offering a $500 prize to the company enrolling the most new men by July 1. This was going to take some doing in Company E, which had dwindled down to nothing and was at present a myth.

New York, although expecting the unusual from Fisk, seemed uncertain how to take his rise to a colonelcy. It caused more comment than the elevation of General Grant to the command of all Union armies during the war. Some newspapers regarded it as the biggest joke since Daniel Drew endowed a theological seminary, while others viewed it as perilous rather than funny. What was Fisk doing— getting ready to stage a military coup d'état? Some thoughtful people recalled his frantic scramble to gather an army during the A. & S. hostilities the previous year and laid this new move to a determination on his part not to be caught short again when a crisis loomed. He was said to be the first person in history to hold simultaneously the titles of colonel and admiral. There was speculation as to whether this new command did not imply some betrayal of his former dedication to the sea, and whether he should properly be addressed as Colonel-Admiral or Admiral-Colonel. Fisk, enjoying the fuss, was measured once again by Tailor Bell, who, wiseacres said, had to use an extra-long *elastic* tape to gauge his girth. Bell fitted him with a uniform heavily festooned with gold braid which, one writer affirmed, cost a cool $2000 and was as gorgeous as a Mexican general's.

Fisk had compiled a list of 200 Erie and Opera House employes who were clearly able to shoulder a musket. He approached them with arguments about a man's duty to his flag, the rugged delights of soldiering and the many social diversions enjoyed by members of the Ninth. These representations were so convincing, coming as they did from the man who held their jobs at his pleasure, that few could resist them. There was a rush of Erie personnel to the colors, one of the recruits being Henry Page, business manager at the Opera House, who never suspected he was taking a fatal step. The colonel announced that the first moonlight parade would take place April 14, right down Fifth Avenue.

To Fisk, Fifth Avenue represented the last and most important citadel of success, the only one he had failed to storm and capture. He had whipped Wall Street, subdued Erie, triumphed over the theater, won wealth, power and intimacy with the mighty, and still Fifth Avenue turned back all his attacks. It was the street of fashion, shaded by huge ailanthus trees, lined from Washington Square to Fifty-ninth Street with the homes of the elect. Sixth Avenue had the shopping bazars, Ninth Avenue had the new and noisy elevated railway, Park Avenue was a grubby street filled with the din of Commodore Vanderbilt's trains, and Fifth Avenue stuck up its nose in the midst of it all, conscious of its quiet elegance. To Fifth Avenue, Fisk was the mortal enemy who must be kept out at all costs. He would have dearly loved admittance there—on his own terms—but this was a dream never to be realized, the terms being unacceptable. Since all of the Fifth Avenue gentlemen's clubs excluded him, he had joined with Gould, Mayor Hall and others in the formation of the Blossom Club in a former mansion on Fifth near Twentieth Street, where the sitting room was adorned with a large portrait of Boss Tweed.

On the night of the 14th, he led his regiment down the avenue, a figurehead colonel on display, with Braine behind him giving the marching orders. The band was execrable, the uniforms shabby, and grandees in the clubs along the way gazed down on the commander with contempt. It was noted that scattered cheers came only from the Blossom Club.

A lover of bands, Fisk aimed to improve the Ninth's if he had to hire an entirely new one. His advent as colonel had not only astonished the town but also injected a new element of interest into the regiment itself. Even the men in the ranks could see that he took his new duties more seriously than anyone had expected or even desired, and was determined to make his command the best in New York regardless of effort or cost. He promptly gave Braine and several other officers good Erie jobs. Out of the great Fisk coffers came money for new uniforms for the whole regiment. He lured a platoon of his skilled Opera House musicians into the colors, rebuilding the band virtually overnight. Recruiting was going on at a merry clip. Company E, reborn, was manned largely by Erie personnel and was christened the Fisk Guard. By May 13, when Colonel Fisk and his command were the guests of Impresario Fisk at a special showing of *The Twelve Temptations* at the Opera House, the regiment had swelled to almost 500 men.

The colonel, in full panoply with sword and white kid gloves, his red mustaches waxed to points fit to run an enemy clear through the body, greeted his soldiers as they filed into the lobby clad in their new dress uniforms—dark blue trousers with broad gold stripes, blue coats with gold lace, dark red epaulets. The Ninth had never had it so good. "In an anteroom hard by," a reporter noted, "a corps of attentive waiters were kept busy icing champagne and dispensing it freely to all who called." There were plenty of calls. What other regiment offered free champagne? In the midst of this gaiety the colonel's brow darkened when a constable walked up and handed him a familiar paper—a summons. It turned out to be a suit by a grocer over a $41.25 butter bill. To a man who had been and was being sued for millions, a lawsuit for a mere $41.25 over a prosaic

item like butter was a studied affront. In a rage, he threw the
summons on the floor and ground it under the heels of his
shiny new fifty-dollar military boots.

"It is a trick," he snarled, "to insult me in front of my
men!"

Loyal members of the Ninth advanced on the constable
with such menacing aspect that he made haste to leave, but
aside from this unfortunate incident the party was a huge
success. Fisk and his officers retired to the Erie box, where
they got a fine view of 100 Beautiful Young Ladies high-
kicking over their heads and the colonel unloaded a joke
on Braine: "That," he said, "is one movement the Ninth
cannot perform, I'll bet." Down below, the soldiers admired
the stage waterfall, cheered the Demon Can-Can and kept
the waiters so busy that the regiment was in fairly ragged
formation when it left the Opera House after the show.
"After the performance," says a historian, "he [Fisk]
entertained his officers and some of his chief *danseuses* at
a sumptuous entertainment in his elegant banqueting hall."

Fisk next scheduled a grand ball for the Ninth at the
Academy of Music for May 27, inviting Boss Tweed and
other luminaries. On the 27th he sent Tweed a worried
note:

"My dear Tweed: . . . I have all my arrangements for
the Ball made for this evening, the Squire [Peter B.
Sweeny] will be there, and also the Governor & Staff. I
have just heard that you were not coming but I don't think
this can be possible; and it would be a great disappointment
to me not to see you there. . . ."

Tweed failed to show up, but the Academy was a gorgeous place nevertheless, with a décor of stars and flowers
and catering by Delmonico's. The colonel entertained Governor Hoffman and other notables with a private supper in
the prima donna's room at midnight at which mutual toasts
were drunk. "Mr. Director-Admiral-Colonel Fisk returned
thanks in a neat speech," noted *Leslie's*, "in which, replying

to some jocose allusions to his rotundity, he signified his intention to procure a *curved* musket to correspond to the proportions of his figure." Other National Guard groups in New York sneered at the Ninth and its tinsel colonel, suggesting that the regiment had traded its soul for tainted wealth, but there may have been envy mixed in with the jibes, for the men of the Ninth were discovering delights never before known in soldiering.

It was at this time that Commodore Vanderbilt, still angry because of the loss he had taken in Fisk and Gould's Black Friday operations, and still being sued for millions by the pair, dealt them a mighty blow. He reduced the Central's rate on cattle between Buffalo and New York from $160 to forty dollars per carload. Although Erie would lose heavily at the forty-dollar rate, Fisk and Gould felt they had to meet the reduction. No sooner had they done it than the Commodore, with the air of a man who has led his enemies into a trap, lowered his rate to one dollar a carload.

One dollar a carload! Vanderbilt's moneybags could stand it, but Erie would be ruined. Fisk and Gould went into anxious conference, Gould tearing paper into bits. It was Fisk who saw that the Commodore, instead of backing them into a corner, had presented them with a glorious opportunity.

Erie did not reduce its rate further. Fisk got on the telegraph to the road's Buffalo agent, ordering him to buy all beef cattle available in his area and ship them to New York on the Central. The agent rounded up 6000 head. Soon the Central's eastbound freights were choked with livestock, losing money on every carload—a loss Vanderbilt shrugged off on the theory that he was giving Erie the *coup de grâce.* Erie meanwhile carried almost no cattle but was handling other freight at gratifying rates, and Fisk, having temporarily gone into the beef business, was disposing of his livestock to New York commission merchants at a handsome profit, thanks to the Central's philanthropic tariff. Not until several days later did the Commodore discover that instead of smiting "them blowers," he was subsidizing them. "He very nearly lost his reason," said one observer, and hurriedly pushed the rate back to the old figure.

Irked at the necessity of traveling to Long Branch in boats he considered shabby, Fisk had spent $94,000 the previous winter for the former Stonington steamer *Plymouth Rock*. He had the 345-foot vessel refitted for the 1870 season into a floating hotel with thirty-two apartments, a restaurant and a splendid bar finished in white marble and lined with mirrors. Fisk's likeness was painted "in rich colors" on each side of the ship's boiler. Thereafter he sailed to the New Jersey resort in style, sometimes accompanied by Miss Mansfield, who, although her affections had strayed, liked Long Branch and other luxuries so well that she found it expedient to postpone a final break while she parleyed for her future security. The colonel-admiral, a confirmed hotel greeter ever since his boyhood when he worked at Brattleboro's Revere House, stood by the gangplank when the boat docked and passed pleasantries with everyone who came off. Two years later, long after Josie had quarreled irrevocably with Fisk, she gave a revealing bit of testimony when questioned in court.

"Was he [Fisk] hospitable and generous in character?" an attorney asked her.

"Well, I always thought he was very open hearted," Josie conceded.

"Had he many friends and acquaintances?"

"A great many."

"And exchanging acts of courtesy and kindness?"

"Always," Josie replied.

Now, in 1870, she was telling Fisk he was anything but generous and open-hearted—was, in fact, a defaulter to his obligations, depriving her of moneys justly due her. Never, in her infatuation for Ned Stokes, did she forget that Stokes had trouble enough supporting his own family, that he had a wretched habit of losing money on the horses and was a slender reed for a non-earning young lady to lean on. She was not ready to sacrifice diamonds for love, wanting both. All that summer she was waging a cold war, applying constant pressure, running the gamut from tears to threats, importuning Fisk for the sort of competence any lady expected. Fisk, still resisting, was occasionally exiled from her home at 359 West Twenty-third, taking refuge with Valet Marshall at his own diggings at 313, returning when the storm cleared. To bolster her case, Josie accused him—possibly with some truth—of having affairs with Nully Pieris and Mlle. Montaland. The galloping Red Knight, invincible in Wall Street, seemed unhorsed and bereft of shield in Twenty-third Street.

That summer he learned, doubtless from friends aware of it for some time, that his bosom comrade Stokes had been seen suspiciously often at 359. Incredulous, he must have investigated and found cause for alarm. Yet the exalted Fisk ego came to his defense. Certainly it was in character for a ladies' man like Stokes to be smitten by Josie. But that Josie should prefer Stokes to him, Prince Erie—unthinkable! He was an unhappy man nevertheless when he wrote her August 1 at Long Branch:

> My dear Josie: I send you letter I found to my care on my desk. I cannot come to you to-night. I shall stay in town to-night, and probably to-morrow night, and after that I must go East. On my return I shall come to see you. I am sure you will say, "What a fool!" But you must rest, and so must I. The thread is so slender I dare not strain it more. I am sore, but God made me so, and I have not the power to change it.
>
> Loving you, as *none but you,* I am, yours, ever, James.

In analyzing the famous Fisk-Mansfield correspondence, which contains unfortunate lacunae, some reading between the lines is required. Having informed Josie that he would be out of town, Fisk apparently detailed friends or operatives to keep a close watch. On his return he found that Nully Pieris, whom he now suspected of being in league with Josie, had driven to a telegraph office on Broadway and sent a message to Stokes, who was conscientiously following the horses at Saratoga Springs: "Pay no attention to former despatch. Come on first train." Fisk, suspecting that Josie had inspired the telegram, taxed her with deceit in a note reading in part:

> . . . Comment is unnecessary—a plotting house, and against me. What have "I done" that Nully Pieris should work against my peace of mind? Yours truly, ever, James.

Yet this mistrust, rather than causing an immediate break, was to lengthen out into a series of white papers much like those between two quarreling nations seeking to make known their stand while trying to avoid open war. Meanwhile, life went on and Colonel Fisk had a job to do, arranging the summer encampment for his regiment. As always during peacetime, the military establishment had tended to diminish the stress on the stern rigors of drill in favor of more social activities—a drift with which the colonel was in hearty accord. The place where the regiment would camp came to him in an intuitive flash. Long Branch! The soldiers could go in Fisk's own boat, enjoy the hospitality of his favorite hotel, the Continental, and the colonel would have an opportunity to show off his revitalized command to the gay resort crowd. While Long Branch was not without distractions, and a fair comparison today would be to send soldiers to Las Vegas for undisturbed training, the Ninth cheered the idea.

The regiment now had ten well-filled companies totaling almost 800 men—a gain of some 300 percent in the four months since the new leader took over—but New York was still inclined to snicker rather than admire. Prominent among the belittlers was the city's famous Seventh Regiment, which had a fine war record, had kept many veterans on its roster and was known for spit-and-polish discipline with a minimum of monkey-business. To the veterans of the Seventh, the Ninth was known as the Opera House Army, Fisk's Footmen, and by other names even less flattering, so that the feeling between the two outfits was not cordial.

On August 20 the Ninth left the armory in fine array, led by the colonel. "Prince Erie rode a splendid sorrel," noted the *Herald*, "and sat in the saddle as gracefully as though he had come fresh from Haguenau's bloody field." The men crowded aboard the *Plymouth Rock*, enjoying the white marble bar as they sailed out into the bay. Fisk, who had been studying up on the command routine, now was able to start and stop the regiment unaided. However, when the boat docked at Sandy Hook and the men flocked ashore, it took more complicated orders. The colonel made a valiant attempt to command the maneuver, with Lieutenant Colonel Braine at his shoulder murmuring instructions, but the formation dissolved in such confusion that Braine had to bellow "As you were!" and take over. The regiment pressed on to Long Branch and pitched tents in the outskirts, a place Fisk named Camp Gould to honor his Erie colleague. Although the men slept under canvas, they made no pretense at mess-kit stoicism, taking all their meals on linen tablecloths at the Continental.

While one historian says the excursion "turned into a monumental week-long drunk," this is an exaggeration. There was the usual skylarking to be expected on such an expedition, but in the main the colonel kept his men fairly well in hand, paying the fines for a few who had disagreements with the police. He had made elaborate preparations for the most magnificent encampment in Ninth annals, bringing along not only the regimental band but also the bands from two of his ships, the *Plymouth Rock* and *Bristol*. He had invited Governor Hoffman down to review the regiment. It happened that President Grant was then vacationing at his Long Branch cottage. While Fisk had disliked Grant ever since Black Friday—a feeling entirely mutual— and the *Tribune* even reported with a shudder that he openly thumbed his nose at Grant's passing carriage, this probably was mere rumor, for he invited the President to join Governor Hoffman in reviewing the unit. This may not have been the sole reason why Grant left Long Branch, but the fact is that he *did* depart for Newport August 23, undoubtedly with a sense of relief. Governor Hoffman could hardly ignore an invitation from one who had contributed so liberally to his campaign, but he had presidential aspirations and he seemed to feel that close identification with Fisk might be politically hurtful. When he came, it was with a small entourage and the air of a man eager to finish his chore and begone. He reviewed the Ninth, then rushed off with almost indecent haste, saying he was too busy to stay for the regiment's grand finale, a ball at the Continental.

Although aware of some snubs, the Ninth got a rousing reception when it paraded through town, the band was given free beer by the colonel, and even if the grand ball fell somewhat flat because of the failure of invited bigwigs to come and the presence of only one girl to every five troopers, it was an outing they would never forget. When they returned to New York on August 29, the colonel was beaming despite a face peeling with sunburn, and the regiment marched so smartly up Fifth Avenue that it actually drew cheers. "Indeed, the march was a perfect ovation from beginning to end," said the *Herald* approvingly. ". . . The Seventh has need to look to its laurels."

Since an ovation was something Colonel Fisk rather enjoyed, it is safe to say that he forgot for the moment the pangs in the region of his heart.

20
Stale Beer and Rotten Cheese

HELEN JOSEPHINE MANSFIELD, an unemployed actress in 1867 who owned only one passable dress and was behind on her rent, had made such effective use of her arrangement with Fisk that by the fall of 1870 she was living on a scale equaling that of some of the most famous courtesans of France's Second Empire. While an audited account of her personal and capital gains is unavailable, a description of her improved condition would have to include the following properties and perquisites:

A $20,000 equity in her four-story house.

Ownership of its improvements, furnishings and silverware, worth $65,000 by her own estimate.

A collection of gowns, furs and similar finery that would have done credit to a Fifth Avenue grande dame.

An impressive assortment of jewelry.

Three house servants to wait on her.

A carriage and coachman at her call.

A private box at the Grand Opera House.

Frequent all-expenses-paid trips to Long Branch.

Free transportation on the Erie Railway or on any of Admiral Fisk's steamers.

Some of the items represented privileges which would continue only at Fisk's pleasure. Others were outright property, hers to do with as she pleased. Bored with Fisk as she was, had she told him so frankly and put a quick end to their affair, it is safe to say that she could have realized at least $75,000 by the sale of her assets—a substantial fortune at that time sufficient to keep her in comfort, if not luxury, the rest of her days. Miss Mansfield preferred to eat her caviar and have it too. For a solid year, after being smitten by Stokes in the winter of 1869-70, she continued to enjoy the Fisk bounty and ask for more. When he balked at this, she intimated that she was privy to Erie and Tweed Ring secrets that would embarrass him if made public.

On September 11, 1870, their differences caused Fisk to pack up with Valet Marshall and retire to his own rooms, either voluntarily or on request. In a bitter letter he addressed her shortly thereafter, he touched on the threats she had made:

> As far as the great exposure you speak of is concerned, that is a dark entry upon which I have no light; and as I fail to see it, I cannot, of course, understand it.

In a revealing passage, he made plain that he regretted the disrepute that kept him out of the best circles, and blamed it—surely not with entire justice—on Josie:

> ... All this time I showed ... you, nothing but kindness both in words and actions, laying at your feet a soul, a heart, a fortune, and a reputation, which had cost, by night and day, twenty-five years of perpetual struggle, and which, but for the black blot of having, in an evil hour, linked itself with you, would stand out today brighter than any ever seen upon earth.

The colonel did not underestimate himself. He sent back a ring Josie had given him, saying, "Its memory is indecent." He went on:

> I had a few pictures of you, but they have found a place among the nothings which fill the waste-basket under my table ... I fain would reach the point where not even the slightest necessity will exist for any intercourse between us. I am in hopes this will end it.

For all this blunt talk, Josie knew her man, knew that her hold on him was secure. She replied softly, saying that his letter was cruel and unwarranted. Then she returned to a Mansfield theme as recurrent as the familiar trumpet-blast in Beethoven's Fifth:

> You have told me very often that you held some twenty or twenty-five thousand dollars of mine in your keeping. I do not know if it is so, but that I may be able to shape my affairs permanently for the future [I point out] that a part of the amount would place me where I would never have to appeal to you for aught. I have never *had one dollar from anyone else,* and arriving here from the Branch, expecting my affairs with you to continue, I contracted bills that I would not otherwise have done . . . After a time I shall sell my house, but for the present I think it best to remain in it. The money I speak of would place me where I would need the assistance of no one.
>
> . . . I am sorry that your association with me was detrimental to you, and I would gladly with you (were it possible) obliterate the last three years of my life's history; but it is not possible, and we must struggle to outlive our past. . . .

Fisk, who had called her Dolly and Dumplings, still had enough humor to give her a new nickname in keeping with her desire for a "settlement": Lumpsum. He replied with some logic:

> . . . Have I not furnished a satisfactory mansion for others' use? Have I not fulfilled every promise I have made? Is there not a stability about your finances to-day (if not disturbed by vultures) sufficient to afford you a comfortable income for the remainder of your natural life? You say you have never received a dollar from any one but me, and you *will never* have another from me, until want and misery bring you to my door, except, of course, in fulfillment of my sacred promise, and the settlement of your bills up to three weeks ago, at five minutes to eleven o'clock.

Keeping close tab on Stokes, Fisk had learned that he had been forced to pawn his gems, possibly because of misplaced confidence in a horse. Taking this as his text, Fisk wrote that Josie was saying figuratively of Stokes:

"Why, man, how beautiful you are to look at, but nothing to lean on." And you may well imagine my surprise at your selection of the element you have chosen to fill my place. I was shown to-day his diamonds, which had been sacrificed . . . at one-half their value . . . You will, therefore, excuse me if I decline your modest request for a still further disbursement of $25,000. I very naturally feel that some part of this amount might be used to release from the pound the property of others, in whose welfare the writer of this does *not* feel unbounded interest.

While the Fisk-Mansfield correspondence lacks the literary distinction of the letters between the Brownings, and is of interest chiefly to illuminate the motives of two quarreling sinners, there is a superficial polish to both Fisk's and Mansfield's missives suggesting that neither of them did their own writing. Fisk may have dictated the gist of his messages to his private secretary, John Comer, allowing Comer to weed out the more glaring grammatical errors. It was later speculated that Stokes, a smooth fellow with words, may have been Josie's epistolary tutor.

The letters continued, with Fisk as always protesting too much. Had he sincerely wished to end the affair, he could have done so with a word. He kept the line of communication open, sending his valet to Josie with further unnecessary representations of his position, replete with such phrases as "the holy feeling I once had for you," and "We have parted *for ever*." Implicit in them all was his forlorn hope that they had not parted forever. He had agreed to pay Josie's bills up to "five minutes to eleven o'clock" on September 11. He was indignant when she used a sly trick on him, coaxing merchants to put earlier dates on bills incurred after the 11th. He ended up by paying them. He even achieved a momentary attitude of detachment toward Stokes, writing Josie:

> . . . Cling to him. Be careful what you do, or he will be watchful. How well he knows you *cheated me*. He will look for the same.

For Fisk to lose Josie to Stokes after the whole town knew he had set her up in luxury would be a supreme humiliation, a standing joke at Delmonico's and every drinkery along Broadway, a subject for delighted insinuation in the press, a belly-laugh for all of New York, a defeat so mortifying that even the brassbound Fisk could scarcely walk abroad without shame. Undoubtedly this was in his mind, but beyond the mere matter of public derision was a fact even more pathetic. He was still infatuated with Josie.

The lady knew it just as surely as she knew that Ned Stokes wanted to get his diamonds out of pawn. She played on Fisk's weakness, not with great skill, for no artistry was necessary. A few soft words by mail, then her gracious permission for him to visit her, and she had disarmed the colonel of the Ninth.

On November 7 he sent her $500.

On November 10 he sent her $300.

On November 19 he sent her $500.

At this time the imported company was on the Opera House boards with the Offenbach operetta *Les Brigands,* a satire on the world of finance fully appreciated by Bandit Fisk. On November 14 the bemused opera-bouffe lover wrote his Lorelei:

> Dear Dolly,—Do you really wish to see a "brigand" at your house to-night? If so, what hour, or from what hour and how late shall I call? for I might be able to come at eight, or, perhaps, not until ten. Say what hour, and how late is your limit after the time you first say.

On January 1, 1871, James Fisk Jr. climbed into the handsomest of his six carriages and was whirled away by four high-stepping horses, with four footmen in flamboyant livery riding outside. As so often happened when he drove abroad, he was in reality taking others for a ride. He was paying his New Year's calls in the self-effacing Fisk tradition. At each stop the footmen descended with a purple-and-gold carpet which they unrolled from carriage to door. They stood at attention, two on each side, as the master, blazing with diamonds, strode inside to pay his respects. This was the sort of display that made cultivated New Yorkers writhe, while the more free-and-easy yeomanry laughed at it because Fisk laughed at it himself at the same time as he enjoyed it, and it seemed the logical self-expression of an eccentric who had made himself a distinctive part of the city.

Yet the "Erie-pressible" Fisk exhibitionism, as one newspaper termed it, far more than being merely vulgar, was an outrage on good public relations that raised still further the choler of those who felt themselves wronged by the company. It was painful to Jay Gould, who had long since given up trying to slow down his gaudy partner. Creaky Erie had rolled up a good profit of $4,106,450.77 the previous year, but its common stock was selling at 21½, its lowest in a decade, and icicles were not forming in hell, for there would be no dividend—all because, as Fisk explained it, the road was still suffering from the monstrous Vanderbilt swindle not yet punished by the courts. A man named John Peck joined the army of stockholders who were suing the company for a dividend they thought due them. Many of the road's workmen, who labored a twelve-hour shift for $1.62 a day, had not been paid since November. A reporter went over to the Erie Jersey City yards and talked to a brakeman who discreetly refused to give his name as he described the hardships of life without a paycheck.

"And how could it be otherwise," the brakeman demanded, "when so much money goes for women, wine, horses and opera houses, full of disreputable actresses and dancing girls? Why, they tell me that Fisk was at a ball the other night and that he had a big woman on his arm . . . and they say that every bit of her dress was covered with pearls and her hair was full of diamonds—diamonds, by G—d! diamonds; and if you come down here a little way I'll show you a family who have had only one loaf of bread between five persons in two days. . . ."

Fisk had his usual faculty for brushing such remote unpleasantness aside as he dashed from house to house to wish his friends a prosperous New Year. What really worried him was Josie, who seemed unable or unwilling to slam the door on Ned Stokes.

Although the relations between Fisk and Stokes had grown strained, they had not yet reached open warfare. For months they had conducted cautious negotiations in an effort to solve both their amorous and business differences in secret. On one occasion they called in Judge Barnard, a close friend of both, as arbiter. The three men parleyed for several hours in Josie's gilded parlor, but this was one instance when Barnard's favorite weapon, the injunction, was of no use at all and he had to fall back on wisdom, which proved unavailing. Twice Josie called on Boss Tweed, once traveling to Albany to visit him and ask him to persuade Fisk to accept the Mansfield terms in the controversy. Tweed, who could make mayors and governors, found this problem too much for him. The Fisk-Stokes quarrel was rendered all the more delicate by the vulnerability of both contenders. While Fisk's affair with Josie was New York's best-known scandal, the newspapers thus far had avoided open mention of it—a condition of semi-secrecy Fisk wished to preserve, not only to spare his wife but also to shield the already bespattered Erie Ring from further odium. Stokes seemed less concerned about his wife's feelings than in maintaining his profitable connection with Fisk in the refinery business and in protecting his social standing, which was precious to him and would be wrecked if his liaison with the notorious Mansfield woman became known.

To muddy the picture further, the gay Stokes was said to be paying attentions to Mlle. Aimée, the Opera House star, as well as to a Thirteenth Street beauty named Amelia Graham, while there were still rumors that Fisk had more than an impresario's interest in the brunette Céline Montaland, the prima donna who sang the role of Fiorella in *Les Brigands*. Those who worried about mere love triangles could take heart from the multilateral Fisk-Stokes involvement.

It appears that in November, 1870, Josie persuaded Fisk that she had cast off Stokes, thereby bringing in $1300 in largesse in twelve days. However, there were later disagreements, Fisk once visiting her house only to find that she had thrown his galoshes out the door and wanted none of him. He was still friendly enough with Stokes to discuss his problems with him.

"See here, Ned," he said plaintively, "she won't even let me leave my gum shoes in the house!"

It was a remark that would haunt him. Later, he became convinced that Josie was not only seeing Stokes but was funneling some of the Fisk funds his way. He was tormented by the suspicion that he was subsidizing his own rival, who now enjoyed the freedom of the mansion he had built for Josie. Striking back, Fisk cancelled the verbal agreement whereby the Brooklyn Refinery Company received preferred rates via Erie and also supplied the road with its oil. Since it was this arrangement alone that made the refinery profitable, Stokes' handsome income was wiped out. He had taken more than $90,000 out of the refinery in a year and a half—a good return considering that Fisk had supplied the capital and Stokes had been so preoccupied with gambling and women that he had done little actual work.

The Erie withdrawal was so disastrous to him that he arranged a meeting with Fisk at Delmonico's, where he made a sporting proposition. Why not put it up to Josie— let her decide which it would be, Fisk or Stokes? Fisk, unaware that the cards were stacked against him, was willing. The two rivals took a hansom to the Mansfield residence and put the question to her.

Josie, who may have been coached in advance by Stokes, took a line of peacemaking and masterly impartiality. It was ridiculous, she said, for two grown men to quarrel in such a schoolboy manner. She liked them both, and there was no reason in the world why they could not all be friends.

"It won't do, Josie," Railroader Fisk insisted. "You can't run two engines on one track in contrary directions at the same time."

But she was determined to do just that. The meeting ended on this equivocal note, leaving Fisk with the unhappy feeling that the issue was being evaded and he was being cozened. Still he seemed confident that if Stokes' financial props were kept out from under him, he would soon cease to be a serious rival. So the Erie custom was still withheld, the business of the refinery ground to a halt, and by the year's end Ned Stokes was in desperate straits.

Shortly after New Year's, he went to the Devoe Manufacturing Company and collected $27,500 the Devoe firm owed the Brooklyn Refinery, keeping it as his own. Hearing of this, Fisk exploded. On January 7, 1871, he swore out a warrant charging Stokes with embezzlement. Late that evening—a Saturday—Stokes was lounging in the gorgeous bar of the Hoffman House at Broadway and Twenty-fourth Street when a pair of deputies arrested him and whisked him off to the Ludlow Street Jail.

It was Samuel Bowles all over again. Stokes was able neither to reach friends who would loan him money nor officials empowered to bail him out. He was forced to stay in jail over the weekend, missing his daily manicure and the scented Florida water with which he was wont to bathe. When he was released on bail Monday morning, he was bent on vengeance. It appears that he did some talking to newspaper friends, for a ditty about Fisk's cast-out galoshes appeared in the public prints, reading in part:

> *The heart that once on Erie's walls*
> *The soul of greatness shed,*
> *Now sits as sad in Erie's halls*
> *As if that soul were fled.*

> *So sleeps the pride of former days;*
> *So glory's thrill is o'er*
> *When Josie, in her altered ways,*
> *Throws gum shoes out the door.*

New Yorkers guffawed over a cartoon of Fisk, weeping into his galoshes. The time of mediation had passed. It was James Fisk Jr. *vs* Edward Stiles Stokes, and no holds barred. When Stokes came up for trial on the embezzlement charge before Judge Dowling, he won a technical victory. Dowling ruled that while the Brooklyn Refinery Company was corporate in form, it was in reality a partnership, and that under the law appropriation of company money by a partner did not constitute embezzlement. Stokes walked out of court with a triumphant grin on his handsome face. Thinking to consolidate his gain, he dispatched eighteen men to the refinery to repel all invaders and to convey some $50,000 worth of oil away for sale. Fisk, toughened by combat in the A. & S. war, sent a larger force across the East River. They made a frontal assault, battered down the door, threw out the Stokes defenders and took possesion of the works. Stokes retained an attorney, Thomas W. Pittman, to devise legal action. He published an announcement in the *Herald* simultaneously aimed at quieting his creditors and warning Fisk of exposure unless he backed down:

". . . I shall show to the public, if it becomes necessary, the animus behind the scene and which has caused this litigation. The Brooklyn Refinery Company are now heavily indebted to me and I hold their obligations for a very large amount—in all to a sum over $100,000—and other obligations to a large amount are daily accruing. I am ready and willing to give real estate security to the amount of the entire capital stock of the company for any indebtedness that may be found against me. . . ."

The *Herald*, possessor of the keenest journalistic nose for scandal of its day, caught the scent and decided it was high time to give its readers the lowdown on *l'affaire* Fisk-Stokes-Mansfield. A reporter called on Stokes, who was conferring with Lawyer Pittman at the Coleman House, and found Stokes dressed to the nines as usual in a "black overcoat with handsome sealskin facings" and wearing "beautiful moss agate sleeve buttons." Pittman opened the assault.

"I wonder how the newspapers can be humbugged into believing that there is anything in this bloated fellow Fisk," he said. "I have tested him, and I've found him as thin as a sheet of ice in a tumbler that's been standing in a bachelor's chamber during a frosty night."

"I don't for the life of me see," quoth Stokes, "how men of brains like Sweeny and Tweed can tolerate such a fellow. He's never had anyone to give him a good square stand-up fight until now. I shall push him to the wall this time sure. Unless he keeps very quiet I shall sue him for libel, and then we will see how he likes that. . . Jay Gould is tired of Fisk, for he is always getting Gould into hot water. . . ."

"Fatty Fisk is trying to beg off as well as he can now," Pittman chuckled. "You may bet that this thing has shaken him all to pieces . . . He is frightened to death lest Mrs.

Mansfield should tell all she knows about the Erie business. She was over with him that time in Jersey City at Taylor's Hotel . . . and she can smash him when she likes. It makes me laugh to hear how ready he is to whine when he's caught."

"Come, Tom, let's drop poor Fisk for a while," Stokes suggested. "I may say, however, that all my claims have been settled with the firm of which I was a member, and I can say that I have been paid $50,000, as Fisk has been very glad to settle. They put up a job to arrest me at eleven o'clock at night and to keep me in all Sunday night so as to disgrace me. But what has been the result? I have come out all right, and New York is laughing at Fisk as it never laughed before. . . ."

The reporter, with tongue in cheek, asked Pittman what he thought of "the morals and religious opinions" of Fisk.

"Good God, sir!" the lawyer exploded. "You are jibing me. Morals! The man never had any; hasn't got any now, and will never have any this side of the bottomless pit. As for his religious opinions, they don't amount to a glass of stale beer or an ounce of rotten old Dutch cheese. I believe that he pretends to be a kind of a sickly Congregationalist, but he'd swing his coat inside out any day for a bad half dollar if he thought he could play it on a car conductor and beat the poor snoozer out of forty-five cents change in good money."

"You're pretty hard on Fisk, Tom," Stokes reproved. "But I think he deserves it all."

". . . Yes, sir," Pittman went on, warming to the task, "he has done more to debauch American morals and American youth than any man in the city. Why, every Yankee boy from the part of the country from which Fisk hails, on hearing of this bloat becoming so conspicuous in the newspapers and getting so much money and coming Sardanapulus and Belshazzar with his harlots over the people of New York—why, the innocent little boy in Yankee land,

with his stomach full of beans and his head full of Ralph
Waldo Emerson, wants to go and do likewise, and become
another Jim Fisk or a 'Prince Erie' or an 'Admiral of the
Sound Steamboats.' Faugh! It makes me sick. He'd be shot
in any other country."

"What do you think of the physical courage of Fisk, Mr.
Pittman?" inquired the scribe, thoroughly enjoying himself.

"I have never seen a bigger coward than that same Fisk.
He'll weaken like a dog if you kick him, but if you stoop
to him he'll sit on you."

The *Herald* man, who knew a good burlesque when he
saw one, grabbed his hat and hurried to Josie's mansion. He
was admitted by a servant, and as he waited in the hall he
noticed the thick rugs and rich appointments. "All the
accessories that wealth and refinement could suggest," he
noted in impetuous prose, "were heaped in this palatial
apartment with a reckless profusion worthy of a squander-
ing Goth or predatory Hun." When he was ushered into
the dining room, where Josie and her cousin, Mrs. Williams,
were enjoying dessert, he was inspired almost to poetry:

"This [room] had been fitted up in the most gorgeous style. The ceiling and walls were painted and
frescoed in the highest style of art; panels adorning the
walls with trophies, game, birds, fish, and other indications
of a refined taste, were as thickly strewed in the room as
leaves in Vallambrosa . . . There were chairs around the
table, caparisoned as if they had been intended for King
William . . . These chairs had been pressed by the gawky
form of Graf Von Fisk, and in the pillowy folds of the
sofa the luxuriant limbs of the railway *impresario* had re-
clined, and on the mat at its side the modern Menelaus had
sobbed his heart wildly away before the unrelenting glances
of the modern Helen, most destructive and seductive of her
sex. In this saloon Menelaus Fisk had encountered the
fiery assault of Achilles Stokes, and had been vanquished

by his death dealing spear . . . It was here that great Achilles had rested on his ensanguined lance, as his foe, the hero of a hundred illicit fights, lay prostrate before him. . . ."

Almost ignoring Marietta Williams, the reporter bent his attention on Josie Mansfield, who was clad in white silk.

"She was tall and shaped like a duchess. Her skin was as fair in fibre and hue as the lily itself. Over a fair white forehead hung a mass of jet, silky black hair, and from her small, seashell-like ears depended a pair of hooped rings. Her hand, white and smooth, which she offered to the reporter as she rose gracefully from the table, was a hand from which a cast could be taken. The lady's eyes were of a peculiar gray, and lambent like the phosphorescent streaks of light that follow the wake of a ship in mid ocean. When she rose the folds of her dress fell in undulating waves to the richly carpeted floor."

Transfixed by this beauty, the newsman, who was well grounded in the classics, was reminded of what Oliver Cromwell said when he landed in Ireland and gazed down on the level from a height: "This is a country worth fighting for." He asked her for a statement.

"Well, I don't know that I can add anything to the comments and statements that have been made in the papers for the last few days," Josie said. "There has been a great deal stated that was false about me, and some little truth. I suppose it has made me somewhat notorious, and that I may have lost my reputation by the business. But I cannot blame myself for anything but my acquaintance or intimacy with Mr. Fisk. I do not wish to say anything unless he provokes me to a quarrel, and then I am perfectly sure that I can defend myself, or do more than that. I know Mr. Stokes very slightly."

The reporter let that pass. He asked whether the house was a gift from Fisk.

"Nothing of the kind. The money which bought this house was made by me in Wall Street, through a mutual friend, a third person, whom I do not wish to name . . . The money for the house and furnishings and frescoing which I have expended amounted, including repairs, to sixty-five thousand dollars and over." She added, as if to explain her disagreement with Fisk, "While acquainted with Mr. Fisk I was always supplied with silks, wines, food and everything that I could desire; but he would never allow me any freedom."

"He wanted to keep you dependent on him entirely," the reporter suggested, "fearing he might lose you?"

"Perfectly so," Josie nodded. "Fisk . . . said one day, 'Josie, I'm making a good deal of money in the street, and I might as well make a dollar or two for you, and I can use your money to advantage through a friend.' And so he did, I'll say that for him. But he always wanted to keep me dependent. He had an atrocious taste in purchasing, and when he made me presents he used to select the loudest shawls and jackets and dresses that he could find for me. In his own person he was very neat and clean always."

The newsman tried a new tack. "Mrs. Mansfield, do you think that Fisk is insane, from your knowledge of the man?"

"It's more than possible," she conceded. "The disease is hereditary in his family. His father was insane." She mentioned one annoying Fiskian foible. "He keeps his business engagements punctually enough, but he has kept this table waiting dinner for as much as five hours at a time, and during evenings he would issue a lot of the most crazy orders for things he wanted. . . ."

"Don't you think Montaland is a coarse person in her way?"

"I do not. I think she is very nice and pretty. I was present at her dinner the night he told her that he could have New York called 'Fiskville' if he so desired. That was like him all over."

The reporter remarked on how amusing it was that Fisk had been "sobbing at your feet to be taken back."

"I don't know about that," she smiled. ". . . The funniest thing, perhaps, is about his gum shoes." She made it clear that she preferred to be known as Helen Josephine Mansfield, without the name of her former husband. "I would not give Frank Lawlor the satisfaction to think that I bore his name. It would please him too much." Then, with charming frankness, she went into a bit of personal history.

"Frank Lawlor used me wrong and I came to New York and captured the landlady and the woman who was in the house with him at the time. Fisk was jealous and he got me to buy this house down here, so that he might always have me under his hand and near those whom he trusted. Jay Gould always disliked and hated me because he believed I had so much influence over Mr. Fisk . . . Mr. Fisk never goes in the street at all without a man to watch him, and he always kept a man in this house at seventy-five dollars a month just to watch the house. When I went to a public place of amusement there were always at least twenty men whom I knew I could put my hand on at a moment's notice whom Fisk had detailed for the purpose. . . ."

"Mrs. Mansfield," the reporter put in, "can you inform me who were the partners, the men behind the screen in the Erie Railway during its numerous vicissitudes?"

"Oh, yes; you mean the persons with whom he has divided the spoils of war? I know all about that matter, but you must excuse me . . . I do not care to betray any confidence placed in me by Mr. Fisk."

Just to make sure that Fisk understood her power over him and her firm alliance with Ned Stokes, Josie fired a parting shot as the delighted newsman left:

"I don't wish to take any step further unless I am provoked. Then I am ready for Mr. Fisk, if he makes the advance against me or lays a finger on any friend."

One suspects that Josie and Stokes had got their heads

together in advance and invited the *Herald* to interview them individually, for the story contained precisely the propaganda they wished to impress on Fisk. The statements of both of them contained bald threats of exposure and blackmail. Undoubtedly they thought that the newspaper, in return for their revelations about Fisk, would treat them sympathetically as his victims. They must have been affronted when the *Herald*, in its January 18 issue, handled the whole affair in uproarious burlesque style as given here, impaling Mansfield and Stokes on shafts of satire as merciless as those aimed at Fisk, and setting the pace with a riotous quadruple headline:

F I S K I A N A
"Menelaus" Fisk, "Belle Helene" Mansfield,
"Achilles" Stokes and "Ulysses" Pitt-
man in an Infernal Quadrille.

How Fisk and Stokes Quarreled, Fought
and Did not Bleed About a Lady
Fair With Jet Black Hair.

The Wrath of Erie and the Humors of Stokes
—Sage Advice by "Ulysses" Pittman—
War to the Knife All Round.

Stokes must have been aghast at the depiction of him as the new favorite in the Mansfield boudoir. Yet the message of menace got across to Fisk when he read the story. He saw Josie in a new light as a woman who not only made no pretense of virtue, but made no *pretense* of any pretense, an adventuress who had armed herself by tossing away what few shreds of semi-respectability still clung to her and publicly challenged him to battle. Her weapons, he well knew, were the letters he had written her and her asserted knowledge of Erie-Tammany secrets that would be ruinous if she exposed them. Fisk was already being blackmailed. Josie and Stokes had made good use of the *Herald* interview to hint at what they might tell unless he met their terms. If he had any further hope of winning back La Belle Helene, he must have given it up then and there.

As interested Manhattanites waited for more, the quarrel vanished from the newspapers in a lull that betokened movements behind the scene. Josie meanwhile had loyally supplied Stokes with ammunition by giving him the Fisk letters. Stokes, it was said, sent an emissary to Fisk demanding $200,000 as the price of silence—a price Fisk refused to pay despite his yearning to get back the missives. Stokes, hounded by debts, finally agreed to sell his share in the refinery to Fisk for a fair price. To keep their private differences out of court, the two rivals settled on Lawyer Clarence Seward as impartial arbitrator to decide the matter once and for all.

One cardinal point Prince Erie insisted on—that Stokes surrender to Seward the letters which would be a weapon so long as he held them.

So Seward took custody of a parcel of letters which were, and would remain, as troublesome as they were uninspired. After deliberating, the lawyer gave his decision. Stokes was entitled to no further payment in the refinery transaction, he said, since he had put nothing into it. However, he could keep the $27,500 he had already withdrawn and receive an additional $10,000 for the indignity of his weekend imprisonment, plus $5000 for attorneys' fees. Seward then handed the letters over to Peter Sweeny for safekeeping and left for Europe. Stokes, despite his earlier demand for $200,000, signed a paper declaring that he did "remise, release and forever discharge" Fisk from further obligation.

Menelaus and Achilles had reached a truce, but were watching each other warily for the next move.

21
Fisk at Bunker Hill

AFTER the emergence of the Mansfield scandal into the open, a change came over the attitude of the New York press toward Fisk. Seldom thereafter was he treated with the dignity one would expect to be accorded an entrepreneur so versatile that he combined the functions of colonel, admiral, impresario and railroad mogul. He was regarded as a sort of civic clown, an incredible compound of fraud and farce who was counted on to furnish a laugh a day for the newspapers. His vulnerability was comforting. Comment true or false could be made about him with virtual impunity. He was public property, easily the most notorious man in the nation, the subject of more newspaper lineage than anyone in the country with the possible exception of President Grant.

He had no privacy except when he was behind locked doors, and even then rumor made merry with him. Reporters dogged him, seeking the latest Fisk *bon mot*, the latest gossip, the latest humiliation. The unhappy denouement of his affair with Josie was considered the most side-splitting joke within memory. He could not complain, having laid himself open for this treatment, and on the surface his urbane jollity seemed unruffled. No one would have guessed that his booming laugh concealed inner sorrow, nor would he give any but his closest friends the satisfaction of knowing that he had a heart like ordinary men and it was bleeding.

Always a hard worker, he managed to keep some control of his business enterprises as he beat off the Stokes-Mans-

field sortie. He astonished theatergoers by presenting Offenbach operettas not with one prima donna but three, Mlle.
Aimée taking the lead role in the first act, Mlle. Silly in the
second and Mlle. Montaland singing the third. Planning to
send the opera troupe on a summer tour, he was incensed
when he tried to engage the Philadelphia Academy of
Music and the sedate Philadelphians, knowing him by reputation and regarding opera bouffe as almost equally sinful,
sent their regrets. He reached down into his fathomless bag
of invective and hurled a Fiskian bolt, calling the Philadelphians a crowd of *"benzine galoots."*

He shrugged off still another lawsuit against Erie, this
one brought by a group of English stockholders. Ebenezer
Hoar, attorney for the Britons, charged that Fisk and
Gould "have made away with $20,000,000 in a single year."
The way these two had swallowed up Erie while shareholders vainly tried to curb them moved Hoar to apt meta-
phor. "The only analogy I can think of," he said, "is that
story of Baron Munchausen, whose horse was attacked and
eaten up by a bear, until the Baron found himself riding
the bear."

Fisk, who would have found Munchausen excellent company, was still strewing largesse on the Ninth Regiment, of
which he was truly fond. "His growing stoutness annoyed
him greatly," Actress Clara Morris recalled, "yet he was
the first to poke fun at what he called his 'unmilitary figure.'" Although he was no all-out trencherman, he did
enjoy rich food that made it ever harder to get into Tailor
Bell's magnificent uniform. "It takes two men's best efforts,
while I hold my breath, to clasp my belt," he complained.

Although the motives behind his selection as colonel of
the Ninth had been largely mercenary, he had saved the
dying outfit and given it vigorous health. The once-a-week
soldiers found that in addition to mere cash, he poured into
the regiment the warmth of an amiable personality, a leadership that was novel even if not precisely military, and also

instilled a joyful feeling in the ranks similar to the antici-
patory spirit of youngsters on Christmas Eve. Who could
tell what events stupendous or madcap would happen next
day or next week with Colonel Fisk commanding?

The papers could laugh at him, but no one could say he
did not get things done. True to his promise, he had rebuilt
the regimental band in less than a year into an organization
of musical brilliance. He had landed one of the best band-
masters in town in Signor Carlo Patti, but not even Patti
was up to the exacting Fisk standards and was succeeded
by Carl Bergmann, the renowned conductor of the Phil-
harmonic Society. One by one the sour-note blowers had
been replaced by well-paid professional musicians. Fisk
even lured Jules Levy, acclaimed as the finest cornetist of
the day, into the fold by paying him $10,000 a year, an
unheard-of salary for part-time work. By the spring of
1871 the Ninth Regiment Band, 100 strong and arrayed
in new scarlet uniforms bought by Fisk, was playing Sunday concerts at the Grand Opera House to enthusiastic
dollar-minimum audiences. The colonel-impresario advertised it sweepingly as "Without Exception THE FINEST
BAND IN THE WORLD—100 SOLOISTS." Listeners
had to admit that he was not far wrong, although quibblers
pointed out that what he had done was to organize a crack
professional band and give it the regiment's name. Nully
Pieris, who had convinced him that she was not in league
with Josie, often appeared as soloist with the band.

On May 31 occurred one of New York's most prodigal
affairs of that or any other year, the marriage of Tweed's
daughter Mary Amelia in a $5000 wedding gown to Arthur
Ambrose Maginnis. Fisk and Gould were somewhat per-
functory in their observance of the event, Fisk presenting
the bride with a $500 silver ice bowl with polar-bear handles
and Gould making do with a miserable set of silver nut-
pickers costing only $200. Still, the young couple got an
encouraging start in married life, receiving $700,000 worth

of gifts from public officials and contractors doing business with the city. Police Superintendent James Kelso was noticeably embarrassed because his gift, an ice bowl with polarbear handles, was identical with Fisk's. Although Judge and Mrs. Barnard were niggardly, giving only a gold locket, Peter B. Sweeny made up the deficit with a gold bracelet encrusted with diamonds, and other jewelry valued at $40,-000. Andrew J. Garvey, grateful for plastering work, gave a huge silver coffee urn, salver and goblets. James H. Ingersoll, happy to be supplying furniture and rugs for the new courthouse, bestowed a sickle-shaped brooch with sixty diamonds. Gifts from hundreds of other admirers included a $5000 parasol and filled a room to overflowing in the Tweed Fifth Avenue mansion with so many gems and complete silver services that the bride and groom had stock enough to open several large jewelry stores.

Yet the atmosphere was not as gay as it might have been. Some citizens had come to the belief that the Tweed regime was not honest. The New York *Times* was assailing the Ring daily with accusations of corruption. Thomas Nast, the biting cartoonist for *Harper's Weekly*, was caricaturing Mayor Oakey Hall as "O. K. Haul" and depicting the Tammany chieftains as civic vultures. Although the critics had no proof of fraud, there was uneasiness among the braves, some of whom realized the impolicy of parading that $700,000 in wampum before a public already wondering where the money came from. The *Times* ironically headed its story on the diamond saturnalia "From Poverty to Splendor," and the Brooklyn *Eagle*, after asking rhetorically where the Tweed millions were made, answered its own question: "They were made in politics, by a few short years' occupancy of moderately-salaried offices."

Signs were visible that the solidarity of the Ring was cracking, one of them coming only a few weeks earlier when the long-delayed lawsuit of Fisk and Gould *vs* Commodore Vanderbilt over the "big swindle" of 1868 had finally come up before Judge Barnard. Barnard, who since his conversion had made no decision unfavorable to Erie, whittled a great pile of shavings as he listened to the tales of Vanderbilt's crimes recited by Erie's eminent David Dudley Field. Then he decided for the Commodore, uttering words of deepest treason.

"There was no fraud whatever," he said.

Attorney Field reeled out of the courtroom like a man stabbed by his own kin. This was such a stunning about-face that knowing observers laid it either to (1) Barnard's belated sensitivity to the rising public disgust at his habit of seeing everything Erie's way, or (2) a Vanderbilt bribe so enticing that the judge could not resist. The decision may even have been hurtful to the unoffending Mary Amelia Tweed, for who knows but what Fisk and Gould might have been more generous in their wedding gifts had Barnard forced Vanderbilt to pay them the $4,500,000 they claimed he had extorted from them?

That summer, Fisk lived alone at 313, having been permanently expelled from 359 along with his gum shoes. To make him even lonelier, the opera bouffe troupe, including Mlle. Montaland, was now on tour and would not return, which made the services of the interpreter, Georges Barbin, no longer necessary. Yet he had taken such a liking to Barbin that he kept him on at full salary, living in as a sort of general handy man but actually serving as companion. Fisk could not abide the thought of breakfasting alone, having no one to talk to. Barbin now sat at table with him while Valet Marshall served as cook and waiter, the Belgian on the receiving end of a stream of the master's conversation.

He made frequent trips to Long Branch, where he foregathered with his half sister Mary Grace and her husband, George Hooker. He still often called Mary Grace by her baby nickname, Minna. One of the most winning of his qualities was an affection for relatives and friends so deep and genuine that he could not do enough for them. Although Mary Grace, the soul of probity, must have known that her half brother was not always above reproach, it was his warmth and kindness that was nearest to her and made her regard him with something close to reverence. The Hookers named their baby son James Fisk Hooker, and Mary Grace defended and praised Fisk for a half century after he died until her own death in 1922.

Other Fisk friends at Long Branch were the society gambler, John Chamberlain, and the Morse family, whom he was still helping financially. Mrs. Morse and her daughters had recently returned from Europe, where she had been successfully treated for a serious eye ailment, with Fisk paying the bills. He was defraying the educational expenses of her two daughters. Her son John Morse was on the Erie payroll. All this came about not only because of Fisk's long friendship with her late husband but also because her elderly mother had loaned him money during an earlier stock market crisis.

There were rumors in Manhattan that Ned Stokes was estranged from his wife. Mrs. Stokes, possibly taking offense at the racy newspaper stories about her husband and Miss Mansfield, had sailed with her daughter for Germany "for her health" with funds supplied by her father. Lucy Fisk, perhaps for similar reasons, had also gone to Europe. Stokes had moved into the fashionable Hoffman House, taking the best suite despite a bristling array of debts. In an effort to recoup, he had resorted to some questionable practice at the racetrack in Providence, causing the Narragansett Racing Association to bring charges aimed at ruling him off the turf. He was telling his friends that Fisk had swindled him in the refinery settlement and that he intended to get much more out of him—$200,000 or so.

Meanwhile Colonel Fisk had opened a brisk skirmish with the city of Boston. Conceiving the idea of showing off his regiment and band to his friends in the Hub, he sent a committee of three officers to clear the way for the entry of the Ninth into Boston in celebration of Bunker Hill Day. The committee presented the following Fisk letter to Mayor William Gaston:

> Dear Sir: This will introduce to you Major J. R. Hitchcock, Captain A. G. Fuller, and Lieutenant A. P. Bacon, officers of my regiment, and the Committee appointed by the Board to visit your city, and confer with you in regard to a proposed trip on the 17th of June, *prox.* They are empowered to make all arrangements in behalf of the Ninth Regiment; and I would respectfully ask that the hospitality of the city be extended to the regiment.

The arrest of Samuel Bowles and other acts of Fisk had not endeared him to proper Bostonians. When Mayor Gaston presented the proposition to the Common Council, several aldermen said they would sooner invite the plague and the subject was quickly tabled. The Boston *Advertiser* snorted that "The action of the Colonel of the Ninth New York Regiment, in asking for an official reception of his corps by the City of Boston, marks a new era in the history of effrontery. Such compliments are generally supposed to be tendered by the host, rather than asked for by the guest. . . ." Fisk was finding the *galoots* of Boston even more *benzine* than the Philadelphians.

"Well," he said, "this is what you may call an attempt to snub me; but I think I can stand it. It ain't always the same dog that's the under one in the fight, and I've knowed the sickest horse cured. I'm going to Bosting, boys, as sure as Satan, and the Ninth is going along!"

One of his officers pointed out that further requests would probably bring only further insults.

"Look a-here, Doc," Fisk replied, banging the desk. "I've set my heart upon this trip; and I'll make it, by the Eternal, if I have to take the regiment on in citizens' clothes, and send the arms and accoutrements by express. We can ship

the muskets and things in coffins, you know, and consign
'em to an undertaker . . . I'll try a little more persuasion.
May be they'll mend their old tin oven, and not put on any
more airs. . . ."

He went over Mayor Gaston's head and wrote the governor of Massachusetts, who quickly granted permission to
parade in Boston. Triumphantly Fisk gave the mayor the
back of his hand, informing him of the governor's consent
and asking "that you will relieve the Common Council
from further consideration of the subject, as their action or
inaction is a matter of perfect indifference to the gentlemen
under my command."

This hauteur was premature, for he discovered that while
the governor could permit entry into the city, only the
mayor held jurisdiction over Boston Common. The colonel
felt that only the Common would give his regiment the
setting and audience it deserved. His "perfect indifference"
gave way as he backed down and addressed the mayor once
more:

> Dear Sir,—As I am informed that your city ordinances
> prohibit the entry of any regiment upon Boston Common
> without permission from the Mayor, I respectfully request
> permission for the use of the Common by the Ninth Regi-
> ment, N. Y. S. N. G., on the 17th, for a dress parade, and
> on the 18th for public religious services.

The mayor and aldermen enjoyed a chuckle over Fisk's
discomfiture. They relented to the extent of permitting
the use of the Common on Saturday, June 17, but still denied
it for Sunday on the ground that the crowd and confusion
attending such a military display would be a desecration of
the Sabbath.

"When the Ninth Regiment wants to pray," the colonel
growled, "I'm damned if it won't do it!"

With time growing short, he wrote the mayor of neigh-
boring Charlestown, asking permission to use Monument

Square for religious services. The Charlestown authorities, suspicious of any prayer meeting sponsored by the irreligious colonel, refused. Nevertheless the Ninth, 733 men strong, with 100-man band and thirty-man drum corps, embarked on one of Fisk's Sound steamers on June 16. They were delighted to be met next morning by Boston's Fifth Regiment—an honor they had never been accorded by their disdainful fellow units in New York.

The Ninth made a splendid showing in the Bunker Hill Day parade, with Fisk in the van on a fine black charger. Yet the New York *Herald* could not take him seriously, remarking, "Although a bit too small in stature to appear to great advantage on horseback . . . still he bestrode the animal with a kingly grace and looked every inch of what he is reported to be—a man fit to command any army of which he could obtain control." That evening an estimated 50,000 Bostonians cheered as Fisk himself, without benefit of Braine, barked the commands that sent his regiment through a sparkling dress parade on the Common. But it was the band that sent the spectators into transports, with the London-born Levy sporting a monocle as he blew his cornet as only he could do. Boston, it was admitted, had no band in the same class.

The colonel was a happy man, his circus blood coursing to the plaudits he lived for, his inner being warmed by the knowledge that the people of Boston were giving him a royal welcome regardless of the chill mien of the city fathers. What a pity that Lucy was in Europe, unable to witness this triumph!

On Sunday morning, when he planned to hold regimental services in Franklin Square, he was faced by crisis—a drenching rain. Surely, jokesters suggested, the great Fisk could cause the rain to stop with a sweep of his hand. He could not, but he acted quickly, rented the Boston Theater, moved the whole regiment there from the St. James Hotel in omnibuses and invited all and sundry to attend. He badly wanted a sizable group of Boston celebrities to surround him with importance on the stage. The celebrities, however, were cool and the only one he won over was his old friend and former boss, Eben Jordan.

For all that, the regiment's chaplain, sandy-bearded Rev. Edward O. Flagg, led divine services, the band played sacred music, and Colonel Fisk wound up the proceedings with a speech in which he thanked Boston and forgave the city officials, saying, "We will cherish no bad feeling." The Ninth left for New York in high spirits, feeling that they had won the battle of Bunker Hill and also that they had the craziest, most wonderful colonel in Christendom.

The Colonel's
Combat Fatigue

IT WAS Fisk's habit to pass around a box of Park & Tilford's perfectos at staff meetings, so that his deliberations with his officers took place under a fragrant blue cloud. He had no reason to expect that his military service would involve the kind of smoke caused by hostile gunfire. The year 1871 was full of unpleasant surprises for the colonel both in love and war. It was as bad for his good friend Boss Tweed. Tweed, already beset by enemies, added to his own troubles and those of Fisk by a spectacular bit of mismanagement in a matter with which neither of them had close acquaintance, namely, religion.

It was the custom of New York's Irish Orangemen, Protestants all, to parade on Orange Day, July 12, the anniversary of the Battle of the Boyne in 1690 when Protestant King William of Nassau defeated Catholic James II of England. This was a celebration distasteful to the city's Irish Catholics, who far outnumbered the Orangemen, with whom they had feuded for 181 years since the battle. The Irish had always demonstrated against the parade. In 1870 they had gone a good deal farther than that, charging the Orangemen and bringing on a pitched battle that left five dead and scores injured—an affray that further impaired the relations between the two groups. Now, in 1871, there was loose talk among the Irish that if the parade were held, every vile Orangeman in it would be exterminated.

Remembering the previous year's clash, Mayor Hall sought the guidance of Tweed and City Comptroller Richard "Slippery Dick" Connolly. These three were perhaps no more concerned about public safety than about their good standing with the heavier voting elements in the population. Irish Catholics and Germans comprised such an immense number of voters that Hall, despite his English Protestant ancestry, had always been careful to attend their national celebrations and praise them in well-turned speeches—a trait so marked that some wiseacres called him "Mayor Von O'Hall." Votewise, the Orangemen were negligible. After some discussion among the three, it was decided to ban the parade. Knowing that this would cause resentment among the city's Protestants, the mayor tried to dodge the onus by having Police Superintendent Kelso issue the order forbidding the Orangemen to march.

Both Tweed and Hall were astonished at the storm of protest. Newspapers and clergymen demanded to know what had become of the constitutional right of free assembly, and whether New York was being dictated to by a mob. Was Hall taking his orders from Dublin? It was recalled that Mayor O'Hall had sported a bright green suit and a sprig of shamrock as he reviewed the St. Patrick's Day parade only four months earlier. Mayor Von Hall had likewise partaken of sauerkraut at German festivities. Now he was accused of hiding behind Kelso's coat-tails, denying the Orangemen the right to celebrate their traditional anniversary. Catholic Archbishop John McCloskey himself bravely defended the Orangemen's right to march, and the tumult grew.

It became audible in Albany, where Protestant Governor Hoffman, although he was Tweed's man, saw that Tweed was sponsoring an injustice. On top of that, Hoffman, who had visions of succeeding Grant in the White House, was not forgetting that the preponderance of the voters in the nation, unlike New York City, were Protestant and might turn against him should he permit the suppression of the Orangemen. The governor hurried to New York on July 11 to point out these larger considerations to Tweed, Hall and other Tammany leaders. The Boss, nominally a Protestant, saw his point. Still, there was also the possibility that the Irish, jubilant at the prohibition of the parade, would be angrier than ever if the ban were lifted. Not until midnight did Hoffman have his way. He issued a statement:

"I hereby give notice that any and all bodies of men desiring to march in peaceable procession in this city to-day, the twelfth instant, will be permitted to do so. They will be protected to the fullest extent possible by the military and police authorities."

All question of motive aside, Hoffman's move was a courageous one, for he knew he was courting trouble even though he was right in principle. He ordered the paraders surrounded by such a wall of armament that any citizens contemplating violence would be discouraged. He called in Colonel Fisk and the commanders of four other National Guard regiments, along with Kelso, to perfect the defense plans, depriving Fisk and his colleagues of all but a few hours' sleep that night. The governor's order appeared in the morning papers, causing wrath among the Irish. Feeling they had been cheated, they vowed to take the suppression of the heathen Orangemen into their own hands. A mob of them stormed the armory on Avenue A, aiming to seize the muskets kept there, and were turned back only after some stout clubbing by the police. Most of the Irish stevedores at Piers 14 to 19 quit work and prepared for battle. Arms and green ribbons were handed out at Hibernia Hall, a green-painted structure on Prince Street also housing a well-patronized gin mill, until another detail of bluecoats raided the place. An orange-clad dummy was hanged in front of Owen Finney's saloon on Spring Street. Several scores of muscular sons of Erin toiling in the quarry at Central Park got news of the governor's order and quit work in a body, taking with them handy iron tools and heading downtown for the scene of the parade, stopping at grog shops on the way to nurse potheen along with their grievances.

Some officials, nervously recalling the Draft Riots, wondered if they had the makings of a city-wide insurrection on their hands. Superintendent Kelso and General Shaler, who was heading the National Guard forces, were at police headquarters on Mott Street, keeping in telegraphic contact with every precinct station, ready to send reinforcements wherever needed.

With the parade scheduled to start at 2 o'clock, a few Orangemen were collecting at their meeting place, Lamartine Hall, on Eighth Avenue and Twenty-ninth Street, guarded by 500 policemen. The governor's revocation of the ban had come so late that many of them were unaware of it and had scattered to their homes, while others were so intimidated by the warlike atmosphere that they voluntarily relinquished the privilege of marching. Not until 11 o'clock did the Orangemen decide to go through with their ceremony even though they would have only a corporal's guard wearing the colors. The line of march would start at flag-bedecked Lamartine Hall, proceed down Eighth Avenue to Twenty-third, turning at Erie's Opera House corner to reach Fifth Avenue and thence continuing downtown.

Fisk was at the Ninth's armory on Twenty-seventh Street that morning with Major Hitchcock, giving the regiment marching instructions. The men were told that missiles might be thrown at them, but were warned to stand firm and not to fire unless ordered to do so. For many members of the Ninth, including the colonel himself, whose previous military experience had been gained in the benign surroundings of Long Branch and the Academy of Music, this was something new and perhaps a mite frightening.

Toward 1 o'clock Fisk got word that a large body of Orangemen planned to come over from Jersey City via the Erie ferry to bolster their New York brethren. Gover-

nor Hoffman had already ordered that no outsiders be permitted, knowing there would be trouble enough protecting
the city's own paraders. The day was growing hot, so Fisk
left his hat, coat and sword at the armory as he got a carriage
and rode to Castle Erie to telegraph Charles McIntosh,
superintendent of the Erie ferries in Jersey City, to stop the
boats until the crisis was over. He had trouble reaching
McIntosh. Fuming at the delay, he saw that it was well after
1:30 when he put through the message and dashed out to
hail a hansom.

There were none in sight. Most hackmen being Irish, by
this time they had stabled their rigs and were out gathering
brickbats to throw at the Orangemen. Fisk, to whom his
personal appearance was as important as the fate of his
eternal soul, had a painful decision to make. He had to walk.
If he went to the armory to retrieve his raiment he would
be late for the parade. If he walked directly to the parade's
starting point six blocks north, he would be on time but
would appear before the public in humiliating deshabille.
Duty won out over pride. He headed up Eighth Avenue
at a smart trot for a fat man on a hot day. Ahead of him he
could see the units of the procession getting into formation.

It turned out that only ninety-four of the hardiest of
the Orangemen were marching that day. The cavalcade
was headed by a force of 250 policemen, followed by the
crack Seventh Regiment, then the Orangemen, flanked on
the left by the Eighty-fourth Regiment and on the right by
the Twenty-second, with the Sixth Regiment, Fisk's own
Ninth, and another battalion of policemen bringing up the
rear. Unlike ordinary parades, this one sought not display
but concealment. Being entirely surrounded by soldiers
and policemen, the Orangemen were virtually invisible from
street level, paraders behind a screen, marching for no
other reason than to proclaim their right to march. Broad
Eighth Avenue, lined on both sides by grubby four-story
buildings, was packed with humanity on the sidewalks, in

the windows, even on the rooftops, many of them wearing green ribbons, hooting and jeering but so far hurling nothing more than insults.

A few blocks away, Fisk was suffering grievous loss of dignity as he lumbered up the street in his shirtsleeves, puffing and perspiring. The sidewalks were so crowded that he had to take to the pavement. Bystanders eyed him scornfully, shouting suggestions that he get a horse. A few, seeing by his trousers and boots that he was of the military, flung rocks at him, but he reached the head of the column unscathed, his shirt soaked with sweat, his lungs wheezing. He threaded his way through the ranks until he reached the Ninth and was greeted by his men. He had only a minute or two to catch his breath before the parade, five blocks long, got under way. Fisk, heretofore the most splendid colonel in the city, led his regiment bareheaded, coatless, dirty-faced and carrying a sword borrowed from Major Hitchcock.

The band struck up a tune somewhere in the bowels of the procession, and the hidden Orangemen, their gay regalia going to waste, held aloft orange banners and a large transparency reading, "American Freemen, Fall In!" The paraders were lost among five regiments of infantry and 600 billy-swinging policemen, a guard totaling over 3000 men, making more than thirty protectors for each Orangeman. It did not seem too many, considering the ill will of the spectators. The Celts along the walks broke into such a clamor of jeers and catcalls that the band was drowned out. Snatches of insult such as "Bloody traitors!" and "Cowards hiding behind the soldiers!" were heard along with curses in Gaelic and English.

A shot rang out as the caravan moved southward, but apparently did no harm. Missiles began to fly—stones, eggs, garbage. Colonel Fisk was becoming acquainted with some of the less romantic aspects of soldiering, but he knew that a few veterans of the Ninth had received even more hostile receptions at Antietam and other places he had read about. He marched stiffly on, his gaze straight ahead. A crew repairing Twenty-seventh Street had left a large stock of cobblestones, so ammunition was all too handy for the insurgents, who seemed fully as antagonistic toward the soldiers as toward the Orangemen themselves. The police in the van had to charge a determined group of rock-throwers, but the procession moved on. Cunning Hibernians on the rooftops were dismantling mouldering chimneys and tossing bricks down on the paraders. One man was felled like an ox by such a missile, and to the marching thousands the thought of bricks dropping on them from a four-story height was unnerving.

The parade came to a stop when a solid mass of demonstrators blocked the way near Twenty-third Street. The police advanced with swinging clubs to clear a path. The members of the force, most of them good Irish Catholics, were true to their duty for all that. During the halt, a shot was fired from a window, wounding a soldier in the Eighty-fourth Regiment.

The men of the Eighty-fourth, who had already taken a punishing shower of stones, were shaken. Some of them, furious, fired back into the crowd. Like an echo came a rattle of gunfire farther up the street. Bullets plowed into Fisk's regiment. Private Henry Page, the Opera House business manager, fell dead, a *Times* reporter noted, "the top of his skull being entirely shot away, and the brains being scattered over his comrades." Private Walter Pryor collapsed with a mortal stomach wound. Sergeant Samuel Wyatt, who had emerged from the Civil War unharmed, crumpled to the pavement, slain by a peacetime bullet. Several other men were hit. One company of the Ninth got out of hand, broke ranks and fired a volley into the mob. Other regiments, their discipline snapping, began shooting.

Citizens more or less innocent fell wounded or dying on both sides of the street. Screaming, terrified spectators ran madly for cover, and there was panic on Eighth Avenue.

Scores of fear-stricken people, seeking only safety, bolted through the interval between the Sixth and Ninth Regiments—right where Colonel Fisk stood, trying to control his men. They bowled him over like a tenpin and trampled him under foot, bruising him painfully and breaking Major Hitchcock's sword in several pieces. When the crowd passed, he tried to get up but could not. His ankle, he bellowed, was broken.

The colonel lay helpless on the cobblestones, his shirt dirtied and torn, his waxed mustache frayed. Around him were dozens of soldiers and civilians lying in pools of blood, some quiet, some groaning. The shooting ended as quickly as it started. Eighth Avenue was a scene of carnage which no one who saw it was likely to forget. "The gutters of the street ran with blood," one observer recorded, "and . . . the dead bodies were piled one upon the other." A group of Fisk's soldiers had their hands full carrying the weighty colonel up the stairs to a second-floor doctor's office nearby. There they left him, for the parade was starting again, massacre or no.

The doctor, finding Fisk's ankle not broken but dislocated, jerked it back into place, bound it up and loaned the patient a cane. By this time the parade had passed on and a bitter crowd of Ribbonmen, some with friends or relatives among the casualties, were looking for vengeance. The fat colonel whom they had seen carried up the stairs seemed as good a quarry as any. Fisk limped over to the window. He saw soldiers guarding the wounded and dead. He also saw an ominous-looking body of civilians gathering in front of the building.

"That damned Fisk is in there," they shouted. "Kill the villain! Hang him!"

The colonel's martial spirit vanished, as he would have

put it, to where the woodbine twineth. His tin oven had already been battered enough. He made a strategic movement to the rear via the back stairway. He hobbled down an alley with considerable speed for a wounded man, the pain in his ankle assuming less importance because of hoarse shouts behind him. The alley was too open a place, affording a good line of fire. He flung away his cane, mounted an empty keg and hoisted his portly figure over a fence.

The retreat of Colonel Fisk through the back yards between Eighth and Ninth Avenues never got into the Official Records but was fraught with hazard as he dodged clotheslines, ashcans and privies. Breathing hard, dripping with sweat, he finally burst into the back door of a tenement and collapsed gasping on a chair. The startled householder, taking pity on him after hearing his story, gave him a mouldy old coat and hat by way of disguise. Feeling safer, Fisk took to the open again, proceeding westward with caution until he gained Ninth Avenue, where he saw a carriage and hailed it. To his surprise, its occupant was Jay Gould, who took one glance at the evil-looking figure and urged the driver on.

"Hold on a minute!" Fisk roared, identifying himself.

Gould recognized his grimy partner and took him aboard. They drove to the Hoffman House, which turned out to be a poor choice because the parade soon passed nearby on Madison Square and a crowd of shouting Irishmen gathered outside the hostelry.

To the colonel, now clearly a victim of combat fatigue, every Celt was an enemy with a rope. He escaped by the back door, got a carriage, caught the next boat to Long Branch and did not remove his disguise until he reached the friendly asylum of Borrowes' Hotel Continental. There a *Sun* reporter found him later, drinking lemonade and surrounded, the newsman reported, by a "bevy of females," and "a beautiful girl was fanning him."

The parade ended without a single Orangeman scratched,

but the morgue wagons and ambulances were so overburdened with other casualties that grocers' and butchers' carts had to be impressed into service. Among the police and troops were four killed and twenty-four wounded. Forty-one citizens were killed—one of them ten-year-old Mary Ann York, who had made the mistake of wearing an orange dress—and sixty-one wounded. Some were unoffending spectators cut down by wild bullets. Only the crack Seventh Regiment had kept its poise throughout, possibly in part because it sustained no serious casualties. Fisk's Ninth, with two dead, one dying and four wounded—not counting the colonel's ankle—had suffered by far the worst among the soldiery. Some of the Ninth's men bitterly blamed these losses on frantic shooting by the Sixth Regiment. The police accused the military of "reckless, wholesale shooting," laying the casualties among the bluecoats to wild shots from soldiers' guns. It was charged that an officer in the Eighty-fourth, which started the shooting, was "staggering drunk." The confusion would never be straightened out, but the whole city, shocked at the toll, blamed the administration. Among the unlisted wounded were Boss Tweed, Mayor Hall and Governor Hoffman, whose political ambitions had been shot in the vitals.

Three days later the Ninth Regiment suffered still another fatality in the person of Sergeant Edward Gaffney. Gaffney, an Irish Catholic, had stayed home on the day of the parade for religious reasons. Hearing some reflections on his courage as a result, he cut his throat and bled to death.

Meanwhile, Colonel Fisk was still at the Continental, favoring an ankle that was already famous. News of his exit from New York in disguise caused scornful comment. Rumors flew about the time of his departure, the exact status of his ankle and the nature of his disguise. It was said that he had been too terrified to appear in the parade at all; that he *had* been in the parade but had fled at the first shot; that his ankle was no more injured than Mayor Hall's;

that he had fainted from fright and been carried away; that he had escaped to Jersey concealed in an old woman's Mother Hubbard, etc.

"The Colonel's valor is equal to his piety," sneered the *Times*. ". . . He has shown that he can fight and pray, and, when needful, run away in a manner surpassed by few soldiers of any age." "Jim Fisk's Wonderful Wound," head-lined the *Herald*, while the *Tribune* subtly made mention of his "wounded (?) ankle." Although pained at these imputations of cowardice, unlike Gaffney he did not cut his throat. His ankle *was* badly injured, he said testily, and sent out an official communique via a *Times* reporter:

"His ankle is greatly swollen, compelling him to send for physicians, who pronounce his wound still dangerous. The Colonel expresses his deepest regret at not being able to attend the funeral of the dead heroes."

He must also have regretted that his wound was in the ankle, which, although similar to the trouble experienced by storied Achilles, seemed an absurd thing to lay low the puissant commander of the Ninth. Lieutenant Colonel Braine and Adjutant Edgar Allien hastened to Long Branch to commiserate with their chief, make plans for the funeral of Page and Wyatt, and also to counter the rumor that the colonel had run like a rabbit. Perhaps Braine and Allien could hardly blame him for his undignified back-yard flight, but they must have been irked that he continued his retreat clear into another state, which was so hard to explain convincingly to scoffers. A second communique was issued that day:

"Lieutenant Colonel Braine takes occasion to deny that Colonel Fisk did not command the regiment, and asserts that Colonel Fisk did his full duty to preserve the public peace and was foremost in the fray . . . Colonel Fisk did not leave New York until he was informed that his command was on the march to the armory and that the mob had been checked. Colonel Fisk is confined to his room on account of injuries received, and will not be able to leave before a week."

The colonel was still fretting at Long Branch, with his half sister Mary Grace Hooker to comfort him, when the combined funeral of Page and Wyatt was held in New York. The regiment's Chaplain Flagg, who officiated, did not forget him. "From your generous and gallant commander downward," he told the men of the Ninth, "you have shown most commendable bravery."

But the *Times* had another word for Colonel Fisk:

"Perhaps of him it may one day be said that he was first in war, first in peace and first in the pockets of his countrymen."

23 *Those Dreadful Billets-Doux*

The City Hall was full of thieves,
As autumn forest full of leaves.

WHILE Boss Tweed was pondering the wisdom of that
$700,000 wedding, and the unsuspected political repercus-
sions in an innocent parade, a couple of disgruntled ex-con-
federates gave him the finisher. They managed to smuggle
copies of city records out of Comptroller Connolly's office
and take them to Publisher George Jones of the *Times*.
Jones long had been publishing accusations. Now he had the
proof he needed.

He also had something rare in that gluttonous era—the
stamina to withstand one of the biggest bribes ever offered.
Tweed's henchman Slippery Dick Connolly, hearing of the
defection, tried to buy Jones' silence for $5,000,000. "I
don't think the devil will ever make a higher bid for me
than that," said Jones. Cartoonist Nast, whose caricatures
were damaging to the Ring, likewise proved that honesty
was not dead. Offered $500,000 to "take a trip to Europe,"
he stayed in New York and kept right on drawing.

The Ring, described in a Nast cartoon as "True as Steal,"
had indeed been stealing so systematically in every city department that its total loot was later estimated at something
near $200,000,000. Its *chef d'oeuvre* of larceny was in the
new courthouse, now nearing completion. This building,
originally planned for a total cost of $250,000, had so far

cost the taxpayers $11,000,000. Daily the *Times* ticked off the facts:

Andrew J. Garvey had been paid $2,870,464.06 for plastering.

The courthouse thermometers cost $7,500.

Tweed's own printing company received $186,495.61 for an order of stationery.

Three tables and forty chairs cost $179,729.60.

John H. Keyser, the Ring plumber, collected $1,149,-874.50 for plumbing work.

James H. Ingersoll, an old friend of Tweed's, received $4,829,426.26 for supplying carpeting.

These were only a few of the examples listed by the *Times*. Wiseacres got busy with pencils and figured that Ingersoll could have covered the lower half of Manhattan Island with a high grade of Brussels carpeting for $4,829,-426.26, and that Garvey must have applied his plaster six feet thick and used gold mesh for reinforcing. The citizens, although their own apathy was largely to blame, were not amused. At long last a reform movement was on the march. Tweed, hoping to weather the storm, was so badgered by newsmen that his temper overrode wisdom and he uttered his famous retort: "Well, what are you going to do about it?" A new Nast cartoon showed Hoffman as President in 1872, a mere shadow behind the vast frame of Tweed, with a Cabinet including Admiral Fisk as Secretary of the Navy, fast-figuring Comptroller Connolly as Secretary of the Treasury and Andrew Garvey manning a bucket of plaster as Secretary of the Interior.

Fisk lingered at Long Branch, nursing his wound, visiting with the Hookers and Morses and donating a $3000 purse at the nearby racetrack. A reporter spied him at the Continental "in command of a small regiment of feminines," noting that although he did not join in the dance he walked "without limp or halt." The colonel had a magic faculty for enjoying himself despite mounting woes. The Mansfield scandal had spread in such widening circles that, like a small boy caught in naughtiness, he wrote to his wife in Europe confessing his errors and begging forgiveness.

Being blackmailed now from two sides, he saw that his only chance to beat back the Mansfield-Stokes onslaught was to admit publicly his affair with Josie. This was a necessity so painful that he kept delaying. The lady was now bringing suit for $50,000 she claimed he owed her, the amount having doubled in a year. As for Stokes, he was taking action to have his previous settlement with Fisk set aside, declaring that Lawyer Seward "betrayed my confidence by making an award in the interest of Fisk." Stokes wanted $200,000 more. While both of these suits were ostensibly of a business nature, Josie's concerning funds she said had been invested for her, and Stokes' relating to the Brooklyn Refinery, it was well known on all sides that the plaintiffs' most dangerous weapons were the Fisk *billets-doux*.

The letters had gone on an interesting tour. Josie had given them to Stokes. Stokes had surrendered them to Lawyer Seward. Seward, on compromising the quarrel, had handed them over to Peter Sweeny—a friend of Fisk's—for safekeeping. Josie and Stokes had been careful to make copies, but nevertheless were serving Sweeny with papers demanding the originals back. Exclusive control over the letters was basic in their strategy, for the newspapers were itching to get them and once they were published their value as a threat against Fisk would be lost.

The many-sided affairs of Fisk were keeping scores of lawyers occupied and in funds. In addition to separate suits against him by Josie and Stokes, he was still being sued by the English stockholders. He was defendant in a suit brought by one John Ponton, whose boat had been rammed by Fisk's *Bristol.* He was being sued by Isaac Davis and sixteen others for alleged swindles perpetrated on them in the Black Friday uproar. Several lawsuits still pended from the

Mast Hope wreck. There were others, probably many others. Fisk himself admitted he did not know how many there were, saying at one hearing, ". . . there are suits against me wherein large amounts are claimed; some gold suits are pending; I don't know how many suits there are against me, nor the amounts claimed against me."

Still, he was trying to keep posted on them, conferring daily with tall, blond Attorney William Morgan, who served as his legal intelligence arm. Among Morgan's duties was to keep him informed as to the status of old lawsuits still in progress, new ones about to come to court, and threats of future ones which might or might not be settled out of court. Lawsuits were so common that he took them as part of the day's work, giving them an allotted portion of his time and no more. The disastrous Chicago fire that burned much of the city to the ground came during this welter of litigation. Fisk staged two benefit performances at the Opera House for the stricken Chicagoans and found time to drive his coach-and-four around New York to pick up donations of food and clothing, filling a special Erie train sent westward with succor. "*His* relief train must be rushed through first," Clara Morris noted. "*He* must beg personally."

At the same time, on October 10, Erie held its annual election, at which Fisk and Gould took occasion to answer complaints by the British stockholders and others that the Classification Act by which they held office for five years deprived the stockholders of their rightful control. It was farthest from their intention, said Fisk and Gould, to stay in power unless they were wanted.

". . . we now lay before you our resignations as Directors of the Corporation," they said in a statement, "a trust which we shall not again take up unless freely restored thereto by the vote of the stockholders."

They then left the room, but did not take their gum shoes with them. The stockholders present, carefully rigged in advance, voted them back in for a five-year term, thus adding another year to their incumbency and extending their control to 1876.

While other legal actions were routine to Fisk, not so the Stokes and Mansfield suits, which hurt his pride and menaced what shreds of privacy remained to him. Above all he was bitter at the alliance of his former mistress and former friend against him, and their use of letters he considered sacred. For a year he had been in constant retreat before Josie's assaults, giving ground, paying money, hoping to win her back. Now all that was over. At last the colonel was fighting, and the methods he used were no more delicate than hers.

His lawyers dredged up every fact available about her scandalous background, doubtless learning things he had never known himself. Her former husband Frank Lawlor, now a theater manager in Albany, was interviewed. Lawlor told how D. W. Perley had been blackmailed in California by Josie's stepfather after Perley had been found semi-clad in Josie's company. Whether or not Josie was innocent in that instance—and her entire innocence seemed hard to believe—the blackmail idea may have been born in her then. A statement was taken from Annie Wood, the Thirty-fourth Street madam who had introduced Fisk to Josie in 1867. Miss Wood related how her friend Josie, destitute at the time, had asked her to arrange the meeting, having heard of Fisk's free-handedness with $100 bills. Nully Pieris was persuaded to tell what she knew of the Mansfield-Stokes blackmail plans. Fisk lured away Richard E. King, a young Negro who had worked for a year as waiter in Josie's menage, and got an affidavit from him, doubtless paying him well.

"When I went to live at the house of Mrs. Mansfield," King's statement read in part, "I was told to keep away from John Marshall [Fisk's valet], and all Mr. Fisk's party, and Mr. Fisk, and have nothing whatsoever to do with them, and that was a condition of my keeping my place. When I went there to live, I found that Mr. Stokes and Mrs. Mansfield were living there together as man and wife. . . .

"The principal subject of conversation between Mrs. Mansfield, Mr. Stokes, and Mrs. Williams . . . was the manner in which they proposed to make money out of Mr. Fisk by means of letters from him to said Mansfield . . . by selling the same to newspapers, or compelling him to pay them money to prevent the same from being made public, and they said they could get a large amount of money out of Mr. Fisk in that way."

The imbroglio was now developing such a head of steam that those of Fisk's closest friends who knew the comparative innocence of the letters suggested an obvious remedy: Let him publish them himself, thereby disarming his enemies at one stroke. This he could not bring himself to do.

"They may curse me for this, and damn me for that, and ridicule me for something else," he said, "but, by the Lord, this is my *heart* that you want me to make a show of, and I won't. "

Jay Gould, who had shrugged off Fisk's eccentricities for four years, was aghast at the flood of scandal pouring on his partner and splashing on Erie and Gould himself. With the Tweed Ring reeling, Erie's staunchest protector was gone and the reformers were now snapping at the Erie Ring. Just when the corporation needed to put on its most pious front, its vice president was dragging it into a morass of muddy publicity, carrying his quarrel with the wretched Mansfield woman into the courts, where she could say all sorts of things injurious to Erie.

Gould was doubtless tearing paper into bits. It did him no good, for Fisk was determined to fight it out even though his private judge had turned traitor. Judge Barnard, foreseeing Tammany's downfall, had run full circle in his career of fraud by the most fraudulent gesture of all, an effort to appear virtuous, even granting an injunction injurious to Tweed himself. When Stokes' suit against Fisk came to court, it came before Judge Daniel Ingraham, a comparatively honest man. Claiming that the Fisk-Mansfield correspondence contained evidence about Brooklyn Refinery affairs, Stokes managed to pry it loose from Sweeny and give it to Judge Ingraham. The judge apparently found nothing incriminating about it, for he read it, listened to the evidence, denied Stokes' appeal to reopen the refinery claim, and handed the letters back to Stokes' attorneys.

The terrible-tempered young dandy was furious at his defeat. It meant that unless he could get a rehearing on some technicality, he would get not a dollar more out of Fisk legitimately. But he still held his trump card—the letters. Fisk, who had developed such a fixation on this tender point that nothing else seemed as important, had won the decision without regaining control of his heart's outpourings.

His next move was to bring an action before Judge Calvin Pratt in Brooklyn, claiming that Stokes had given the letters to a Brooklyn newspaperman for publication. He asked for an injunction forbidding Stokes or anyone else from publishing them, declaring that to do so "would expose to public observation all his [Fisk's] private concerns."

The newspapers had been watching this skirmish with delight. "Fisk Begs The Law To Save Him From Being Scandalized," the *Herald* headlined, describing the correspondence as "a pillar of fire by night and a column of smoke by day to the redoubtable Fisk." Both Josie and Stokes, in legal complaints, by word of mouth and every other means of publicity, had insisted that the Fisk letters contained not only personal matters but also "inside" secrets of Erie and Tammany crimes. There was a general feeling that Fisk was fighting their publication not merely to preserve his privacy but to keep himself out of jail.

In Brooklyn, however, Judge Pratt proved almost as amenable to Fisk as Barnard once had been. He issued an injunction restraining any person from publishing, copying, reading or repeating the contents of the letters. Pratt was so accommodating that he appointed J. D. Tuthill to take custody of the correspondence—an interesting choice since Tuthill was an employe of Erie and of Fisk. Although banned, the missives already had a respectable circulation, having passed from Josie to Stokes to Seward to Sweeny to Ingraham to Stokes to Pratt to Tuthill, with no one knows how many side trips along the route.

Fisk's friends now suggested that, having won his point, this was the perfect moment for him to publish the letters voluntarily, thereby spiking his enemies' guns and demonstrating his own comparative innocence. Gould must have urged this advice on him strenuously, for rumor was rife that Gould as well as Fisk was compromised in them. The hard-pressed colonel, who had kept copies and knew that Josie, Stokes and possibly others likewise must have copies —knew also that there was no telling how long the Pratt injunction would hold—did some painful soul-searching. At last he agreed. He told his secretary, John Comer, to make transcripts of all his epistles to Josie and send them to the newspapers. Along with it he prepared a statement to the public, reading in part:

> This will amuse a great many heartless people, but I am satisfied to let them laugh. For much that I have done, I have been justly blamed, and have been ridiculed for much more. In this correspondence, which was an insult to one of the purest women that ever lived [his wife], I have been more guilty than in anything else. I have sought and obtained the forgiveness of my wife. Now let the world laugh.

Then, in an unwise moment, he changed his mind. Had he gone ahead with this laudable resolution he would have saved himself a mountain of trouble, would have won some sympathy from a public now suspicious of him—might even have lived to a ripe old age. Fisk, so long impervious to insult, had grown sensitive to newspaper ridicule of his private life. His vanity was wounded by his loss of Josie to Stokes—a defeat that publication of the letters would bring to the joyful attention of every citizen in the land, as well as visit the ultimate humiliation on one citizen of Boston, Lucy Fisk. Fisk had no one but himself to blame for the pass he had come to, and yet his friends sympathized with him in his extremity.

On October 27, 1871, Boss Tweed, who had quietly been transferring his property to relatives, was arrested for fraud. He was freed on $1,000,000 bail, most of it furnished by Gould. It was rumored that the Elegant Oakey was going crazy, tearing out his hair by handfuls. Andrew Garvey, the Prince of Plasterers, took a fast train to Canada. The brother of Peter Sweeny boarded a boat for Europe. Elbert Woodward, a Tweed underling, likewise sailed for the Continent. On October 31, Deputy Sheriff Judson Jarvis walked into Fisk's Opera House office.

"Mr. Fisk," he said, "I have an order for your arrest."

Fisk laughed heartily, according to the *Tribune*, "as though the joke was too good to pass with ordinary merriment."

"So it's Mansfield again, is it?" he said. "Well, I have bondsmen here."

He furnished bail, bade Jarvis adieu and went on with his work, which was indeed necessary, for Erie could have been getting little of his attention in these stormy times. Next day, Josie assailed him in a letter addressed to him but printed in the *Tribune* and all other large papers and intended solely for newspaper publication. The *Tribune*, always Fisk's enemy, said archly that the letter had come "from an unknown source," knowing perfectly well that it came from Miss Mansfield herself, although she had expert help in its composition. It read:

> Sir: You and your minions of the Erie Railway Company are endeavoring to circulate that I am attempting to extort money from you by threatened publication of your private letters to me. You know how shamefully false this is, and yet you encourage and aid it. Had this been my intention, I had a whole trunk full of your interesting letters, some of which I would blush to say I had received. If you were not wholly devoid of all decency and shame, you would do differently. . . . Unfortunately for yourself, I know too well the many crimes you have perpetrated. Was it not only recently you bought over my servants, a negro boy, Richard E. King, also my cook, and bribed them to perjure themselves to aid you in your villainy? . . . You surely recollect the fated Black Friday—the gold brokers you gave orders to to buy gold, and then repudiated the same, because, as you said, they had no witnesses to your transactions. . . .
>
> It is an everlasting shame and disgrace that you should compel one who has grown up with you from nothing to the now great Erie impressario to go to the courts for a vindication of her rights . . . It is only four years ago since you revealed to me your scheme for stealing the Erie books; how you fled with them to Jersey City, and I remained there with you nine long weeks, how when you were buying the Legislature the many anxious nights I passed with you at the telegraph wire, when you told me it was either a Fisk palace in New York or a stone palace at Sing Sing, and if the latter would I take a cottage outside its walls, that my presence would make your rusty irons garlands of roses, and the very stones you would have to hammer and crack appear softer under my influence. You secured your Erie palace, and now you use your whole force of Erie officials to injure and slander me. It is indeed heroic, and worthy of the hero of the memorable 12th of July last.
>
> I write you this letter to forever contradict all the malicious, wicked abuses you have caused to be circulated, and

at the same time fully state that I am willing to leave all matters in dispute and difference—and forever settle any further controversy—to our respective counsel. . . .

If you feel your power with the Courts still supreme, and Tammany, though shaken, still able to protect you, pursue your own inclination. The reward will be yours. . . .

Helen Josephine Mansfield

Grand Duke Alexis of Russia was scheduled to visit New York soon, but the excitement over his coming paled beside that blown up by Miss Mansfield. The lady once again demonstrated the cool maneuvering of an adventuress who cared not a rush about her own reputation but was interested only in money. As propaganda the letter showed able strategy, implying a knowledge of Fisk's "crimes" and making the most of his connection with whipped and bleeding Tammany. The *Tribune's* Horace Greeley, to whom Fisk was the living antichrist, began a sustained assault on him. Possibly Greeley, irked because the *Times* had scored a beat in its exposure of the Tweed Ring, was determined that his own paper should win credit for slaying the Erie dragon.

". . . it is a positive happiness," crowed the *Tribune*, "to behold in one week William M. Tweed, the master, and James Fisk, Jr., the man, in the Sheriff's hands." "DOWN WITH THE ERIE ROBBERS!" it headlined, demanding that the letters be published because they contained "well-nigh evidence enough to send half the Erie rogues and perjurers to State Prison." The Stokes-Mansfield lawyers meanwhile applied to Judge John Brady in Manhattan for an order lifting the ban on the publication of the correspondence. Probably never since creation did so many judges, lawyers, newspapermen and interested citizens expend so much effort and money over letters of so little literary or evidential value.

In answer to Josie's lawsuit, Fisk submitted the affidavit

of Richard King as evidence that he was being blackmailed. While he *was* being blackmailed, the King affidavit has a spurious ring. It seems doubtful that Josie and her lover would discuss their shakedown plans before the servants, and the disappearance of King after signing the affidavit makes it appear that it was contrived and paid for by Fisk to manufacture proof of a plot whose existence he too well knew.

The publication of the affidavit made the combustible Stokes all but burst into flame. The job of squeezing more money out of Fisk was proving harder than he had anticipated. Worse yet, gobs of the dirt flung in the Fisk-Mansfield alley brawl were sticking to him. Proud Ned was at as much of a disadvantage as a boy in spruce Eton collar and white stockings fighting with grimy street urchins. He had his social standing to worry about—something neither of the other combatants could lose, since they had none. Much as he enjoyed Josie's charms, this was an aspect of his life he had meant to keep secret. Now even the *Tribune* was calling him Fisk's "too successful rival," the whole town was gabbling about his freedom of the Mansfield boudoir, and his reputation was suffering.

He sued Fisk for libel. At his instigation, Josie also swore out a warrant charging that in the King affidavit Fisk had done the impossible—damaged her good name.

Two more lawsuits . . . Fisk, apparently unperturbed, went about his business as usual. Learning that his Brattleboro friends, the Mixers, had become parents, he sent Mrs. Mixer a fine baby carriage with leather cushions and fringed canopy—a relic still on display in Vermont. He donated $2000 to the New York Association of German Musicians. His outward aplomb, as well as his solvency, must have been maddening to the nervous, debt-ridden Stokes. On the evening of November 9, 150 grateful German bandsmen marched to Fisk's home and serenaded him with Weber's "Der Freischütz" overture, attracting 5000 spectators. Fisk peered through the shutters, then came out on the porch amid cheers, beaming at his audience.

"From all this demonstration," he said in part, "I have no doubt that the people expect the Grand Duke Alexis, and I am sorry to be so poor a substitute. The musicians of New York have always been my intimate friends . . . and I have merely done what I could by giving what little I could from what little I have."

The crowd guffawed at this implication of poverty. One bystander yelled angrily, "Well if ye're not poor now, ye soon will be." Fisk, ignoring the gibe, accompanied the bandsmen to Castle Erie, where they all had a splendid collation, compliments of the Erie treasury.

A week later, a fire that broke out in the basement printing room in the Erie building was quickly extinguished. Jokesters in Wall Street had a good laugh about that. Naturally, they said, the overworked presses had got red hot and caught fire from printing all that spurious stock.

24 *Washday in Yorkville*

MAGNIFICENT MANSFIELD
The Falstaffian Fisk Routed Horse, Foot
and Dragoons by the Late
Partner of His Joys.

The Dirty Linen of a Lifetime Washed
Publicly in a Police Court.

WITH this triple-bank headline did the irrepressible *Herald* mark the first head-on collision of Mansfield *vs* Fisk before Judge B. H. Bixby at the Yorkville Police Court on East Fifty-seventh Street on November 25, 1871. People fought so hard to get in and view the fray that one woman fainted on the stairway, an elderly gentleman had his spectacles broken and a squad of policemen had to restore order. Reporters were there by the dozen with pencils sharpened and ears flapping. The city's newspapers might disagree in politics but they joined unanimously in the journalistic pastime of making fun of Fisk, the fat rascal who could be ridiculed with such safety, the terror of Wall Street who turned out to be such a jackass in love.

The *Herald,* a sheet lean on principle and long on scandal, had sent its most gifted satirist, probably the same bard who had sung earlier of the joust between Menelaus Fisk and Achilles Stokes. Now he had shifted from the Greek to the Roman era and—as was apt to happen in the *Herald*—he sometimes became so convulsed by the fun of it all that he forgot the facts. As the drama unfolded, he dashed off vivid prose:

"Two great forces met yesterday . . . in the Yorkville

Police Court. These two colliding forces were Marc
Antony Fisk, Jr., who has offered up an entire railroad,
with all its rolling stock, and an opera house, together with
a fleet of Sound steamboats, at the feet of a woman who
once toyed with his well-waxed mustache, and Cleopatra
Helen Josephine Mansfield, the beautiful and gorgeous
heroine of Jersey City and the owner of the palace in
Twenty-third Street. . . ."

Fisk, properly for one steaming into such a battle, arrived
in his admiral's uniform. "His mustache bristled ferociously,
in the fashion of General Boum, and a big diamond pin
shone out of his fat chest like the danger light at the Sandy
Hook bar," continued the *Herald* scribe, who then turned
his similes on another combatant:

"The exquisite Stokes was all glorious in a new Alexis
overcoat of a dull cream color. An elegant diamond ring
glowed on his little finger like a glow worm in a swamp,
and a cane was swung carelessly to and fro between his
manly legs. Stokes looked so handsome that Mrs. Mansfield found it quite impossible to take her eyes off his face,
while she directed only withering glances of contempt at
the agonized Fisk."

If it made any difference, this was Josie's libel suit, not
her action to recover $50,000 she said Fisk withheld from
her, which would come later. Appearing in her behalf were
Assistant District Attorney John Fellows and Lawyer John
McKeon, while Fisk was represented by William A. Beach,
Charles Spencer and the faithful Thomas Shearman. David
Dudley Field, who had suffered criticism and even heard
some talk of disbarment because of his long labors for Erie,
evidently decided that to appear in court *vis-à-vis* the Mansfield woman would be injurious to his dignity. Besides,
Field was busy beating off the English stockholders. Fisk's
lawsuits were so varied that his defenders tended to become
departmentalized, each group of attorneys specializing in
one type of action. Only the previous day he had testified

in a Black Friday suit, and within another week he would once more do battle with the British and also appear in answer to one of Stokes' suits. But today the foe was Mansfield, who, sitting beside her cousin, Marietta Williams, moved the *Herald* man to searching description:

"Mrs. Mansfield looked so lovely that she created quite a flutter . . . This lady . . . is now well known from Maine to Oregon from her connections with Marc Antony Fisk and Octavius Caesar Stokes. She is much above the medium height, having a pearly white skin, dark and very large lustrous eyes, which, when directed at a judge, jury or witness have a terrible effect. Her delicate white hands were encased in faultless lavender kid gloves, and over her magnificent tournure of dark hair was perched a jaunty little Alpine hat, with a dainty green feather perched thereon. Her robe was of the heaviest black silk, cut à la Imperatrice, and having deep flounces of the heaviest black lace over Milanese bands of white satin. At her snowy throat the only article of jewelry on her person, a small gold pin, glistened and heightened the effect."

Josie was coolness itself as she took the stand and answered questions fired at her by Attorney Spencer, one of them relating to her age. "I will be twenty-four years of age on the 15th of December next," she said, thereby differing with other authorities, who added it up to at least twenty-eight. The strategy of the Fisk lawyers was to demonstrate that she had no reputation to lose. Declaring that she was blackmailing Fisk, Spencer introduced the King affidavit and proposed to show that she had had previous experience in extortion by delving into the Perley scandal in California—a move Attorney Fellows strenuously opposed. "The question is whether her veracity is to be confounded with her chastity," Fellows complained, as if she possessed either. But Spencer had his way, and Josie was forced to testify about this piquant episode in her life.

"Can you not tell me," Spencer asked, "whether in San

Francisco a pistol was pointed in your presence at a man's head. . . ?"

"There was a circumstance of that kind happened," she admitted.

"Was it a man by the name of D. W. Perley?"

"Yes, sir."

"Was it pointed at him by a person of the name of Warren [her stepfather]?"

"Yes."

"Did he [Perley] sign a check before he went out?"

"Yes, I believe he did."

However, she denied that there was anything improper between her and Perley, or that Perley had been clad "only in his shirt." Although the legal limits to the questioning left the incident hanging in mid-air, spectators gained the impression that the check was not in payment of an ordinary debt and that Perley had indeed been blackmailed, whether or not Josie had knowingly trapped him. She admitted meeting Fisk at Annie Wood's house. Here she may have repented her earlier *Herald* interview in which she said, "While acquainted with Mr. Fisk, I was always supplied with silks, wines, food and everything that I could desire," for now she portrayed herself in a new role—a woman of independent means gained through stock speculation.

Fisk had only been a friend, she suggested, and had never paid her a penny. Her money came rolling in as a result of lucky speculations in her behalf conducted by one Marston, a friend of hers and Fisk's. Right from the start, during her stay at the American Club House on Broadway, she had paid her own way. She even made a pretense at virtue, claiming that her expenses during the exile at Jersey City were not paid by Fisk but that "the money, I suppose, came from the Erie Railway." Lawyer Spencer made short work of that.

"Where were you staying in Jersey City?" he demanded.

"Taylor's Hotel, where I had a suite of rooms."

"Did anybody occupy them with you?"

"All the time, do you mean?"

"You know what I mean."

"Mr. Fisk did, sometimes."

"Anybody else?"

"During the day," she said, "it was used as a sort of rendezvous by the officers."

"During the night only by yourself and Colonel Fisk?"

"Yes, that is all, I think."

She was forced to admit that her "stock winnings" were paid to her personally by Fisk, that Fisk aided her in buying the Twenty-third Street house, that Fisk paid for the furnishings. She likewise conceded that she had given Fisk's letters to Stokes "because he told me it would benefit him in the case that was pending between him and Mr. Fisk"—an admission damaging both to her and Stokes, showing them to be working in concert against Fisk. Josie was on the stand for three hours, and while her poise was as spectacular as her beauty, the *Herald* was incorrect in saying that she had routed Fisk "horse, foot and dragoons." On the contrary, when court adjourned her veracity looked as shopworn as her chastity, and Ned Stokes was grim as he strode out.

Unlike most men, who would have sought seclusion during the breathing spaces between such scandal, Fisk had an India-rubber ability to rebound from his troubles. Between court appearances, the colonel took his staff and the entire Ninth Regiment Band, along with Cornetist Levy, to serenade Grand Duke Alexis at the Hotel Clarendon on Union Square. After the band played Meyerbeer and a Russian hymn for the royal visitor, Fisk went inside, chatted genially with Alexis and told him grandly, "I . . . extend to you the freedom of everything I own on the American continent."

The duke, who may have read the papers, did not return the compliment. When he gave a great ball a few days later at the Academy of Music, Colonel Fisk was not among the 1000 guests invited. Nor was Admiral Fisk asked to attend a more intimate affair given for Alexis at Delmonico's by the seafaring men of the New York Yacht Club.

To Ned Stokes, accustomed to deferential treatment in the society columns, the newspaper burlesques of his affair with Josie called for some reply. To point out his own rectitude and the innocence of his relations with her, he prepared another propaganda blast. On November 27 he sent a letter to all New York papers of large circulation, submitting a counter-affidavit by Maggie J. Ward, Josie's cook. Mrs. Ward deposed "that said Fisk repeatedly sent for me and asked me to swear to certain matters about Miss Mansfield and Edward S. Stokes." Like Josie, Stokes sought to purify his cause by aligning it with the forces of decency fighting the Tammany-Erie minions:

"The lying affidavit of Richard E. King, the negro hireling of James Fisk, jr., who is now a fugitive from justice, submitted in the criminal suit of Mansfield agt. Fisk, jr., and in which my name was devilishly and maliciously introduced, was designed solely to intimidate and deter me from the further prosecution of my suits against Fisk . . . I don't mean to be deterred either by his blackmail or his violence.

"James Fisk, jr., has for the past four years defied all law through his connection with a demoralized Ring. I mean to determine whether, under the new administration of affairs, he still has the power to distort justice, and with his braggadocio beard an injured and outraged public, whose money he has used not only to debauch society, but to enable him to retain possession of a stolen railroad. . . ."

As one observer truly said, Stokes had brooded so long over losses in money and repute that "it became a monomania with him." Possibly by this time he wished he had never gone to court about it, but he was too proud—and too broke—to quit.

25

A Special Stinkpot

IN CONSIDERING the Fisk-Stokes-Mansfield controversy, which George T. Strong called "a special stinkpot," the relatively honest observer seeking for the right is struck by the scarcity of virtue on any of the three sides. None of the trio was blameless, nor could their testimony be believed without reservation. To find the truth amid such triple-decked bamboozling was asking a lot of a police court judge. The exact nature of the private relations among the three for more than two years was unknown except to them. The whole quarrel was so complicated and so corrupt that it furnished in social intercourse a close parallel to what the Tweed regime meant in politics—namely, it was blemished all the way through.

Yet even in sin there are degrees of guilt. Of the three, only Josie Mansfield, who had risen from poverty and amassed a fortune at Fisk's expense with no more effort than to manipulate her luxuriant eyelashes, could be said to be without reasonable complaint. Josie's glamorous exterior concealed the instincts of a hog at the trough. Stokes, although he had fattened on the Fisk oil arrangement until he stole the colonel's mistress, had one legitimate grievance—his two-day stay in jail at Fisk's instigation. But he had been paid $15,000 for this inconvenience, and had agreed to a settlement on that basis as well as to surrender the letters he now sought to publish. Fisk's money, which the pair were scrambling for so indelicately, was in large part stolen from the Erie stockholders. Each side in the quarrel was ready to resort to any chicanery to defeat the other.

Still, if in this three-cornered riot of delinquency it is possible to find one character worthy of sympathy, it would have to be Fisk. He had lost his pretty plaything, he had become a national laughingstock, he had paid out thousands and was fighting on the defensive, seeking to keep from paying more and from having his intimate letters published before the world. Although it was a trifle late in the day, he had shown manliness in begging his wife's forgiveness, something the egocentric Stokes would never do.

Even Jay Gould, the faithful husband whose only backstreet love was speculation, could sympathize with his partner. Yet to Gould, as president of Erie, Fisk and his everlasting scandals were more of a disgrace than the corporation could bear. Erie was in dire trouble, virtually bankrupt. It could find few buyers for a bond issue it floated. Years of neglect for maintenance had left the road in parlous shape. On one day, December 4, a worn-out locomotive exploded at Hawley, Pennsylvania, blowing out the roundhouse roof, and rotten rails gave way near Rutherford Park, New Jersey, wrecking a freight train. It was only through sheer luck that neither of these mishaps involved passenger trains and that dozens were not killed.

This internal decay worried Gould less than the menace from without. The English stockholders were showing frightening strength. With reform in the air, he was giving thought to changes in the Erie directorate that would lend it an aura of respectability, restore its credit and mollify the critics. He asked for the resignation of Tweed as a director and got it. But how could Erie attain any good repute with Fisk still vice-president, and Mansfield still telling the world how she had been virtually an ex officio director herself?

To Gould, Josie represented a ghastly executive error come home to roost. She should never have been allowed to accompany the directors to Jersey City in the first place, nor to live next door to the New York offices, nor to enter-

tain Erie leaders at her home and hobnob with them at the
Opera House and Long Branch. The scheming wench had
become identified with Erie. She was conferring a bad
name on the railroad as well as on Fisk. Gould, who had
disliked Josie all along, had Fisk to blame for this scandal
coming at a crisis in the corporation's affairs. Fond as he
was of his plump partner, Erie had to be cleansed or his
own control would topple.

On December 1 Fisk was in Boston, where he must have
had painful admissions to make to Lucy, recently back from
Europe. Returning to New York, he went ker-plop into
more trouble. Stokes and Josie were appearing in Judge
Brady's court, demanding that the ban on the letters be
lifted. Shouted Josie's attorney, Samuel Courtney: "The
man [Fisk] whose public career, whose every-day, open
exhibition of his life is as notorious as the career of any
common prostitute known to the police—that man comes
here and asks the extraordinary relief of not having his
crimes exposed. . . ."

Judge Brady took the case under advisement. Hard upon
this, the jury in the Black Friday lawsuit of Davis vs Fisk
and Gould decided in favor of Davis. Three of the jurors
said they had been approached by furtive strangers offering them fat bribes to hold out, one of them whispering,
"Name your sum for a disagreement; money is no object."
David Dudley Field protested that his clients would never
stoop to such tactics, called it a plot to discredit them and
asked that a mistrial be declared. The sixteen other plaintiffs in Black Friday suits, gleeful at Davis' victory, were
clamoring for their day in court against Fisk and Gould.
The suit of one of them, John Trevor, got under way. In
still another court the English stockholders were pressing
their suit against the same pair. Peter B. Sweeny, Fisk's old
Tammany friend, suddenly departed for Canada, where he
wrote back solemnly, "I came here simply for my
health. . . ." One-legged General Daniel Sickles landed in

New York from Europe, and although he was not saying so, he came as attorney for still another group of English stockholders aiming to flay Fisk and Gould. Erie was so short of serviceable locomotives that there was a disastrous freight blockade at Port Jervis, where "the sidings were packed with trains for miles." A citizen of Binghamton wrote in to complain that the Erie depot there was not only unswept but was "frequented by lewd women."

Fisk was a man who liked action, but possibly this unbroken fusillade grew provoking. One breathing spell was given him. His next court appearance in answer to Josie's libel suit was postponed until January 6. Meanwhile, court officers instituted a search for the famous letters, which had last been left in the hands of John D. Tuthill at 213 West Twenty-first Street. A police sergeant spoke to Mrs. Tuthill, who said vaguely that she believed her husband was "somewhere in the country," and had no idea if or when he would be back. There was dark speculation that Fisk had probably paid Tuthill's passage to Tanganyika, but this really made little difference since Miss Mansfield and Stokes had certified copies and at least one New York newspaper likewise claimed to have copies. Already Greeley's *Tribune* had been daring enough to print a couple of minor excerpts that were reasonably correct. By this time the letters had been in so many hands that there is no telling what ignobilities might have been perpetrated with them, but there is a suspicion that Josie and/or Stokes may have furnished the texts to the *Herald* at a price, for publication as soon as the injunction against it was lifted.

For weeks the *Tribune* had taken the stand that the free publication of the letters was as vital to the nation as the right to vote, and was getting almighty impatient with Judge Brady for his delay in releasing them. Now the *Tribune* flew into a rage at a new rumor: that Fisk had gone to Boston not to see his wife but to dicker with certain well-known financiers of that city who were compromised in the letters. These financiers, said the rumor, were so aghast at the threat of publication that they paid Fisk a king's ransom in blackmail so that he could make an out-of-court settlement with Josie and thus destroy the incriminating correspondence forever.

"Fisk, jr., has robbed the woman whom he seduced," complained the *Tribune*, ". . . and now that he is on the eve of being forced by law to settle with her or go to jail, he attempts by his guilty knowledge of other men's secrets, gained by criminal association with them, to force them to pay his debts . . . Now let Judge Brady dissolve the injunction, and the letters will be spread before the people, to whom, in view of the startling crimes they expose, they really belong. . . ." So many bigwigs were tarred by the letters, the *Tribune* said, that Fisk "has the whole gang of rogues in his power. Unlike some of his associates, his character for some time has been such that the scandal of belonging to the Ring seems his nearest approach to respectability." Fisk, the newspaper said, "is open to conviction on a score of charges," and added later, "As long as he was content to amuse with his buffoonery, this fellow was half endurable, but when he comes with his purchased testimony to confuse justice he becomes an insufferable nuisance of whom we demand to be rid."

Fisk's old tin oven was catching it for fair. Unlike in earlier skirmishes, he issued no statements, perhaps feeling that the condition of his reputation was beyond his poor power to add or detract. He was busy trying to keep his railroad running, and also with a grand gala holiday entertainment at the Opera House, where the Ninth Regiment Band played on Christmas Eve with four soloists and Mr. and Mrs. William Florence took over the next night with *The Ticket of Leave Man*. Possibly he had little part in the statement by Gould, published December 29, that Erie business was now good enough so that a payment of three and one-half percent on the preferred (not common) stock would be made for the last half of 1871. This, the first public report about Erie earnings since Fisk and Gould took over, was such a transparent bid to regain lost goodwill that it aroused general sarcasm. "It . . . is designed to blind the stockholders," the *Tribune* said, while the *Herald* commented, "But the people want to know when Fisk and the others are going to resign."

Gould was taking care of that. He was planning a wholesale housecleaning of the directors, not including Director Gould, who meant to retain control. There was a story that he nervously manufactured confetti as he broached the subject to his partner.

"Gould, blurt it out," Fisk said with considerable emotion. "Don't be afraid of hurting my feelings. Blurt it out!"

"The time has come," Gould said, "when we must set our house in order . . . the only thing that can prevent utter annihilation for the whole of us is your resignation as Vice-President of the Company."

On December 31, 1871, Fisk resigned as vice-president, remaining as comptroller and a director but knowing that his days as Prince Erie were numbered. While it was a bitter blow, it was one he could hardly feel undeserved. His sins were coming back to plague him with such Biblical inevitability that it was petty anticlimax when Erie Engine No. 105 jumped the track near Hackensack, crushing the fireman's foot, and one Charles C. Allen brought suit for $50,000 against Fisk and Gould, charging false arrest in one of the many gold litigations.

Yet even as Fisk's marble palace crumbled about him, he retrieved one victory from the ruins. On January 5, 1872—the same day that Erie's Orange County Express jumped the track near Turners, New York, wrecking the engine and terrifying a score of passengers who were lucky to get off with mere bruises—Judge Brady denied Stokes' plea to make use of the letters. The judge pointed out that he had earlier entered into a settlement with Fisk, surrendering the letters "for a valuable consideration," and now was seeking to default on his own agreement.

For Stokes, the decision was disastrous. He had one thing in common with Fisk: Josie Mansfield had brought him trouble. In a year's time he had paid, or owed, $38,000 to at least five different attorneys in his various actions against Fisk. So far he had got nothing for his pains but a load of debt and a mangled reputation. In addition, the grand jury was weighing Fisk's charge of blackmail against him —a charge he might later have to fight in court. The young man from the Hoffman House was very nearly raving.

26 *Such a Good Boy!*

"Colonel Stokes was, as usual, fashionably attired," said the *Herald*, "wearing an elegant overcoat of Ulster frieze, with light pants and an immaculately polished pair of boots. He seemed more anxious than is his wont. . . ."

This was at the Yorkville Police Court on Saturday, January 6, 1872, where the case of Mansfield *vs* Fisk was coming up for its second hearing, proving untrue the rumors of an out-of-court settlement. Fisk was not there, his testimony being scheduled for a later session. He was recovering from a minor bilious attack, something unusual in one so robust even though his difficulties were enough to upset a Neanderthal stomach. Doubtless he was glad to escape another rencontre with the woman who had shamed him.

"The voluptuous charms of Miss Mansfield," the *Herald* went on, "were splendidly set off by a dress of black silk, velvet jacket, jockey hat and illusion veil." Her pretty cousin, Marietta Williams, was with her. But the star of the day was Fisk's attorney, silver-haired William A. Beach, a fellow who knew precisely how to insult an adventuress.

He insulted Josie with pitiless politeness, dragging her through her career with Fisk since its inception, pointing out her economic gains, asking questions that painted her as a vampire not satisfied with blood but wanting flesh as well. She lost the poise that had marked her previous testimony. Her voice began to falter as she answered: "I don't remember anything of the kind . . . I did not ask Miss Wood to introduce me to Fisk . . . The meeting was accidental . . .

No, I have no recollection . . . I have never shown a disposition to blackmail him. . . ." Finally the superb Mansfield burst into tears, and had to fight to regain her composure.

"Stokes stalked through the room gloomy, and perturbed-looking," wrote an observer, "evidently ill at ease." Josie got a needed respite when Mrs. Williams took the stand to tell how respectable the Mansfield household had been and to defend her cousin's character. "Her general habits—" Mrs. Williams began, when Beach cut her off.

"I don't mean her general habits," he said dryly. "That would involve an extensive range of inquiry."

Spectators roared as Stokes glowered and Josie again dove into her handkerchief. Fisk's turn would come later, but now it was Stokes who mounted the stand, struggling for urbanity. For him, everything had gone wrong since he first took up the cudgels against Fisk. Undoubtedly he had counted on a handsome settlement out of court, but somehow that had not come to pass and here he was, placed in this embarrassing juxtaposition with Josie and with Beach doing his level best to show that he had spent much of his time for the past two years sleeping with her and spending Fisk's money.

Right at the start, in answer to a question, he made it clear that he did not hold with old-fashioned convention in regard to the relations between the sexes. Nevertheless, he insisted that his friendship with Miss Mansfield was an entirely innocent one, and that when he visited her, Mrs. Williams invariably sat there between them like a duenna. He denied that he had managed the household and comported himself as if he were married to Miss Mansfield, although he conceded that he had discharged her coachman, a man named Steers, saying, "I did it for Miss Mansfield." He stayed there overnight, he said, "only when it was very stormy," and he did not relish Beach's suggestion that the weather must have been inclement much of the time.

Stokes' self-control was shaky by the time adjournment came at 1 P.M. The titters that swept the courtroom indicated disbelief that he and Miss Mansfield had enjoyed only the delights of conversation. It took no great penetration to divine a general opinion that Josie was little better than a selective prostitute and that he had played the ignominious role of fancy man, sharing the luxuries she had wheedled from Fisk. Rumor had it that one week hence Beach would question him about other disreputable friends as well as about his humiliating scrape at the Narragansett racetrack. "Stokes' own counsel," one narrative says, "informed him . . . that his case was hopeless and must be abandoned."

Ned Stokes borrowed Josie's large carriage—the one Fisk had given her—and drove downtown with his attorney, John McKeon, and Assistant District Attorney Fellows to Delmonico's for oysters and ale. Josie, taking Fellows' rig, was driven home with her cousin. At Delmonico's, as Stokes and his legal companions were quaffing ale at the bar, Judge Barnard strode in. The handsome judge was in hot water, his betrayal of Tweed having come too late in the day, and proceedings for his impeachment were advancing. For all that he was still the breezy man about town. He saw Stokes, McKeon and Fellows, all of whom he knew. He had a bit of news. The grand jury, he was told, had just returned an indictment against Stokes and Miss Mansfield on Fisk's charge of blackmail.

Stokes at this moment was somewhat separated from the others at the bar, and they later said they did not know whether he had heard the judge. In any case, he left abruptly and hailed a carriage on Broadway. "Hoffman House," he said to the driver, Lawrence Corr. Corr drove up Broadway and stopped at the hostelry on Twenty-fourth Street, where he waited while Stokes went inside. Coming out a few minutes later, he told Corr to take him to 359 West Twenty-third—Josie's address.

Fisk meanwhile got news of the morning's testimony from his legal bird dog, William Morgan, who had attended the hearing. He could scent victory in this skirmish—a prospect that must have given him satisfaction even though he was in retreat at all other points of his complicated battle line. Rising late, he had found his health almost restored. He had breakfasted with Georges Barbin, then had Valet Marshall help him into fancy attire topped with a black, scarlet-lined military cloak, silk hat and gold-headed cane. He went to his office to attend to the company payroll and another matter far out of the line of duty. While the investigation of the Tweed Ring continued, the reformers had taken care to prevent further robberies with an injunction tying up city funds so effectively that the police, among other municipal employes, were not being paid—a salary blockade that had many of them in straits. Fisk, who knew scores of policemen by their first names, was arranging a $250,000 personal loan to pay them.

As he worked at his desk with Secretary Comer, his friend John Chamberlain, the Long Branch sportsman and gambling impresario, strolled in. Chamberlain was a skylarker who made his living by betting on everything from the deuce of spades to Wall Street stocks, and he often consulted with Fisk about the latter. During the off season he operated an elite gambling place at 8 West Twenty-fifth Street, only a few blocks from the Opera House.

According to his later testimony, Chamberlain chanced to look out the window around 3:30, just as he was leaving. On the street he saw a horse-drawn coupe containing Ned Stokes, a fellow gamester he knew well. The carriage was crossing Eighth Avenue, going west on Twenty-third Street toward Josie's house. Stokes was craning his neck to look upward, straight at Fisk's windows.

A few minutes later Fisk washed at his $1000 nymph-ornamented sink, donned his military cloak, clapped on his top hat, stopped at the Opera House bar for a lemonade, then left to pay a visit to the Morses. Mrs. Morse, with her elderly mother and two daughters, were staying at the Grand Central Hotel at Broadway and Amity Street, an ornate hostelry that could boast that President Grant had once slept there although it had been completed only the previous year. The Bostonian Morses, to whom he had long played fairy godfather, were also good friends of his wife Lucy, and he had often been their host in his Opera House box. He got into his waiting carriage, driven by his colored coachman, Francis Houseman. However, they did not take the most direct route to the hotel, which would have been straight down Broadway from Madison Square. Instead, they drove east to Madison Square, down Fifth Avenue to Fourteenth Street, east on Fourteenth to Broadway and thence down to Amity Street.

Ned Stokes, who in some mysterious way knew or guessed his enemy's destination, took a shorter route. He got out of his cab a half-block from the Grand Central and made the rest of the distance on foot at a fast clip, dressed in his double-breasted gray overcoat, top hat, and carrying a cane. Richard Wandle, a gambler who knew Stokes by sight, happened to be lounging in front of the hotel at about 4 P.M. He saw Stokes coming at what he later described as "not quite a run, but between a run and a fast walk." The young sportsman was so intent on his mission that he bumped into a lady on the walk and, forgetting his usual courtesy, did not even stop to apologize. He darted into the hotel's ladies' entrance on Broadway, something gentlemen were not properly supposed to do. John Redmond, a young Irish porter, was just inside the door, but since he was atop a seven-foot ladder cleaning the gaslights, he did not bother to steer him to the main entrance. Stokes hurried up the stairs, disappearing from view. Hotel employes later recalled him "pacing back and forth" in the upper lobby.

Ten minutes later, Redmond was off his ladder but still tidying the hall when Houseman drove up and Fisk got out, walking in the same entrance. *He* was not supposed to use that door either, but he was a regular visitor, a man so free with jokes and tips, so accustomed to making his own rules, that Redmond would not have dreamed of correcting him.

"Hello, John," he said. "Is Mrs. Morse in?"

"No, sorr, she's gone out an' the oldest girl's gone with her," the porter replied. "But the other wan is in her grand-mother's room, sorr."

"Tell her I'm here and ask whether she can see me."

So saying, Fisk headed upstairs to wait in the second-floor sitting room. Redmond put his cleaning cloth in his pocket and started to follow.

Fisk was halfway up, the boy a dozen steps behind, when he became aware of a figure at the top of the stairs. He looked up. It was Stokes, aiming a revolver at him.

Thomas Hart, a bellboy on the second floor, saw Stokes standing there, gun poised, and later testified that he said, "I've got you now."

The two men on the stairs were only a half-dozen steps apart. Fisk was trapped between two walls, at point-blank range. The fat colonel made a target that could not be missed. Stokes fired twice in rapid succession.

"For God's sake," Fisk shouted, "will anybody save me?"

John Redmond later was somewhat vague as to what he was doing at this moment. Possibly he had scrambled down-stairs to get clear of the bullets. Fisk staggered and grasped the handrail, but did not fall. A contemporary drawing shows him reeling on the stairway, silk hat flying, cape out-flung. As Stokes vanished into the upper corridor, Fisk recovered himself enough to walk down the stairs. By this time the sound of the shots attracted a swarm of hotel employes to the ladies' entrance. A group of them helped the wounded man up the stairs, where the odor of gunpowder still lingered, and into Room 213, which was vacant.

Bellboy Hart meanwhile followed Stokes at a safe distance, saw him cross the second-floor lobby, pause at a sofa, then go down the main staircase to the first-floor lobby. As he turned into the saloon, Hart pointed him out excitedly to H. L. Powers, manager of the hotel. Powers took after him with a small posse of citizens, shouting "Stop that man!" They caught up with him in the barber shop at the Mercer Street entrance, where several patrons with lather-covered faces stared in amazement from barbers' chairs as he was seized without resistance. Officer Henry McCadden, called from his beat nearby on Mercer Street, arrived to make the arrest official. He found no weapon on the prisoner.

Dr. Thomas H. Tripler, the house physician, reached Room 213 on the double. He found Fisk on his feet, blood streaming from his right arm. Fisk said he was also wounded "in the belly." Tripler put him in a sofa, gave him some brandy and water and dressed the arm wound. He cut away the shirt and found a bullet hole above the navel. He probed the wound to a depth of four inches, but the slug was deep in Fisk's bowels and could not be found.

"Doctor, if I am going to die, I want to know about it," Fisk said. "I am not afraid to die, but then if I am going to die I would like to know beforehand."

"Colonel, you are not going to die tonight," Tripler replied with more assurance than he felt, "and not tomorrow either, I hope."

Police Captain Thomas Byrnes entered the room with Stokes in tow. Byrnes later said, "Mr. Fisk laid there as if he had no pain at all." Stokes, an observer noted, "wore a rigidly dignified air, with a face perfectly immovable, expressive only of intense passion strongly suppressed."

"Colonel Fisk, you see this man," Captain Byrnes said. "Was it he who shot you?"

Fisk nodded. "Yes, that's the man who shot me. That's Stokes."

As the prisoner was taken away, Fisk asked, "When can Lucy get here?"

A telegram had already been sent to Lucy. The hotel personnel worked off its hysteria by sending messages broadcast. Coachman Houseman went flying back to Castle Erie to spread the news. Doctors were summoned as though they could heal the wounded man by sheer weight of numbers. Dr. Tripler was joined by Dr. Frank Fisher, then by Fisk's personal physician, Dr. John P. White, then by Drs. James R. Wood, Theophilus Steel, Lewis Sayre and Enos Foster. Seven doctors could do no more than one. They gave the patient chloroform and tried more ineffectual probing.

Newspaper city rooms were electrified when the tidings reached them. Fisk, who had furnished them with so much intriguing copy for four years, had done it again, this time by getting shot by his rival. Reporters, friends and curiosity seekers stormed the Grand Central. Guards had to be posted to keep the sickroom from invasion. Fisk was moved to a bed in adjoining Room 214, which connected with 213 by sliding doors. Gould arrived, George and Mary Grace Hooker, David Dudley Field, Thomas Shearman, Boss Tweed, Attorney Morgan, dozens of other friends. Uptown, Gambler John Chamberlain reacted skeptically to the report that Fisk had been shot. "I'll lay $500 against $100 that it's false," he said.

A *Herald* reporter dashed to the *palais* Mansfield and watched Josie go pale when he told her what had happened.

"[Stokes] must have been insane!" she gasped. ". . . I wish you to understand that I am in no way connected with this sad affair." Then she uttered priceless irony. "I have only my reputation to maintain."

At the hotel, Tweed insisted on sending for his own physician, Dr. John Carnochan, who arrived to make it eight. "Fisk maintained his composure," a reporter noted, "the muscles of his face never quivering. . . ." The squadron of doctors were cheery at the bedside but gloomy elsewhere. "Your client had better make his will," Dr. Wood said to David Dudley Field.

Stokes' gun, a four-chambered Colt, was found tucked into a sofa in the second-floor lobby. The bloody slug that had pierced Fisk's arm was picked up at the foot of the stairs. Attorneys Field and Shearman sat at Fisk's bedside, assuring him that the will was merely a wise precaution. Another precaution was the removal of his huge shirtfront sparkler, diamond cuff links and gold watch, given to Manager Powers for safekeeping. He dictated his will, swearing to his estate as "not exceeding one million dollars," appointing his wife and Eben Jordan executors and leaving the bulk of it to Lucy, with generous bequests to his parents, his half sister and the Morses. In the outer room Gould sat quietly until "everyone was suddenly startled by seeing him bow his head upon his hands and weep unrestrainedly with deep, audible sobs."

Tweed, still at liberty on bail, went in to sit with the patient. Many of the Boss's cronies had fled the country, but he had stayed to face the music. Fisk gave him a feeble smile.

"Well, William," he said, "you have had a great many false friends in your troubles, but I have always stood by you. I'm afraid that you're going to lose another friend."

"Are you in any pain, Colonel?" the fallen Boss inquired.

"When you were a boy did you ever run away from school and fill yourself with green apples? I feel just as I used to feel when I filled myself with green apples. I've got a belly-ache."

The cautious Tweed gave thought to possible embarrassing evidence. "Don't you think you had better send for Comer to take charge of any private papers that you may have in your pockets?"

"No, I have no private papers with me," Fisk grinned. "They are all public papers and I don't care who sees them."

It was the colonel's last joke. The public papers he referred to were fifteen $100 bills still in his wallet. His jocularity must have been chilled when an official with an ominous title—Coroner Nelson W. Young—arrived to take an ante-mortem deposition, but he refused to give up hope. To Young he gave a statement describing the shooting and identifying Stokes as his assailant which according to law would be accepted as truth only if he believed himself dying.

"Do you believe that you are about to die from the injuries you have received?" Young asked.

"I believe that I am in a very critical condition," Fisk replied.

"Have you any hopes of recovery?" the coroner pressed.

"I hope so."

The words invalidated the statement, but Young could do no more. At the Opera House the Florences were appearing that evening in "The Colleen Bawn." There was talk of suspending the performance, but many tickets had been sold and the show went on, although one observer reported, ". . . it is doubtful if 'Colleen Bawn' ever received a more mechanical representation."

In the hotel lobby, "it seemed as if the whole [Ninth] regiment had assembled," many of the soldiers muttering dark threats against Stokes. In the city rooms, newsmen were working on the biggest story in years, taxing their adjectives to do it justice and to fill not columns but pages in the Sunday morning papers. Cynical reporters agreed that Fisk could do nothing—not even die—in a quiet way.

Had the impresario staged his own shooting with the same care and expense with which he had staged *The Twelve Temptations*, he could hardly have wrung more dramatic sensation out of it.

The newspapermen were aware of an absurd paradox. This night watch—waiting for Fisk to die—had an air of suspense and doom about it much like the night seven years earlier when Lincoln was shot. Who could commit the blasphemy of comparing Fisk with Lincoln, except possibly in native American humor? Yet there it was. Scribes who for months had treated the colonel with the newsprint sneers he deserved, now felt an inexplicable heaviness of heart, as if some great public benefactor were dying and they had in some manner wronged him in his lifetime.

"Never since the memorable night that Abe Lincoln was shot was there such excitement throughout the city," the *Herald* would say, adding about Stokes, "He had very few friends in the city last night . . . The sentiment that was strongest was condemnation of the assassin."

While being escorted to the Tombs, Stokes had asked permission to go into a bar for a drink, which was refused. He remarked that it was exactly a year since Fisk had him arrested for embezzlement. Locked in a cell, he called for cigars and "commenced smoking fiercely, as if for life. Cigar after cigar was lighted and flung away." He spoke to his keeper, asking, "What do you think, is the man seriously injured?"

Fisk, brought up a Unitarian, had taken little part in formal religion, but he had never spoken ill of it and indeed had contributed liberally if sporadically to several churches. He had no spiritual adviser with him during his last hours. He showed no trace of repentance for his misspent life. Undoubtedly Chaplain Flagg of the Ninth would have been there to help him bridge the gap into eternity had not Flagg himself been too ill to get out of bed. As night came Fisk had with him his half sister, Mary Grace, Secretary Comer, George Hooker, Mrs. Morse and a mere four physicians—Drs. Sayre, White, Fisher and Tripler. He complained again of a "green apple belly-ache," and when Dr. Fisher gave him morphia he said, "I am as strong as an ox, and it takes four times as much medicine to affect me as ordinary persons." Outside the door, a flock of reporters smoked and played cards as they waited. One of them, allowed into the sickroom after midnight when the patient was asleep, recorded, "His hair was neatly combed, and even his long mustache was waxed as stiff as when he left the Erie building in the afternoon."

By morning Fisk was in a coma, pulse 130, respiration 18. When Lucy arrived at 6:20 with her companion, Fanny Harrod, after traveling much of the night from Boston, he was beyond greeting them.

"Can nothing be done to save him?" she asked Dr. Fisher.

"Alas! I fear not," he said.

In her eighteen years of marriage to an absentee husband, brunette Lucy Moore Fisk had demonstrated rare understanding and forbearance because she knew him in all his weakness and strength as a mother knows a son. He had kept her in luxury, treated her tenderly, bragged about her to his friends. He had humiliated her publicly as few wives had ever been humiliated. Like a boy, he had begged her forgiveness. Like a mother, she had given it. Now she was able to forget the bitterness and remember only that she had forgiven. She was at the unconscious man's side for more than four hours. When he died at 10:45 she kissed him and said:

"My dear boy! He was such a good boy!"

There was a world of significance in the words. Fisk was a boy who had never grown up, and she had always been a mother to him.

27
Where the Woodbine
Twineth

NEXT day, New York went to far more effort and expense to pay tribute to its most notorious rogue than it had conferred on many of its heroes. As propaganda, the manner of his death could not have been more skilfully contrived. It created sympathy even among some who viewed him with revulsion. Although the colonel had appeared a mite inglorious during the Orange riot, it was agreed that he had met death with admirable courage. The Fisk-hating *Times* called the shooting "brutal and cowardly," and conceded, "There was a grandeur of conception about [Fisk's] rascalities which helps to lift him above the vulgar herd of scoundrels." George T. Strong marveled, "What a scamp he was, but what a curious and scientifically interesting scamp!" The *Herald*, abandoning the Greek and Roman eras, likened his career to a tale from the Arabian Nights. Decent men, said the *World*, had an "instinctive contempt and loathing" for Stokes.

Many humble folk, uninfluenced by headlined scandal, felt that they had lost a friend. Fisk's brother-in-law George Hooker, said one untrammeled reporter, "had become wild from grief and was a raving maniac." Hooker could hardly have been so far gone, but it was true that the whole city went a little wild. Lynch talk became so prevalent among Erie personnel and members of the Ninth Regiment that Police Superintendent Kelso rushed 250 police to guard Stokes at the city prison. A smaller guard was placed at Josie Mansfield's home because of threats against her. Gen-

eral J. M. Varian of the Third Brigade had his staff sweat-
ing over preparations for a military funeral. The Erie board
of directors met under Gould and passed a resolution of
regret. The Erie employes at Buffalo did likewise. The
flag over the Delavan House in Albany was lowered to half
mast, as was the flag at the Revere House in Brattleboro.
Jim Fisk's stepmother, Love Fisk, had arrived from Brattleboro two hours after he died, but she and other relatives
were watchers as New York assumed its right to do him
honor.

Yet there were those who could not forget that the late
colonel had seldom distinguished himself in public service
of any kind—had not even been a good railway executive—
and was famous chiefly for misdoing. The Burlington,
Vermont, *Free Press* suggested that in view of his record,
the safest thing that could be said for him was to repeat
what the Mark Twain character had remarked of a dead
malefactor: "He made a nice, quiet corpse." Officials at the
Stock Exchange, remembering Black Friday, shed no tears.
They were in a dilemma because Henry A. Heiser, a respected member of the exchange, had died the same day
and they did not want to lower their flag lest "the honor
should be attributed to Col. Fisk." They decided to wait a
day to avoid such misunderstanding. Greeley's *Tribune*,
Fisk's old nemesis, thought he had become such an embarrassment to the Erie directors that his death brought
them secret relief: "Mr. Gould, while naturally shocked
. . . would probably, all things considered, be glad to be
rid of such an incumbrance . . . Undoubtedly the present
management will endeavor to hide all their crimes in his
grave."

Clergymen all over the land used the murder as a text in
pointing out that sin inevitably brings retribution. In Brooklyn, Henry Ward Beecher, whose Sunday school superintendent was Thomas Shearman, loosed a triumphant period:
"And that supreme mountebank of fortune—the astound-

ing event of his age: that a man of some smartness in business, but absolutely without moral sense, and as absolutely
devoid of shame as the desert of Sahara is of grass—that
this man, with one leap, should have vaulted to the very
summit of power in New York, and for seven to ten
years [it was less than five—it just *seemed* longer]
should have held the courts in his hand, and the Legislature,
and the most consummate invested interest in the land in
his hand, and laughed at England, and laughed at New
York, and matched himself against the financial skill of the
whole city, and outwitted the whole, and rode out to this
hour in glaring and magnificent prosperity—shameless,
vicious, criminal, abominable in his lusts, and flagrant in
his violation of public decency—that this man should have
been the supremest there; and yet in an instant, by the hand
of a fellow-culprit, God's providence struck him to the
ground! Yet I say to every young man who has looked upon
this glaring meteor and thought that perhaps integrity was
not necessary, 'Mark the end of this wicked man, and turn
back again to the ways of integrity!' "

Fisk would not have minded that nearly so much as the
betrayal by his own Erie stock, which offered him posthu-
mous insult by rising four and a half percent due to a wide-
spread belief that his violent removal promised the road a
better future.

His death left loose ends by the score. Several dozen lit-
igants who had been suing him individually or together
with Gould, found their lawsuits either wiped out or
snarled in confusion. The libel suit of Josie Mansfield, now
staying nervously behind locked doors, was shot full of
holes by Stokes' bullets, as was her action to recover $50,-
000. There was surprise that Fisk's estate was only a paltry
million, most of this represented by real estate and stock.
What had he done with all the millions he squeezed out of
Erie and his other ventures? The only answer was that a
share of it had gone to Lucy, who was now said to be

worth $2,000,000, and that he had sunk the rest on Josie, on luxuries, on lawyers and on charity. The lawyers— how they must have mourned!

There were indeed lessons to be drawn from the violent life and death of James Fisk Jr., but Beecher missed the important one: that Fisk was no isolated freak, no force running counter to his fellow men, but rather was a splendid reflection, a huge photographic enlargement, of the immorality of the time. He was the logical extension of a decadent public state of mind, a national scramble for gain at any sacrifice of the eternal virtues. He was of a piece with the governmental corruption of the Tweed and Grant regimes, the business rapacity of Drew and Vanderbilt, the jocund prostitution of the law by Barnard, which were in the end blamable to the millions who tolerated and supported them. "The Prince of Erie was representative," truly said the *Herald*, sober for a change. ". . . Society needs a general purification." To which the *Times* added, "a vicious state of society . . . has given opportunities to the unscrupulous."

But few were seeking moral instruction. At the Tombs, Ned Stokes made himself as comfortable as circumstances would permit. He was allowed a carpet on the floor, and although the bedbugs were bothersome his meals were good, being brought in from Delmonico's. He had several bottles of his scented bath water. A *Sun* reporter found him wearing a handsome frilled shirt with three magnificent diamond studs. ". . . On the little finger of his left hand he wore a large and costly solitaire diamond ring. He wore a pair of lavender colored trousers [and] a silk velvet dressing jacket, whose sleeves, pockets, collar and lapels were trimmed with pink silk, heavily quilted. His feet were encased in silk stockings, and he wore a pair of slippers richly embroidered with gold lace." The phrase "he wore" was a natural beginning for any sentence relating to him.

Stokes' estranged wife and daughter were in Paris when

they received news of the shooting. Miss Mansfield did not visit him, but Marietta Williams paid a call, certainly carrying a message. Throughout New York there was virtually no other topic of conversation as amateur detectives charted Stokes' movements.

After hearing at Delmonico's about his indictment, he had driven in a rage to the Hoffman House, picked up his pistol, then proceeded uptown gunning for Fisk. He had paused in front of Josie's, said his coachman, but had not gone inside. Lurking around the Opera House entrance, he must have heard Fisk direct his driver to the Grand Central, for Gould said his partner invariably shouted such instructions "in a tone loud enough to be heard across the street." Yet his apparent knowledge that Fisk would use the ladies' entrance—his strategic emplacement of himself and his artillery at the head of the stairs—made it seem that he had spied on his enemy during earlier visits to the hotel, which in turn indicated that the murder, far from being committed in sudden passion, had been planned for days. There was speculation about Stokes' remark that it was precisely a year since Fisk had him jailed for embezzlement. Had a queer sense of melodrama made him hit on the anniversary as the ideal date for vengeance?

Jay Gould, obviously sorrowing, gave a cautious statement about his late partner.

"We have been working together for five or six years," he said, "and during that time not the slightest unpleasantness has ever arisen between us." He laid Fisk's troubles to "an excess of youthful spirits," and said that of late he had achieved a new dignity of conduct. "Since the dissolution of whatever ties had existed between him and Mrs. Mansfield he has been a changed man. He had ceased to practice many of the old habits of which he has been accused, and was in every sense becoming what all who loved him desired he should be."

Fisk's body lay that morning in a gold-handled rosewood

coffin at his rooms at 313, where the weeping mingled strangely with the twitter of a dozen canaries. Boss Tweed, one of the mourners, also had a word to say. Tweed had been struck down by the law rather than by an assassin's bullets, but the final effect would be the same.

"[Fisk was] a man of broad soul and kindly heart," he said. "In his business transactions he was governed by principles which seemed peculiar, without being insincere, and were, perhaps, apparently dishonest, without being otherwise than enterprising . . . He has done more good turns for worthy but embarrassed men than all the clergymen in New York."

It was noted that Tweed spoke as if he had no peculiarities of principle himself. While the physicians could not measure Fisk's soul, they had performed an autopsy and weighed his heart and brain. Both were big, the heart weighing sixteen ounces, the brain a startling fifty-eight ounces, only four and a half ounces less than the record-breaking brain of Daniel Webster. An artist named John Young had taken a plaster cast of his face. At noon the body was carried to the great lobby of the Opera House, which was festooned with crepe and hung with a life-size portrait of Fisk. The grieving grew strenuous as the public was admitted and a long line of citizens formed to view the late colonel, clad in his $2000 uniform with white kid gloves, his sword at his side, his red mustache waxed to perfection. Possibly Charley, who had been Fisk's barber for several years, was jealous of the undertaker's assumption of this rite, for he stopped by the coffin, took the ends of the mustache and twisted them expertly, saying, "One more twirl, dearest of friends, for the last time!"

Outside, a crowd of more than 25,000 surged toward the entrance, blocking all traffic on Twenty-third Street and Eighth Avenue and giving a special detail of police a hard time. "So great was the crush," said a witness, "that five ladies fainted away." Policemen had to brandish clubs to make room for the funeral procession to form in front of the Opera House at 1 o'clock. The cortege that wound its way through bitter cold across town to the New Haven Railway station at Fourth Avenue and Twenty-sixth Street was exactly as Fisk would have wished it—huge, magnificent, military. The shot-torn Civil War battle flag of the Ninth Regiment, draped over the coffin, covered a man who had not fought in that war but had enriched himself by it. Six colonels of New York regiments rode alongside, General Varian to the rear. Among the marchers were the Ninth Regiment, the officers of the Narragansett Steamship Company, a mass of Erie employes, six platoons of commissioned officers of the National Guard wearing crepe on left arm and sword hilt, and a large deputation of German musicians. A quarter-mile of carriages brought up the rear. Fisk's riderless horse followed the coffin, led by a groom, the stirrup hoods reversed, the colonel's boots and spurs attached. The streets were lined with bareheaded watchers as the Ninth Regiment Band—Fisk's own—played the "Dead March in Saul" with muffled drums.

"Never since the martyred Lincoln was borne through New York's streets was so impressive a spectacle witnessed," a reporter commented. It was an anomaly that puzzled Lawyer Strong. "His influence on the community was certainly bad in every way," Strong noted in his diary, "but it is also certain that many people, more or less wise and more or less honest, sorrowed heartily at his funeral. . . ."

Surely there were those among the mourners who felt the incongruity of lavishing this ceremony on such a scandalous, fraudulent man, and sought for reasons why they could with good conscience give him this royal farewell. There were reasons. He had furnished the city with a continuous circus performance for a half-dozen years, and now that the show was over they would miss it. They could forgive him faults they could have forgiven in no one else because he was friendly, because he told such wonderful jokes, because he disliked sham, because he had the common touch and was generous with Erie money. But most of all the reason was simply that they knew him and *liked* him. The warm, magic personality of Jim Fisk had touched them when he was alive, and now that he had gone where the woodbine twineth it lingered after him to belittle his badness.

There must have been many who regretted his strange moral delinquency and pondered what he might have been had he turned his oversized heart and brain to better purpose. The newspapermen would miss him as much as any. Their sheets would be vapid from now on. New York would never be quite the same again. The *Herald* forgot all about Menelaus and Marc Antony and came near weeping in newsprint, voicing a sentiment that was general even if a trifle maudlin:

"His vivacity . . . his incessant, effervescing good humor . . . his bands of music and flocks of canary birds . . . his boyish love of show, of colors and gems and golden braid; that reckless frankness, which made the world the confidant of his business, his dreams and his affections; his insatiable thirst for applause; the world to him a stage, and his whole life, even those phases of life which decorum veils, an acted comedy—no more striking phenomenon of human nature has been seen in our time . . . It is not for us to speak of retribution. And oh, friends, think that the poor always swarmed around his gates and never went hungry away, and that those who knew him best shed tears over his death bed!"

The colonel was placed aboard a New Haven train swathed with crepe even to the locomotive, and was off for Brattleboro, off for home. It was as well that he was not traveling via his own Erie line, for he would be less sure of getting there. The Opera House was dark that night, but Augustin Daly, no admirer of Landlord Fisk, was showing *Divorce* at the Fifth Avenue Theater, with Fanny Davenport, Nellie Mortimer, Clara Morris and others.

Even though she knew, Miss Morris was shaken when she came onstage and faced Fisk's box: "A shiver ran over me—someone . . . had lowered the heavy red curtains and drawn them close together . . . The laughing owner would enter there no more, forever! . . . I never knew a more trying evening for actors, for all knew him well—liked him and grieved for him." Meanwhile a pair of scriveners were working furiously to capitalize on public sentiment, writing a play, *Black Friday,* which would soon appear at Niblo's Garden and would immortalize Robber King Fisk as "Rob King," a lovable scoundrel, Stokes being caricatured as "Dash Hoffman" and Josie as "Violet Spearheart."

The funeral train was met by hundreds of people when it made stops at South Norwalk, Hartford and other stations. Although it did not reach Brattleboro until 11:35, the station was jammed. Many of those present had known Pop Fisk's bully boy as the witling of the Revere House, as the Prince of Peddlers—had held up their hands at the tales of his doings in New York. Now they saw his career run full circle with his return home as a corpse at the age of thirty-six.

The body was removed to Room 1 at the Revere House, the same where Mary Grace Fisk and George Hooker had held their wedding reception. In the morning, citizens flocked in to snow-covered Brattleboro from miles around. "It is wonderful where all the people came from," wrote one reporter. "The principal street presented two long lines of sleighs throughout its whole length, and in the side streets stood unnumbered ox teams, and still they came dashing in. Hundreds arrived from Springfield and Boston and other large cities within easy reach. The hotels were filled to their utmost capacity."

At the services, held on Tuesday, January 9, 1872, at the Baptist Church because it was the biggest in town, the Rev. William L. Jenkins prayed for a solid thirty minutes until listeners began to fidget. Possibly Jenkins felt that it would take some powerful praying to purchase Fisk's admission among the angels. But it was Chaplain Edward O. Flagg of the Ninth, arisen from his sickbed, who preached the sermon. Flagg, an honest man, made no pretense that Fisk was unblemished.

"He who lies before you was no common man," he said. "He was not like the mass. As to his faults, I will not speak of them. A censorious world will do them ample justice . . . When his good qualities are balanced against his bad, I venture to say that we will have at least an equipoise . . . He was magnanimous by nature, and never consulted his means when he wished to do a good deed . . . Colonel Fisk was generous to a fault. . . ."

Then they took Jim Fisk a half-mile up the hill and buried him, along with his colonel's uniform and sword, in the same escape-proof graveyard he had furnished with a $500 fence.

By Way of
a Postscript

THE FISK-MANSFIELD letters—thirty-nine of them—were published in full in the New York *Herald* on January 14, 1872, one week after Fisk's death. Sensation-seekers were disappointed. While the letters gave ample evidence of Fisk's infatuation for Josie and his jealousy of Stokes, there was no compromising mention of any other person or of the Erie or Tammany Rings. The *Herald* did not say how it got possession of them, but there was a suspicion that Stokes had furnished the newspaper with copies of them weeks earlier.

The *Herald* publication was on Sunday. The *Tribune* and *Times* published excerpts on Monday which may have been cribbed from the *Herald*. The *Tribune*, which had long claimed that the correspondence contained evidence enough to send many a rogue to jail, was embarrassed, saying, "They are evidently selected and printed by the friends of the late Vice-President of Erie, and (according to his slayer) do not include those damaging references to public and financial matters contained in other parts of the correspondence. . . ." Stokes, in his cell, said the letters published were only the "unimportant" ones. Gould, on the other hand, vowed that all of the letters had been published. He said Fisk had been anxious to prevent their publication simply because of their personal nature, not because they compromised anyone.

A good case can be made that Stokes was lying and Gould was truthful. Since Stokes had copies of all the letters, if some had been suppressed it seems that he would have taken this opportunity to release those damaging to Fisk.

It is doubtful that Fisk would have been foolish enough to include incriminating business information in his billets-doux. While Josie probably heard enough talk to give her some inside knowledge of Erie-Tammany maneuvers, such hearsay evidence would be of dubious value in court. It would have been perfectly in character for Fisk, with his hatred for Stokes and his extreme sensitivity about his amorous defeat, to spend a fortune fighting publication of the letters merely to protect his own privacy and to check-mate Stokes. Nor does it seem that Josie and Stokes were too high-minded to hint untruthfully that the letters con-tained details of criminal transactions, knowing that this would spur the newspaper demands for their release and at the same time increase the pressure on Fisk to back down and pay heavy blackmail in an out-of-court settlement.

EDWARD STILES STOKES went on trial for murder in June, 1872. District Attorney Garvin demanded that he be hanged, saying, "his hands are stained with blood to the very shoulders." Josie, appearing as a witness for the de-fense, was described by the newspapers as "a modern Desdemona," "a magnificent Medusa" and "this Aspasia," while the prosecutor simply called her "a harlot." The *Herald* said she "took a long, tender look at Stokes, and seemed for a moment to drink in his every feature."

Stokes' defense was a complicated device with many escape hatches. He claimed (A) that he had shot Fisk in self-defense; (B) that he was driven insane by persecution when he shot Fisk; (C) that Fisk died not from the bullet wound but from the excessive probing of the wound by the doctors; or (D) if the doctors did not kill him in this way, they did so by giving him lethal quantities of mor-phine. Josie testified that Fisk kept "eight or ten pistols" and had repeatedly threatened Stokes' life. Witnesses for the prosecution declared that Fisk owned no guns at all.

Stokes said with a straight face that his meeting with Fisk

at the Grand Central Hotel was purest coincidence. As he was walking by the hotel, he related, he thought he saw a woman waving at him from a second-floor window. Believing her to be a woman he had met at Saratoga, he went upstairs and found he was mistaken. He was going downstairs again when he was surprised to meet Fisk coming up. Fisk whipped out a pistol, but Stokes fired first.

Although no weapon was found on Fisk's person or on the stairway, the jury disagreed. At least one juror was suspected of being bribed. At his second trial, Stokes was convicted and sentenced to be hanged. He won an appeal, however, and at his third trial was convicted of manslaughter and sentenced to six years in prison. "Had Stokes been an illiterate laborer," Edmund Stedman commented, "he would have dangled in a noose two months later." His legal expenses depleted his father's fortune, after which he had financial help from his cousin, W. E. D. Stokes, his millionaire uncle, James Stokes, and his old friend Cassius Read, proprietor of the Hoffman House.

In a doggerel ballad about Fisk titled "He Never Went Back On The Poor," which had four stanzas and was published in sheet-music form, Stokes' light sentence got indignant comment:

> *Now what do you think of the trial of Stokes,*
> *Who murdered this friend of the poor?*
> *If such men get free, is any one safe*
> *To step from outside their own door?*

He served four years at Sing Sing, where influence won him favors and he appears to have been treated more as an honored guest than an inmate. But when he was released in 1877, the only person who met him at the gates was Cassius Read. He was something of an outcast, persona non grata at Delmonico's and other places he used to frequent. He suffered from the horrors afflicting some killers, fearing Fisk's ghost and Fisk's friends. He always left a light burning when he slept. "His manner was often described as that of a haunted man," said the *Times*. "He feared assassination . . . He always ate with his back close against the wall so that nothing could pass behind him." Read befriended him, gave him a room at the Hoffman House and eventually took him in as a partner. They quarreled, became involved in lawsuits, and Read, later losing his share in the hotel and sinking into penury, said the younger man had ruined him. Stokes joined a business enterprise with John W. Mackay, the mining operator, which also ended in the courts when Mackay accused him of cheating. Stokes likewise quarreled bitterly with his cousin, W. E. D. Stokes, who had aided him at the time of his trial, and the two were courtroom opponents for years.

Apparently Stokes' wife died or divorced him. He spent his last years in modest circumstances, operating two restaurants in New York. When he died in 1901, aged sixty-one, it was found that he was living with a woman named Rosamond Barclay who claimed they had been secretly married a year earlier.

JOSIE MANSFIELD, unpopular in New York, stayed long enough to testify at Stokes' first trial and to sue Fisk's widow unsuccessfully for $200,000 she claimed Fisk owed her, then took up residence in Paris. Still handsome, in 1891 she married a rich, alcoholic, expatriate New York lawyer, Robert L. Reade, in London, Reade candidly telling a reporter that he married her "because she is the only person who can save me from drink." Drink got him nevertheless. In 1897, when he was declared insane, Josie divorced him and went back home to Boston. Her health failing, she was described as "a semi-paralyzed wreck" in 1899 when she took refuge with a sister in Philadelphia. The record thereafter is sketchy. Shortly afterward, she went with a brother to Watertown, South Dakota, where she was reported in dire poverty in 1909. Just how or when she recovered her health and came into funds is not known, but somehow she returned to Europe to live in the American colony in Paris for many years, dying at the American Hospital there October 27, 1931, having outlived Fisk by fifty-nine years and Stokes by thirty. Apparently she was still coy about her age, given as seventy-eight when she died, which would have made her nineteen when Fisk was murdered and about eleven when she married Lawlor. She was buried in Montparnasse Cemetery in a drizzle with three mourners standing by—two serving women and one unidentified friend.

JAY GOULD, only two months after Fisk's death, was ousted clear out of Erie in a surprise stockholders' coup engineered by General Sickles. A new regime took charge and found the road near financial and operational bankruptcy. The offices were moved from the sinful Opera House back to the old quarters on West Street. It would take years to nurse Erie back to health, but meanwhile Gould showed his magic in other stock operations. He was worth more than $70,000,000 when he died in 1892 at the age of fifty-six.

BOSS TWEED was finally convicted and given a twelve-year sentence. The term being reduced by a higher court, he served one year, then was arrested on other charges. Escaping, he fled to Cuba, then to Spain, where he was caught and returned to the United States. He died in prison in 1878.

JUDGE BARNARD was impeached in August, 1872, stripped of his judicial robes and forever disqualified from holding office in the state. When he died in 1879, $1,000,000 in cash and bonds were found among his effects.

DANIEL DREW, following his stock market defeat by Fisk and Gould, suffered further reverses. After Fisk's death, he took another speculative licking in railroad stocks at the hands of Jay Gould. Characteristically, he kept delaying his promised gift of $250,000 to the Drew Theological Seminary, feeling that he could do better with it in speculation. Instead, he paid $17,000 annual interest on the sum. He went bankrupt in 1875, so the seminary never did get the principal. He resumed friendship with his old enemy, Vanderbilt, during these later years, sometimes playing two-handed euchre with him. The sturdy Commodore left $100,000,000 and a dynasty to follow him when he died in 1877. Drew lived with a son in New York until he died broke in 1879.

LUCY FISK retained an attorney to aid in the prosecution of Stokes and attended some of the hearings with Mary Grace Hooker. Mary Grace was so grief-stricken at the murder of her half brother that she could not bear to stay in New York. She and her husband returned to Brattleboro, where Colonel Hooker became a civic leader and the prosperous owner of an overall factory. Lucy returned to Boston. Having no business sense, she dissipated her fortune in losing investments and unwise loans. Colonel Hooker begged her to allow him to handle her finances, but she declined until most of her money was gone. For years before she died in 1912, she lived with a sister in a South Boston cottage, scrimping along on fifty dollars a month she got in rentals from a few houses she owned in Brattleboro—a purchase Hooker had arranged for her. There is a story that she took to drink in her later years.

Colonel Hooker died in 1902. His wife lived until 1922. Her granddaughters remember her as a charming, naive old lady who regarded her late half brother with unquenchable admiration.

A month after Fisk's death, the 250 canaries belonging to the Narragansett Line were sold at auction by name. Jay Gould brought $8.50; Colonel Fisk Jr., $16.25; and Stokes,

$7.50, the others being knocked down for smaller sums. Fisk's $2,500 music box with the gold-and-silver model of the *Providence* went for $1,500, the buyer being Nully Pieris.

The citizens of Brattleboro collected $25,000 for a monument for Fisk. There was some semi-humorous opinion that the most suitable memorial would be the likeness of an old tin oven entwined with woodbine. However, Larkin Mead, the same sculptor who executed the Lincoln monument at Springfield, Illinois, hewed a shaft of marble with a portrait medallion of Fisk on its face. At the corners of the massive base are four scantily-clad young women representing railroading, shipping, trade and the stage. It is the grandest monument at the Brattleboro Protestant Cemetery, surrounded by the graves of Fisk's parents, his wife and the Hookers. Souvenir hunters have taken most of the fingers and toes of the four young ladies. An elderly Vermonter told this writer: "Never saw a more appropriate monument. Fisk had trouble with naked women all his life, so they put four of 'em over his grave."

APPENDICES

Acknowledgments

MOST of the research for this book was done at the Yale University Library, the New York Public Library, the New-York Historical Society and the Brattleboro Public Library, where many expert librarians were exceedingly helpful. The writer was fortunate in locating three granddaughters of Jim Fisk's half sister, Mary Grace Hooker—Mrs. R. E. Palmer, Mrs. Henry A. Willard and Mrs. Fenton E. Batton—all of whom searched their memories for recollections. In an interview with the writer, Mrs. Palmer recalled conversations with her grandmother, "family talk" about Fisk, and cleared up several points that had been in doubt.

Warm gratitude is also felt for help given in a variety of ways by Mr. Wayne Andrews of New York; Mr. Paul K. Swanson, Librarian, the Brattleboro Public Library; Mr. Richard G. Wood, Director, Vermont Historical Society; Mrs. Marjorie N. Layton, Librarian, Long Branch Public Library; Mr. R. H. Hann, Secretary, the Erie Railroad Company; Mr. Jason Bushnell of Vernon, Vermont; Mr. Robert W. Hill of the Manuscript Division, New York Public Library; Mr. Fenton E. Batton of Wickford, Rhode Island; and Mrs. Walter A. Nelson of Iron Mountain, Michigan.

Bibliography

THE WRITER has sought to present Fisk as a personality, a social phenomenon, a man whose wickedness was emblematic and in some respects almost endemic. There is no pretense at close analysis of his complicated financial maneuvers, which are given only in sufficient outline to explain his motives and actions. Fisk was so wedded to the bizarre that he was a subject of constant gossip which created a sizable apocrypha. The intent here has been to avoid tall stories and to rely on responsible record. All speeches given are direct or indirect quotations from newspapers or other sources. The leading newspapers, which gave Fisk such impolite scrutiny, were scanned from day to day during his New York career. The following sources were consulted:

One Fisk letter at the New York Public Library; one Fisk letter at the New-York Historical Society; and "Jay Gould and the Erie Railway," the manuscript reminiscences of G. P. Morosini, ex-auditor of the company, also at the New-York Historical Society.

NEWSPAPERS AND MAGAZINES

The Brattleboro *Vermont Journal*
The Brattleboro *Vermont Phoenix*
The New York *Herald*
The New York *Times*
The New York *Tribune*
The New York *Sun*
The New York *World*

American Heritage
Frank Leslie's Illustrated Newspaper
Harper's Weekly
The Nation

BOOKS

Adams, Charles Francis, Jr., and Henry Adams—*Chapters of Erie, and Other Essays.* Boston, 1871.

Alexander, DeAlva Stanwood—*A Political History of the State of New York,* 3 vols. New York, 1909.

Andrews, Wayne—*The Vanderbilt Legend.* New York, 1941.

Anonymous—*James Fisk, Jr.: The Life of a Green Mountain Boy.* Philadelphia, 1872.

Anonymous—*The Life and Assassination of James Fisk, Jr.* Philadelphia, 1872.

Anonymous—*The Life of Colonel James Fisk, Jr., With Sketches of Edward S. Stokes, His Assassin, Miss Helen Josephine Mansfield, etc.* New York, n.d.

Anonymous—*Romantic Incidents in the Life of James Fisk, Jr.* n. d., no publisher visible.

Barnard, George G. (subject)—*Proceedings of the Court of Impeachment in the Matter of the Impeachment of George G. Barnard.* Albany, 1874.

Boutwell, George S.—*Reminiscences of Sixty Years in Public Affairs,* 2 vols. New York, 1902.

Bowen, Croswell—*The Elegant Oakey.* New York, 1956.

Breen, Matthew P.—*Thirty Years of New York Politics.* New York, 1899.

Cabot, Mary R.—*Annals of Brattleboro, 1681-1895.* Brattleboro, 1921.

Clapp, Margaret—*Forgotten First Citizen: John Bigelow.* Boston, 1947.

Clews, Henry—*Twenty-Eight Years in Wall Street.* New York, 1888.

Crouch, George—*Another Chapter of Erie.* Pamphlet, New York, 1869.

Field, David Dudley—*The Duties and Rights of Counsel* (Correspondence between Samuel Bowles and Field). Pamphlet, New York, 1871.

Fiero, J. Newton—*David Dudley Field and His Work.* Pamphlet, Albany, 1895.

Fifth Avenue Events—(no author given). New York, 1916.

Flick, A. C.—*Samuel Jones Tilden.* New York, 1929.

Flint, Henry M.—*The Railroads of the United States.* Philadelphia, 1868.

Foord, John—*The Life and Public Services of Andrew Haswell Green.* New York, 1913.

Fowler, William Worthington—*Ten Years in Wall Street.* Hartford, 1870.

Fuller, Robert H.—*Jubilee Jim: The Life of Colonel James Fisk, Jr.* New York, 1928.

Gold Panic Investigation—41st Congress, 2d Session, H. of R. Report No. 31. Washington, 1870.

Grodinsky, Julius—*Jay Gould: His Business Career.* Philadelphia, 1957.

Headley, J. T.—*The Great Riots of New York.* New York, 1873.

Hesseltine, William B.—*Ulysses S. Grant, Politician.* New York, 1935.

Hicks, Frederick C.—*Finance in the Sixties.* New Haven, 1929.

Holbrook, Stewart—*The Age of the Moguls.* New York, 1953.

Hungerford, Edward—*Men of Erie.* New York, 1946.

Jones, Willoughby—*The Life of James Fisk, Jr.* Philadelphia, 1872.

Josephson, Matthew—*The Robber Barons.* New York, 1934.

Kracauer, S.—*Offenbach and the Paris of His Time.* London, 1937.

Lane, Wheaton J.—*Commodore Vanderbilt: An Epic of the Steam Age.* New York, 1942.

Lewis, Alfred Henry—*Nation-Famous New York Murders.* New York, 1912.

Lynch, Denis Tilden—*Boss Tweed.* New York, 1927.

McAlpine, R. W.—*The Life and Times of Colonel James Fisk, Jr.* New York, 1927.

Medbery, J. K.—*Men and Mysteries of Wall Street.* Boston, 1870.

Merriam, George S.—*The Life and Times of Samuel Bowles,* 2 vols. New York, 1885.

Minnigerode, Meade—*Certain Rich Men.* New York, 1927.

Morris, Clara—*Life on the Stage.* London, 1902.

Morris, Lloyd—*Incredible New York.* New York, 1951.

Mott, E. H.—*Between the Ocean and the Lakes: The Story of Erie.* New York, 1899.

Myers, Gustavus—*History of the Great American Fortunes.* New York, 1936.

——— *The History of Tammany Hall.* New York, 1901.

Nevins, Allan—*The Emergence of Modern America,* 12 vols. New York, 1927.

Northrop, Henry Davenport—*Jay Gould.* Philadelphia, 1892.

Oberholtzer, E. P.—*A History of the United States Since the Civil War,* 5 vols. New York, 1922.

O'Brien, Frank M.—*The Story of the Sun.* New York, 1918.

Offenbach, Jacques—*Orpheus in America* (his diary of his American visit, translated by Lander McClintock). Bloomington, Ind., 1957.

Paine, Albert Bigelow—*Th. Nast, His Period and His Pictures.* New York, 1904.

Ruggles, Eleanor— *Prince of Players: Edwin Booth.* New York, 1953.

Sachs, Emanie—*"The Terrible Siren": Victoria Woodhull.* New York, 1928.

Satterlee, Herbert L.—*J. Pierpont Morgan.* New York, 1939.

Seitz, Don C.—*The Dreadful Decade.* Indianapolis, 1926.

Smith, Matthew Hale—*Twenty Years Among the Bulls and Bears of Wall Street.* Hartford, 1870.

Stafford, Marshall P.—*The Life of James Fisk, Jr.* New York, 1872.

Stedman, Edmund C. (ed.)—*The New York Stock Exchange.* New York, 1905.

Strong, George Templeton—*The Diary of George Templeton Strong,* edited by Allan Nevins and Milton Halsey Thomas, 4 vols. New York, 1950.

Supreme Court, County of Delaware—Joseph H. Ramsey against Jay Gould, James Fisk, Jr., and others. No date or publisher.

Van Deusen, Glyndon G.—*Horace Greeley, Nineteenth Century Crusader.* Philadelphia, 1949.

Van Wyck, Frederick—*Recollections of an Old New Yorker.* New York, 1932.

Walling, George W.—*Recollections of a New York Chief of Police.* New York, 1887.

Warshow, Robert Irving—*Jay Gould.* New York, 1928.

—— *The Story of Wall Street.* New York, 1929.

White, Bouck—*The Book of Daniel Drew.* New York, 1910.

Winter, William—*Other Days.* New York, 1908.

Woodward, C. Vann—*The Lowest Ebb* (Article about U. S. Grant in *American Heritage,* April, 1957, Vol. VIII, No. 3).

Writers' Project, WPA, State of New Jersey—*Entertaining a Nation: The Career of Long Branch.* Long Branch, 1940.

Index